FOR BETTER,

Mary Reddrop *trained as a ... worker. She has held senior positions in counselling, super-vision and training in secular and church agencies and edits the newsletter of the Christian Counsellors Association in Australia, of which she was recently made an honorary fellow. She is a member of her parish church council and of the diocesan synod.*

Canon Bruce Reddrop *is a priest in the Anglican Church. After parish experience, he was director of the Anglican Marriage Guidance Council in Melbourne for 28 years, and led the counselling, supervision, training and professional development programmes. He was the founda-tion president of the Australian Association of Marriage and Family Counsellors. He also led the pastoral counselling elements of post-ordination training in his diocese for many years.*

Mary and Bruce *have jointly led counselling and therapy groups, and training groups for counsellors in various disci-plines, including courses for clergy in counselling, marriage counselling and pastoral care.*

They have been married for over forty years, and have two married sons, a grandson and two step-granddaughters.

HANDBOOKS OF PASTORAL CARE
SERIES EDITOR: MARLENE COHEN

FOR BETTER, FOR WORSE

A Guide to Contemporary Marriage Counselling

MARY REDDROP
& BRUCE REDDROP

HarperCollins*Publishers*

HarperCollins*Publishers*
77–85 Fulham Palace Road, London W6 8JB

First published in Great Britain
in 1995 by HarperCollins*Publishers*

1   3   5   7   9   10   8   6   4   2

Copyright © 1995 Mary Reddrop & Bruce Reddrop

Mary Reddrop and Bruce Reddrop assert the moral right
to be identified as the authors of this work

A catalogue record for this book is
available from the British Library

ISBN 0 551 02825–4

Typeset by Harper Phototypesetters Limited
Northampton, England
Printed and bound in Great Britain by
HarperCollinsManufacturing Glasgow

CONDITIONS OF SALE
This book is sold subject to the condition that it
shall not, by way of trade or otherwise, be lent, re-sold,
hired out or otherwise circulated without the publisher's
prior consent in any form of binding or cover other
than that in which it is published and without a
similar condition including this condition being
imposed on the subsequent purchaser.

All rights reserved. No part of this publication may be
reproduced, stored in a retrieval system, or transmitted,
in any form or by any means, electronic, mechanical,
photocopying, recording or otherwise, without the prior
permission of the publishers.

ACKNOWLEDGEMENTS

The warm affection of many people sustained us as we wrote this book. Among friends over many years we are specially thankful for Noël and John Higgins who pray daily for our work, and for Sue Fisher, psychologist and marriage counsellor, who is a long-term partner in prayer with Mary. The Revd Tom Wilkinson PhD, professor emeritus in New Testament, and Olive Wilkinson, MSW and therapist, give us merry companionship and enrich our thinking, and the Revd Roy Bradley, Clinical Pastoral Educator, challenges our self-doubt.

The Revd Robin Payne, lecturer in Old Testament at Ridley College and colleague to Bruce, has made valuable comments on our writing. Other generous friends, competent clinicians, have each read a specific chapter and commented from their perspectives (some of which diverge from ours): Yvonne Bowden, marriage counsellor, Annette Hourigan, social worker, Dr Margaret Payne, gynaecologist, the Revd Grahame Pogue, specialist in groupwork with abusive spouses, and Shelagh Wilken, lecturer in Pastoral Counselling at Kingsley College. We appreciate their interest, and also that of Rae and Peter Alexander whose professional services in typing and computer skills have been of great value.

We thank Marlene Cohen and Christine Smith of HarperCollins for inviting us to write for this series. Our contacts with them have been a pleasure.

In all sorts of areas a man and a woman have to overcome the differences between them to form a unit and a unity. In writing together, no less than in our other activities, we have had to do just that. When two minds work very differently, it is a challenge to bring together in harmony lateral and focused thinking, pragmatics and principles, the profound and the simple, the would-be poetic and the sensibly prosaic. It has been an exasperating task; it has also been fun. We are each thankful for the other's persistence and goodwill, and we thank God for continuing to teach us about the nature of being human.

CONTENTS

FOREWORD

This is a book for clergy written by a clergyman and his wife out of the experience of their long and valued ministry in marriage counselling. It is direct in its approach, often addressing the reader in the second person and so eliciting a deeply personal response.

It is a book written by professionals for those who seek to approach their ministry of counselling in a professional way. As such it calls for careful study and a commitment to be guided by the principles it lays down. Counselling is a demanding ministry and there will be those who will see the commitment it calls for requiring more time than the average parish minister can give. The value of the book for them is that it shows when referral to a professional counsellor is needed.

It is an eminently readable book, generously supplied with case studies which bring alive the theory being presented. All clergy engage in some marriage counselling and all will find here encouragement and help which is accessible at various levels.

I am glad to have been asked to commend this book, and I do so willingly. Mary and Bruce Reddrop are known and loved throughout the Diocese of Melbourne. His nearly thirty years as Director of the Anglican Marriage Guidance Council have equipped him both by experience and study for the writing of this book. That it is, in fact, the joint work of a husband and wife team gives it further authenticity.

I hope that *For Better, For Worse* may become a foundation for the ministry of marriage counselling for many clergy, and that those with whom they work may receive through it enrichment and blessing in their lives together.

Keith Rayner
Archbishop of Melbourne

SERIES INTRODUCTION

The demand for pastoral care and counselling in churches has increased to record levels and every indication is that this trend will continue to accelerate. Some churches are fortunate to have ready access to professionally trained and qualified counsellors, but in most situations this onerous task falls to pastors.

Some pastors* are naturally gifted for the ministry of counselling. Some receive training before ordination and then seek to extend this as opportunity permits through the years. Others have the task of counselling thrust upon them. Most seem to feel some sustained demand, internal or external, to be competent in the field. This series aims to address some of the gaps frequently left in theological training. It is intended to offer support to those entrusted with responsibility for the care and well-being of others.

Comparative studies of healing agencies were pioneered in the United States. As long as thirty years ago The Joint Commission on Mental Illness reported that 42 per cent of 2,460 people canvassed would go first to the clergy with any mental health problem.

Of course there may be reasons other than overtly religious for a preference for clergy counselling. There may seem less stigma in seeing a pastor than a psychiatrist. Also, viewing a problem as a primarily spiritual matter may preclude taking some degree of

---

*The term 'pastor' is used generically here, to include all who have a recognized pastoral role within a local church or Christian community.

responsibility for it and for examining its depths. And, of course, clergy visits are cheaper! Unfortunately, there can be the additional reason that parishoners feel an inappropriate right of access to their pastor's time and skills. God's availability at all times is sometimes confused with ours, as is divine omniscience.

Being a front-line mental health worker can put a pastor under enormous and inappropriate strain. Counselling is becoming the primary time consumer in an increasing number of parish ministries.

Feeling unsafe and inadequate in any situation inevitably produces some form of self-protective behaviour, unless we can admit our inadequacy while retaining self-respect. Religious professionals who are under pressure to function as counsellors but know their skills and knowledge to be in other areas may understandably take refuge in various defences, even dogmatism. The term 'religious professional' is more familiar in some countries than in others. The clerical profession actually preceded all others, in status and in time. 'But what are we professional at?' can be a difficult question to answer. This is especially so when clergy are driven to believe that anything short of multi-competence will let God down.

Pastors may feel obliged not to appear inadequate in the area of counselling because of their confidence that the Bible contains the answer to every human need. And it does, conceptually. The difficulty is not with the Bible nor with the pastor's knowledge of the Bible. Neither of these should be in question. The concern is whether pastors have the additional ability of a clinician. Naming a counselling problem correctly – not the presenting problem but the real, underlying issues and their components – is a refined specialism. Making a faulty diagnosis, especially when God and biblical authority are somehow implicated, is the cause of much damage. Clinical terminology can be applied almost at random but with a surprising degree of assurance. Understanding the Bible, and understanding the complexities of clinical practice, are not one and the same skill. In 1985 a comparative study was conducted into the ability of 112 clergy to recognize 13 signs of suicidal tendencies. (Reported in the *Journal of Psychology and Theology*: 1989: Vol 17: No 2.) It was found that clergy were unable to recognize these signs any better than educated lay people and substantially less well than other mental health workers. This is no necessary reflection on the clergy. Why should they be expected to have this professional ability? Considering them culpable would only be just if they were to assume, or to allow an assumption to go unchecked, that their skills were identical to those of other caring professionals.

One pressure is that graduates of some theological colleges have actually been taught that ordination will confer counselling skills. 'We must insist upon the idea that every man who has been called of God into the ministry has been given the basic gifts for . . . counselling' (Jay Adams, *The Christian Counsellor's Manual*, 1973, Presbyterian and Reformed Publishing Company; Part One, Page 20).

Equating a ministry calling with being a gifted counsellor could be seen to involve some leaping assumptions. These are becoming more apparent as we distinguish what we used to call 'the ministry' from God's calling of *all* believers into ministry. As more work is done on what we mean by 'ordination' more clergy can be released into those areas of ministry for which they are clearly gifted and suited.

Belief that counselling skills are divinely bestowed in conjunction with a ministry 'call' will probably not issue in the purchase of this series of handbooks! Other pastors who believe or fear that neither counselling nor any other skills can be taken for granted, are possibly conducting their ministries under some heavy burdens. This series is written with a concern to address these burdens and to redress some erroneous equations that relate to them. Each author has extensive experience in some avenue of ministry and is also trained and experienced in some aspect of counselling.

These Handbooks of Pastoral Care are designed to aid pastors in assessing the needs of those who come to them for help. The more accurately this assessment can be made the more confident the pastor can be about the form of ministry that is required in each instance. Sometimes pastors will decide to refer the matter elsewhere, but on other occasions there can be a prayerful assurance in retaining the counselling role within their own ministry.

Marlene Cohen
Oxford, March 1994

SETTING THE SCENE

As a guide to contemporary marriage counselling, this book is for the use of a range of marriage counsellors, although it is largely addressed to clergy. Clergy are pastors, ministers and priests. We will more often than not use the word 'minister' to cover all clergy and pastors ordained or otherwise officially appointed leaders; and also people who are not ordained but who are commissioned by their church for ministry.

Mainly we are addressing the needs, in so far as we can, of ministers of local churches or parishes. Reading a book *can not train* ministers or anyone else to be a professional marriage counsellor. However, it *can guide* them in deciding

- how they can minister in a counselling mode to couples who ask for their help,
- how they can increase their skills in marriage counselling,
- how to assess their skills and limitations in counselling couples, and
- when and in what circumstances to refer couples to a professional marriage counsellor.

Possible and Difficult

We begin with two questions, and with brief answers that we will elaborate on through this book. *Is it possible for ministers of churches to counsel married couples effectively?*

Yes, it is possible. But it is difficult: and it is difficult for counsellors of whatever training to counsel couples well. Our experience as trainers and supervisors of marriage counsellors in church agencies and also in private practice tells us how easy it is for any marriage counsellor to focus not on the marriage, but on the individual.

The counsellor, having lost this central focus, tends then to identify more closely with one partner and often loses the other. This is rarely appropriate, and rarely healing for the partners' relationship. And losing the marriage focus is only one of the traps in marriage counselling, however experienced and well-trained the counsellor may be.

Our second question is relevant to the need for oversight of one's counselling (this is another theme we will return to later.) *Is it possible for ministers of churches to have regular and sound supervision of their marriage counselling?*

Some ministers find it so. Increasingly there is recognition of the need in Christian ministry to have regular discussion and assessment of one's work, and this is a form of supervision.

For us personally as professional counsellors, almost weekly supervision is a requirement and a need that we accept and recognize. In the marriage counselling agencies with which we have been associated over many years – both secular and church agencies – the principle of supervision has been increasingly put into serious practice. Most marriage counsellors we know well regard this principle highly.

The Gifts You Bring

You are a minister. The well-being of married couples in your church is of pressing and no doubt prayerful concern to you. Of all people, you will be aware of contemporary pressures on wives and husbands, and of difficulties Christians have (in common with all couples) as they try to sustain buoyant committed marriages. Of all people you will want to be supporting and compassionate and healing to them.

You may have attended courses or workshops in counselling skills, feeling the need to equip yourself better for your ministry; wanting to help people grow in grace and in love for the Lord. Your theological training was, appropriately, in theological categories of thought, not psychological categories. But there is a need for both, although it is your theological training that lays the primary foundations for your understanding of the relation between who God is and who people are.

We don't need to be daunted by either psychology or theology. In so far as psychological concepts are true, they are simply descriptions of how the human nature that God has created works. Theological concepts in so far as they are true are simply descriptions, primarily about the nature of God and his relation to his creation.

Hopefully, your theological education helped you to develop flexibility and to value another person's different, unique journey of faith. If yours was the usual pattern, theological training was followed by your ordination, or your commissioning for ministry.

Ordination and commissioning don't bestow on us skills in tasks like administration, pastoral visiting and leadership of meetings. We learn these abilities and go on developing them. In our contemporary society many of our skills require intermittent updating; even those relating to administration, and certainly those concerned with pastoral care and counselling. We are challenged to keep on monitoring our abilities and enhancing them.

But this is also the era of the quick fix. There are ideas about personality and about healing prayer that sometimes seem to be in this category, promising transformation and empowerment in almost a magical way. God is not the God of cheap grace – the God of the personality fad or of the relationship quick fix. God is the God of life, giving us grace to shape our personal lives and our relationships more and more in obedience to His will.

The most precious and important gift you can bring to the church where you minister is a loving, personal commitment to Jesus Christ and his people. Along with this commitment you can bring the fruits of your theological education. The understanding you bring of your denomination's doctrines and their relation to life can also serve the people well, helping them to be grounded in their church affiliation.

These are attributes that undergird your ministry to people. Counselling is part of ministry in contemporary church life, and perhaps an increasingly important one for all ministers. But if a minister is asked by a church member for counselling on a marriage issue, what then? Marriage counselling is a difficult discipline to do well.

We believe that ministers can do very sound marriage counselling if they have the pre-requisites: not only attributes of the kind we have mentioned, but also the professional discipline necessary to develop their skills; and a suitable temperament as well.[1] Even so, there are some complicating factors a minister must consider. One of them (and we refer to it in several chapters) is availability of quality time, and that depends largely on the minister's scale of priorities. There are other factors also.

Complicating Factors

As a minister, you are relating to your people on a variety of levels and in a variety of roles. This can make counselling a couple in your church a more challenging task for you than it is for many other marriage counsellors. They have contact with clients only in their counselling office and on their phone. They have a specific and limited purpose with people they see: counselling.

[1] See chapters 20 & 21.

In your church you have contact at many levels with couples. You lead them in worship at services. You meet them at church social events. You may even have a couple on the parish council, where you and they have to take part in the vigorous debate that precedes some parish council decisions. Sometimes you and people you counsel will share the same view; sometimes your views will be opposed. In either case, their role and yours in that situation require behaviour that is different from the behaviour appropriate to the relationship you have in counselling sessions. Factors like these put your counselling relationship at risk.

On the other hand, some people seeking help for troubled marriages live out of reach, financially or geographically, of an appropriate counselling agency. Good ministers are likely to be more accessible to them than good professional marriage counsellors. As a minister, you may also bring to counselling a dimension of understanding of what marriage can be that is very valuable to a couple. Not necessarily, however: it depends on the extent to which you can translate that dimension into marriage counselling skills.

Not every effective minister can do this. We admire the one who can say 'Marriage counselling is not what I am suited to do, by my personality and life circumstances.' Some who are supremely confident that they are well suited cannot be convinced that they are not.

This book is designed to help you as a minister to discover and affirm the skills you have, and to encourage you to enlarge and develop those skills through learning and practice.

An important part of your being a marriage counsellor is knowing when and how to refer people whose difficulties are beyond your skills. Some spouses may have emotional disturbance that needs a different kind of help from yours, or a counsellor of greater experience.

The art of making a good referral is discussed in chapter 19 where we consider the reasons for referral, various types of referral, and relationship with the person to whom the referral is made.

Many ministers who counsel couples learn to do this well. Along with learning how to make referrals, they need to develop other skills for marriage counselling, too. The better practised our skills, the better equipped we are to enter the delicate area of counselling a couple or a spouse about a marriage problem. To put this another way, as counsellors we are not to enter someone else's marriage lightly, unadvisedly, carelessly – or over-enthusiastically.

Case Examples

In the dialogues and descriptions of husbands and wives through these chapters, you will inevitably see some similarities to situations in marriages that you are familiar with, including your own. That's because the situations are common ones. If we were to take couples from actual counselling cases and put them in a book we would be breaching confidentiality, so none of the couples as we have portrayed them exist in real life. They are a composite picture of many marriages from our counselling and other experience; or rather, a composite picture of aspects of many marriages.

We have chosen simple case examples, as you will be quick to note. As you compare them with some marriages you are familiar with, you will notice in most of our couples a relative absence of entrenched bitterness, an accessibility of affection to each other, and a will to be honest. Many couples who seek counselling do have these qualities, but others bring such intense conflicts that the counsellor is working with the complexities of very negative, confused relationships.

Part of the task of dealing with complexities is learning from simplified situations and choosing relatively uncomplicated cases. Their value is that they give a framework for understanding basic issues: a framework that offers the counsellor freedom to become aware, with growing experience, of the nuances and complexities in marriages. (When you counsel couples you follow a similar process, abstracting elements in the couple's interaction for them to work with, while being aware that their relationship is more complex than those elements.)

For your reading of the rest of this book, we offer you these caveats: *Be aware of the risks. Recognize your limitations.* We offer you also this encouragement: *Have confidence in what you can realistically do, and in your ability to grow and change (with some pain) as you learn marriage counselling skills.* Eventually you may counsel in a different way from the examples we present, but by developing disciplines and structured approaches that are honouring to the couples you meet with, your counselling is going to be largely for better, not worse.

We invite you to join us in thinking across theological and psychological categories, taking both seriously, as we lead you into considering how far you might be able to equip yourself to help couples living in their contemporary world.

2

INITIAL CONTACT

It had been a good morning service followed by the usual social time in the church hall. Laughter came from the kitchen where the men rostered to serve coffee were washing cups. Groups of chatting people had dwindled to the few who were planning details of a street stall.

Alec, the minister, left cheerfully, his mind on a family he intended to visit. But when Yvette spoke to him at the church hall door about her husband Zach he felt momentarily a weight in his chest and a sense of being cornered. Last time it had been another church member complaining about his wife. 'She spends all our income. She runs up credit we can't manage.' Now it was Yvette saying tearfully, 'Zach never stops arguing and criticizing me. Can you help us? I'm desperate.'

Alec's church was a lively one where a range of people worshipped. Many of them valued him as a spiritual leader and found in him an approachable confidant. But his very approachability and his respect for people's privacy had tended to put him at risk. Not only was he asked often for counselling, but he was tempted frequently to comply with the urgency of people's wish for instant help. It was this that brought a weight to Alec's chest.

However, Alec had already dealt to some extent with what had earlier been a compelling need within himself to meet people's expectations. So he was able quickly to let the heaviness go. He did this by mentally setting a realistic and respectful boundary between

Yvette's needs and his own. He was free then to attend to her request for help in a professional manner.[1]

Making the Appointment

In situations like Yvette's at the church hall, and in most other initial requests for help, Alec follows a well-tried procedure. He responds to the person (in this case Yvette) sympathetically.[2] He ascertains that the arguing Yvette complains about is a chronic problem. Since arguing is a two-person activity, Alec refers to it as 'the arguing' – not, as Yvette implies, something that Zach alone does.

Alec asks Yvette if she is willing to see him in his office where he can give her his undivided attention for a bit less than an hour. This offers Yvette a safety-making, understood structure. There are critical situations where the person should be seen immediately, but usually a marriage conflict is chronic by nature and this is how Yvette has described hers and Zach's.

Alec suggests that their appointment be on Tuesday week in the evening; nine days ahead. This suggestion indicates to Yvette his confidence in her ability to contain her feeling of desperation; and without discounting its importance, he normalizes her situation of marital conflict. In doing this he also checks any tendency to generate drama within himself over her problem.

In the meantime (he tells Yvette), he would like her to think how she will let Zach know that she has spoken to Alec about their conflict. This demonstrates the pastor's respect for the marriage as the couple's domain, and respect for Zach.

Yvette is unwilling at this stage to involve Zach. Alec accepts her refusal without discussion, and the appointment hour with her is

[1]'Professional Christian' has been used sometimes as a derogatory term. But our calling by the Lord *is* our profession, and it includes practising the self-discipline that clarity of thinking and feeling require. We define the word 'professional' then as our calling by the Lord to be his disciplined and trained people.
[2]We use the word 'sympathetically' here in its everyday meaning of responsive kindness. However, counsellors need to understand from inner experience the clear distinction between sympathy and empathy that basic counselling texts describe.

agreed upon. Had Yvette agreed to tell Zach, Alec would have suggested that he see them together, and that she and Zach ring within two days to fix a mutually convenient hour for the following week.

Meantime

Over the next week, as Alec thinks from time to time about the couple he develops a hypothesis about Yvette's wish to see him alone. Based on his present understanding of both Yvette and Zach, it is still only a hypothesis to be tested as the counselling proceeds. The hypothesis relates to how much the couple agree they have a problem, and what stake each has in resolving it.

Though Yvette has initiated the request for help, Alec is aware that she is like all of us when we seek personal help. We bring ourselves to the counselling room partly wanting to change, and partly wanting to be made comfortable without changing. Changing our thinking and our behaviour takes much courage to initiate and continue.

Alec is also aware that it is natural for all of us to blame others when something goes wrong, and that the energy needed for clear thinking and problem-solving can get channelled uselessly into blaming.

True, some of us – instead of blaming others or even along with blaming them – will express excessive guilt and self-blame, perhaps claiming responsibility for the whole difficulty. Alec knows from personal experience that self-blame is not the same as repentance that leads to amendment of life; and that neither self-blame nor mutual blaming provides a pathway into problem-solving between two people.

These are the matters that Alec is aware of as he seeks clarity of focus for his coming interview with Yvette.

Getting Started

Yvette is sitting in a comfortable chair as she talks to Alec in his office. He too is seated, not behind his desk but facing her and at a distance that gives each some space. As he listens to Yvette's account of Zach's critical and argumentative behaviour, Alec is thinking on two levels.

He is considering Yvette's facts: the *content* or *subject* of the conflict:

- what Zach says,
- what she says and does in response, and
- what she is telling Alec about their life style and their respective roles in daily household matters.

He is also considering Yvette's and Zach's *feeling-responses* to each other:

- Yvette's sense of helplessness,
- Zach's anger as Yvette portrays it, and
- the probable underlying sense of helplessness in Zach and anger in Yvette.

These thoughts of Alec's about the couple's feeling-responses are partially informed guesses. However, he will almost certainly be getting a picture *beyond* the story of a persecuting husband with a victim wife. It is a picture of two hurting people desperately trying to keep their lives and their marriage together, in spite of or even *through* their conflict.

Alec is attending carefully to Yvette's story, and his clarifying questions let her know he takes her plight seriously and wants to understand *how it is for her*. At the same time he is listening with the *dyad* in mind, the Yvette-Zach dyad. With the respect he has for the marriage she has brought for counselling, he is not tempted to reinforce Yvette's feeling of being a helpless victim, either by questions or by sympathetic comments; nor is he tempted naïvely to locate the problem in her alone. He 'thinks dyad'. This is an expression we use when encouraging trainee counsellors to remember that a marriage problem involves both partners, even when only one presents it.

Thinking Dyad

Alec is already envisaging Zach in a third chair in the room with them. *The model or paradigm in marriage counselling has to be joint interviewing.*[3] Where Alec does not have both partners present he still maintains that paradigm. It affects all his interventions – his comments, his questions, his requests. This pertains even when the absent spouse remains absent throughout the whole process of the marriage counselling. *The skill of the counsellor lies to a considerable extent in maintaining the paradigm while continuing to be very sensitive to the burdens on the attending spouse.*

While giving Yvette ample opportunity to describe her plight, Alec is also pacing himself and managing the session so that he leaves sufficient time to make sense of the process of this interview and to plan with her what happens next.

Having listened and heard Yvette he asks that she monitor the arguments and criticisms between this and the next session. Will she make mental notes – or better still written ones, of the arguments she and Zach have? Will she note how much of their time together is free from Zach's negative comments? And will she note also what she is saying to herself, and what she is doing, when Zach criticizes her?

In asking Yvette to monitor the marriage conflict, Alec is inviting her to do two things that many people in conflict are not used to

[1] A variety of circumstances related to a couple or perhaps to a counsellor's stage of experience may result in individual interviews taking place, i.e. partners being seen alone. But this does not negate the paradigm of joint interviewing for marriage counselling.

doing: to believe that she can think and assess during conflicts, rather than become swamped in her feelings; and to notice how she manages her feeling-responses. Yvette may protest with Yes Buts, Nevers and Always, saying that nothing positive *ever* comes from Zach and that she can't do anything in response except feel bad.

Alec will recognize such a protest as a defence against wanting to change and move from her victim position. *But he will not confront her defence*, knowing that our defences are important parts of our personal functioning. To confront would be offensively premature and would result in Yvette's reinforcing her sense of helplessness.

To confront Yvette's defence would also force her to step back from the process she has begun, of joining as a client with a respect-fully empathic counsellor. Alec's relaxed response may simply be 'Well, keep your paper and pencil handy and have a go at monitoring yourself. I know you well enough to believe you can do it better than you think you can.'

Considering the Other Partner

Alec will also raise the importance of Zach's presence in the coun-selling sessions, perhaps with an opening comment of this kind: 'It would be good if Zach could hear what you've been expressing to me. Would he come with you next time if he had the opportunity, do you think?' In presenting the desirability of Zach's presence, Alec will have a sensitive awareness of Yvette's position as she experiences it. He will avoid any flavour of hortatory persuasion.

If Yvette refuses to invite Zach, or to let him know she is receiving counselling for their marriage difficulty, Alec considers further the reasons (his hypothesis) why Yvette wishes to continue seeing him alone. There are important implications to be considered if Alec accepts Yvette's refusal. These concern the effects on the marriage of such secrecy; Alec's pastoral responsibility for Zach; and the management of Yvette's transference and Alec's own counter-transference, whether positive or negative.[4]

[4]See split image, transference, chapter 22.

It is possible that Yvette's wish to continue receiving marriage counselling on her own comes out of some dire motivations, conscious or unconscious. But it is dramatic mind-reading for a counsellor to assume these. After all, some of the motivations in any of our choices may be suspect, even our desire to be a skilful marriage counsellor or a soul-winning pastor. Mixed motivations do not explain away the goodness in our motives for choosing a path to take.

Alec has learnt the dangers of mind-reading.[5] So instead of assuming that he knows her motives in not involving Zach in the counselling he takes time to give Yvette information about marriage counselling. He assumes that her wish comes partly from her being uninformed (as most people are) about professional processes in marriage counselling, and a related inability to predict the consequences of having joint rather than individual sessions. For instance, she may be imagining that in joint interviews she will be continuing her role as victim wife with critical husband.

If it appears that Yvette is still requesting individual sessions, Alec has a range of options. His decision will be influenced by the context in which he and Yvette are related as pastor and church member, and part of that context is referred to in what we have said above and will say elsewhere on this subject.

Let's suppose that Yvette agrees now that Zach should be invited. Alec arranges with her to tell Zach that she has seen him and that Alec has suggested that Zach needs to be *taken into account*. She will repeat this explanation when inviting Zach to come with her to see Alec, and she will ask him to ring Alec so a time can be set that suits all three.

Zach may refuse to come with Yvette, and for reasons that seem good to him. It is a blow to learn that one's spouse has talked to the minister about one's perceived failings; and to soften the blow, it will require great sensitivity and respect from the minister in contacts in the immediate time ahead.

[5] See mind-reading, chapter 10 p. 115.

Working with One Partner

In Zach's absence, Alec will still find it possible to counsel Yvette on their marriage. He will not do this by telling her what he assumes to be her defects. Further, he will avoid the trap that many beginning counsellors seem to fall into in such situations, the trap being to let any interview focus on *what the absent partner is doing wrong*.

For the inexperienced counsellor, this trap seems like being empathic, and it is not. In fact it comes close to joining with the partner present in blaming the absent one and expecting the absent one to change! Attempting to counsel a person by focusing on what the absent partner is doing wrong will always appear to that person as a collusion. The person being counselled can easily use the sessions to 'counsel' their partner later, or learn the destructive skill of mind-reading the partner.

In Zach's absence, Alec will not be joining Yvette in this way. As he picks up the to-and-fro of Yvette's and Zach's relating, he will work with Yvette by helping her to focus purposefully on her own part in it. He will also watch for any positive comments she makes about her marriage. He will ask about the good times she and Zach have shared, and get her thinking about what was special for her about those times. But he will also be doing something different that is essential in facilitating the changes Yvette needs to make. He will be taking her resentment seriously.

He will take time to listen and hear as she expresses her resentment towards Zach. 'Resentment is always justified',[6] it has been said, and in a way this is true. Alec will be listening with the true aspect of this in mind. Yvette may have learned very early in life to cover her sense of helplessness with resentment. Helplessness is a very scary feeling; resentment is in some ways empowering. But in the end neither state is constructive in relationships.

If Alec has experienced the genuine empowerment that comes from taking responsibility for his own sense of helplessness, he no longer has to depend on resentment to cover it. He will, then,

[6]Glennon, J., *Your Healing Is Within You*, Hodder & Stoughton, London 1978.

understand something of the purpose of Yvette's resentment. So he will be more able to respond usefully to her expressions of resentment, rather than defensively.

So Alec enters into Zach's and Yvette's marriage as one who facilitates their work of dealing with their very common relationship difficulty. Let's leave him with this task. Later in chapter 4 we will join another minister as he prepares for a first joint counselling session with another couple, Una and Vincent.

3

COUNSELLING AS CHRISTIANS

Biblical Anthropology

'We've come to see you because we want Christian counselling,' said the couple as they sat down in Beryl's study. Beryl felt uncomfortable. She guessed, rightly as it turned out, that this couple had definite ideas on how she should run the counselling session – what she should do and what she should not do.

Beryl was convinced that her counselling was Christian in that

- she espoused biblical values;
- she had a lively faith in Jesus Christ in whom she aimed to live and move and have her being;
- she was committed to Christian values of morality in her life and ministry;
- she saw psychology as a description of how human nature, created by God, works.

Yet this couple seemed to be requesting something different, and that expectation seemed to Beryl to stem from the views of church friends and popular writers. Their sureness that they wanted specifically Christian counselling led Beryl to consider what those specifics might be. She decided to raise it as an issue at her local inter-church group for ministry and pastoral care. We will come to their discussion in a moment, but first let's look at the issue ourselves.

Christians who Counsel

Like Beryl, we too are challenged by people who require Christian counselling and their requirement is one with which we challenge ourselves personally and in discussion groups. As Christians who counsel, and who train and supervise counsellors, we are acutely aware of difficulties around the title 'Christian counsellor'. We see the importance of Christian counsellors being well-trained and competent in the work they do, and thereby witnessing well as servants of the living God. The difficulty is that the title does not clearly indicate the working mode or the skill of the person who appropriates it.

Of course, neither does a generic title such as counselling psychologist, psychotherapist, counselling pastor or social worker, although these usually imply a recognized discipline, or accreditation and membership of a group with a code of ethics. Many Christians with such accreditation would prefer to be known in Christian circles as 'a counselling Christian' rather than 'a Christian counsellor'.

In our own case, we prefer to have people trust us because we are known to be well-trained and consistently supervised in the work we do. We hope too that we are known as people of moral integrity who want to be true to Christian biblical values; to be thoroughly in the world without succumbing to the world's values.

Our concern here is not to be protagonists for a particular name or title. It is that Christians should exercise care and thought as they consider what it means to be a Christian counsellor and do 'Christian counselling'. These terms are not easily defined in a helpful way, as Beryl found when her group for ministry and pastoral care met and discussed the issue. Some members were unsympathetic to her expressed dilemma.

Christian versus Secular

'It's clear what we should be doing as Christian counsellors,' said Charles. 'Secular psychologies can't be accepted and used by God's people. Man-made ideas simply lead us astray when we're dealing with people's souls. We must have a totally scriptural way of counselling.'

Deirdre broke in timidly: 'Charles, I want to be true to Scripture but can you be sure which Scriptures to use for a couple in conflict? They're unique people. They are hurting, they're usually angry too. Scripture can be used like a brick, you know.'

'You're leaving out the Holy Spirit, Deirdre! For one thing, I'm empathic with people. For another, I can trust the Holy Spirit to bring the right Scriptures to my mind as I counsel. I know. I've experienced it.'

'Well,' said Eric, 'it's not Scripture passages so much as a biblical theology we need to live by. As ministers we need the discipline of theology when we counsel. But I respect psychology too and I believe it's valid for us to use the insights it gives. However, it's a completely different frame of reference. In my experience there isn't much common ground between the two disciplines when you're counselling a couple. I think you just have to listen to people and then decide which discipline you use.'

Frances disagreed. 'I've found there's a great amount of common ground. All truth is God's truth, after all.'

'But secular models all reject the fact of sin,' protested Charles, 'so how can they be true?'

'You don't have to take secular psychologists' assumptions about good and evil – or lack of,' said Frances. 'If they're saying something real about the way life is for women and men, then surely we can accept that truth, even if the seculars don't recognize it comes from God? Surely we can learn to understand how they work to bring about healing between men and women, surely we can use their methods just as we do in medical and literary studies?'

'I agree with Frances,' said Giles. 'There has to be a unity between sound theology and sound psychology. There must be, in the nature of things. We need to respect both. What does it matter if a particular psychology was developed by an atheist or a rationalist? Even if in his personal life he didn't live up to what he could understand, he might have grasped a lot more than we do about healing inner conflicts and relationship problems. After all we don't always live up to the Gospel we preach.'

The attitudes expressed in this discussion highlight the challenge we counsellors have as we try to work out a biblical Christian anthropology. A range of views, including those expressed by Beryl's colleagues, is spelt out by Roger Hurding.[1] He identifies such views as 'excluding', 'compartmentalized', 'eclectic' and 'assimilative'.

Hurding also gives a critique of assumptions held about human nature and the processes by which people change through counselling.[2] Though his book says very little about marriage counselling and is not concerned with the how-to's of counselling, his concept of a biblical anthropology is useful for counsellors as they think about their principles and their practice.

Our Multiple Belief Systems

Every counselling Christian and every pastor works from a belief system: actually, from several belief systems. These may be consistent, but human nature is such that there may be inconsistencies in them, even where the person who holds them is a careful and studious thinker. By 'belief system' we mean something more limited perhaps than what some call a world view and some (even more impressively) call *Weltanschauung*.

A belief system has to do with interconnected ideas about how life is and how the world is. For instance, a belief system that holds to the idea of objective values has this as its foundation: that 'certain attitudes are really true and others really false to the kind of thing the universe is and the kind of things we are'.[3]

[1]Hurding, Roger, *Roots and Shoots*, Hodder & Stoughton, London, 1985, p. 265ff.
[2]Ibid, p. 244ff.
[3]Lewis, C.S. *The Abolition of Man*, O.U.P. 1943 and Fount Paperbacks 1978, p. 16.

For us (the authors), that idea accords with our life experience and our counselling experience. We believe that certain values and behaviours are built into reality. This is the way goodness is. This is the way life works. A society cannot make reality different by sanctioning certain forms of greed, intimidation and deceit, or of sexual exploitation and license. The sanctioning does not and cannot unmake what is built into reality. It unmakes the society and itself.

In each Christian who counsels, there is

- a set of thought-out and evaluated theological beliefs about the relationship between God and humankind. There is also

- a set of thought-out and evaluated psychological beliefs about how human nature operates, and principles about how behaviour might be changed. Along with these two systems of belief, there is yet

- a third set by which we carry out much of our living and doing. This belief system is habitual; it is generally not thought-out or evaluated, and it springs largely from our experiences in our family of origin, the family or group in which we spent our childhood. It has been called by various names, names which each usefully emphasize some of its aspects. We shall simply call it 'the third belief system'.

The Third Belief System

Our third system may line up with our thought-out beliefs in a number of respects; in other respects it may be in conflict with them. We are all used to perceiving and identifying this habitual and implicit belief system in other people, as counsellors we need to acknowledge that we too have such a third system; we too are subject to our humanity and to our distortions, as our clients are to theirs.

For instance, Colin is very clear in his faith around repentance, salvation and sanctification; he is committed in his regular prayer and worship; and he is a competent pastoral counsellor who does much excellent work. But Colin gets stuck from time to time with those he counsels; he loses focus and his clients stop gaining clarity of insight.

Colin's habitual system has sentimental ideas about love that sabotage what he understands from his thought-through belief systems. In consequence, he finds it hard to achieve competent limit-setting. This means that at times, instead of showing genuine empathy he acts towards people in a way that they see as extremely loving, caring and understanding. In fact, the sponginess of Colin's would-be empathy at these times debilitates people's self-discipline. It is on self-discipline that genuine self-love and growth depend.

Our habitual belief system will always trip us up some way, because while we can keep it monitored to some extent, we will continue to be somewhat subject to its biases till the end of our lives on earth. But we can be taking care as counsellors to ensure that as far as humanly possible we are working from our other belief systems; those that are consistent with our best understanding of biblical revelation, and consistent with the best knowledge of human nature that psychology and therapeutic theory can give us.

Descriptions of How Human Nature Works

Psychology, in so far as it is true, is a description of how human nature works. Psychology, then, seeks to understand more and more the mechanics of human nature – which comes from God's creation. It is exploring the wonder of what our God already knows all about. God is no more surprised by psychological defence mechanisms or the effects of intermittent reinforcement than he is by the latest discovery of nuclear physics.

Every psychological system and every therapeutic modality is an attempt to describe how human nature works. Inevitably it is partial, limited by its very nature, and distorted by the pre-existing third belief system of its author. All attempts to express biblical understanding are similarly partial and limited by their nature.

Each theorist in the field of human relations and counselling believes in some kind of paradise or heaven on earth: the ideal to be aimed for, and for which his or her method prescribes. 'Self-actual-ization' and 'autonomy' are two of these ideals, but there are many more that come from the belief systems of theorists and colour their presentation; and they may vary according to whether the individual or the couple or the family is the focus.

Sigmund Freud saw the goal of successful psychoanalysis as the ability to love and to work, and also expressed it in terms of giving up the miserable comfort of neuroses to face the ordinary miseries of everyday life. No pie in the sky for Sigmund: just stark reality.

Christian professionals need to recognize that in theorists' desire for the paradise they present, there is some genuine understanding of what people do with themselves and with others in relationships – genuine perceptions about human nature gone askew. We need to respect the information and the good motives they have in presenting their ideals, and value these.

When we counsel people who refuse to lay hold on life, and falsely believe that their compulsive dependency or self-effacement is Christian, we are glad to have Abraham Maslow's concept of a hier-archy of human needs (which includes self-actualization) as we help them to gain health. When we counsel couples where one partner has never owned his separateness, yet believes he is all-giving and all-loving, we appreciate Eric Berne's disciples' use in therapy of the concepts of symbiosis and autonomy.

Where we differ from such theorists' views is not so much in seeing the freedom mentioned as false, as in recognizing that any emotional freedom we achieve is not heaven. Nor is it an end in itself. Even though our newfound freedoms from false thinking and consequent behaviour may be very good for us and for others, we do not live only to ourselves and we do not live only to those around us. *We are called to bring the freedoms we have gained under the Lordship of Jesus Christ.*

Consequently the Christian professional will bring her own views of humankind as she understands it from within her faith. (That faith, ideally, needs to be informed by proper exegesis, worked through in sound theology, tested in experience and evident in the fruits of the Spirit.) Her view of humankind is that people are created in the image of God, and are fallen through sin; that they are redeemable through Jesus Christ and that they are meant for communion with God, who has made them for himself.

From that belief system, she will seek to understand what attitudes and approaches, in any psychological theory, are true to 'the kind of thing the universe is and the kind of things we are', and what parts of these attitudes and approaches cannot be eventually brought under the Lordship of Christ because they go against what is good and true.

Psychology in Pastoral Care

In pastoral care down the centuries, Christians consistently used whatever psychological understanding was available to them.[4] With the burgeoning of psychology as a formal discipline in the twentieth century, some pastoral counsellors found the new expression of knowledge most helpful and also impressive.

So there was a natural tendency to overvalue what they were benefiting from: a tendency that resulted in their disregarding biblical understanding and Christian tradition. Where pastoral counsellors embraced psychological counselling theories without evaluating them in faith terms and in the light of biblical theology, problems and confusion resulted.

In 1970 Jay Adams made a radical contribution in criticizing this tendency and demanding that Christians bring the Bible and biblical understanding back into counselling.[5] We believe he went too far in his rejection of psychology, and that by doing so he disregarded a large part of God's revelation to us through his creation.

We believe that it is better to approach apparently alien ways of

[4] See for instance Clebsch and Jaekle, *Pastoral Care In Historical Perspective*, Jason Chonson, 1975.
[5] Adams, J., *Competent to Counsel*, Presbyterian and Reformed Publishing Co., 1970.

thinking in a spirit of goodwill and enquiry. We can trust that those who think differently from us have goodness in their thinking; and that this goodness, being of God's goodness, is something we need to accept as such. From there we can still be alert to false (unbiblical) premises and conclusions in such people's thinking, and reject these.

Such discernment is fine-tuned by long experience of people promoting their ideas and their therapies, or healing strategies. Discernment is also needed in assessing ideas of Christian counselling and healing. Those who present them may be without benefit of theology and psychological awareness; and alertness to unbiblical premises and conclusions in such formulations of Christian counselling is needed. This is perhaps particularly so in those who are likely to declare 'The Bible says' and believe that we can have paradise on earth — which is not what Jesus believed!

Developing Biblical Anthropology

In our pursuit of an adequate biblical anthropology we have learnt much from secular counsellors. Some of these teachers have shown themselves to be more people-respecting than many Christians are. They have stretched our understanding of human nature, and of the processes of human relating and other human behaviour.[6]

At times it has been important to develop a sharp awareness of their assumptions about the goals of life; to be conscious of where their concepts of a therapeutic heaven differ from our belief that the goal of life is to glorify God and enjoy him for ever. But it has also been important to immerse ourselves in secular disciplines to understand genuinely, and *from the inside*, how they work and how we could assimilate them to increase our effectiveness as therapists.

Over the years, we placed ourselves under the discipline of our teachers and supervisors so that our functioning as counsellors could be regularly reviewed and affirmed or corrected as need be. Over time we did this in some different counselling methodologies, with

[6] Jesus showed himself to be people-respecting, and he taught in a stretching way too.

the aim of serving better the wide range of clients with whom we worked.

We made mistakes as we went. Sometimes we were slow to see the steps necessary in bringing some particular psychological concept under the Lordship of Jesus Christ. Sometimes we chose to use strategies that did not stand the test of time and experience, either theologically or psychologically. But alongside our learning from good teachers of secular psychotherapy, we sought to hold fast only to what was good; and that required vigilance.

So our understanding of biblical anthropology was expanded and corrected as we added to our knowledge of the human nature which is God's creation. This has not placed our faith in Jesus Christ under threat. We do not believe that our faith is so fragile that it will fail when we have to struggle with some new way of seeing things.

God has made his world, and if we are seeking to understand better some part of his creation, we are on his side. God has redeemed his world, and if we are seeking to help someone either to let go false assumptions about redemption or to take up attitudes and behaviours that are closer to a life of goodness and redemption, then we are called to explore and understand all we can about the processes of human nature.

Gradually we have moved, and expect to continue moving, into an integration where we find that at times our theology informs our counselling practice, and at times our counselling practice deepens our understanding of theology, or corrects a shallow or trite aspect of our understanding.

Our biblical anthropology demands that we acquire the best knowledge we can about how human nature works and how people can change their behaviour. It requires that we be consistently under authority, using consultation or supervision to monitor and maintain the way we respect and value the people we counsel. It also requires that we maintain our relationship with our heavenly Father, who is also the Father of those we counsel, whether they recognize him or not; and that we consistently check the anthropology – both explicit and implicit – in our working with people.

In Beryl's ministry and pastoral care group where she raised the question of a couple's requirement of Christian counselling, each member responded according to his or her systems of belief. And Beryl had come to the group with those that were unique to her: her explicit theological system of belief, her explicit psychological system of belief, and her implicit assumptions, which influenced her strongly and which lay mostly outside of her conscious awareness.

Beryl's Third System

Beryl's third belief system, like all 'thirds', was about how life was to be for her and for others, what she had to do to survive well, how she had to relate to others, what she was to expect from herself. Beryl experienced a scared feeling at Charles's definite response ('Secular psychologies can't be used by God's people'). She had felt a little frightened also by the way the couple expressed their definite requirement.

Beryl's response to Charles and to the couple mirrored some of her childhood fears. Her very caring and authoritarian grandmother had never seemed to doubt her own opinions and her definite expectations that Beryl should live by her (Grandmother's) tenets. Beryl had been intimidated by Grandmother's forcefulness of personality, and had felt some element of menace in it. How could she survive if she questioned her beloved Grandmother? Grandmother seemed like God. Or rather, God's image for Beryl took on some elements of menacing watchfulness and demand.

Through her biblical understanding and her experiences of love of kinds different from Grandmother's love, she had formed a much more realistic image of God. It was closer to the images given by her Lord Jesus Christ. However, when confronted by those who (like Grandmother) presented demands in the name of God in a totally dogmatic and definite way, Beryl became uncertain of her own biblical and counselling understanding.

Beryl is now consciously identifying her third system more clearly, and relating it to her biblical and psychological systems.[7] She is less

[7]Discussed further: chapter 8, pp. 93.

likely in future to be intimidated by the definiteness of her colleagues' views, and by the demands of clients. Clients and colleagues alike will benefit from her educated systems. She will be a freer person able to meet them in their 'thirds' as well as in the realities of their faith and behaviour.

In describing childhood influences on Beryl, we are defining as the third system what other writers allude to in asking counsellors to be aware that they bring habitual, learnt attitudes to their work with clients. (Counter-transference is commonly alluded to and is part of these attitudes.)

We are calling it the third system as a simple description of a common phenomenon: a description that can help counsellors monitor and supervise themselves and their reactions even while they are actually counselling; while they are putting into practice their biblical and psychological understandings of themselves and their clients.

4

FIRST JOINT INTERVIEW

David is in his rectory study, setting out three chairs of equal height in the form of a triangle. He is about to see Una and Vincent for the counselling session they have requested. He has arranged to be free from phone calls and other interruptions for the next hour and a half, knowing that this session will take the best part of an hour. After that he will be making some notes and reflecting on the interview.

At the time of the couple's request, David was able, in an easygoing way, to fill some gaps in his information about them. He has these facts at hand:

- the year of their marriage
- their ages and occupations
- any previous marriages
- the names and ages of all children

Knowing them also as parishioners, David now has a fuller context in which to place Vincent and Una. So, when he sits down with this particular couple, the usual preliminary questions and formalities are unnecessary. Counselling, by its professional nature, is a structured task, not an informal talk over a cup of tea.[1] David indicates the

[1] It's surprising that many otherwise careful and sensible people dignify their cup-of-tea-and-talk with the title 'counselling'. Christians, as well as others, bring the high discipline of counselling into disrepute if they take to themselves the title of 'counsellor' without regard for professional standards, ethics and skills.

nature of the task very soon by asking 'What is the issue in your marriage that you're concerned about?'

Una: 'It's a bit difficult to describe. But Vince isn't around when I need him. Or if he is, he doesn't do anything to help. He's too busy being the good guy around the church, being helpful to other people, doing things for them. When I ask him to help around the home, he says he's too busy, or he needs a rest or something'. (*Una starts her statement tentatively, but gathers momentum as she goes along.*)

Vincent: 'That's not fair. I do a lot of things around the place . . .'

Una: 'Yes, but you don't do the things I really need. You don't stop the children from fighting. You don't make them do their jobs.'

Vincent: 'I do tell them to do their jobs.'

Una: 'But you say it too softly. You don't mean it. You don't insist. You let them get away with too much. And when I yell at them, you tell me to calm down, and then the children know you're on their side.'

Vincent: 'I'm not on their side, but yelling at them doesn't get you anywhere.'

Una: 'You're doing it again, Vince, you're blaming me for their behaviour.'

Vincent: 'I'm not blaming you, darling, I'm just saying yelling doesn't work.'

Una: 'You are blaming me. And you always get out of it by saying you're just being sensible.'

Vincent: 'Rector, what's the use? It's always me she blames. We never seem to have a reasonable discussion.'

David's Observations

David listens, building up a picture of the way Vincent and Una relate as they struggle with a particular issue. He observes silently that Una is forthright in stating her concern, and articulate; and her tone is accusing. Vincent, he notes, seems quieter, defending himself with apparent reasonableness; and his tone tends to be placating.

These mental observations of David's are different from interpretations of each partner's *motives*. If David were to jump into an unspoken assessment of motives at this stage, he would lose sight of his counselling task. And he could easily be drawn into the couple's conflict, compounding it by his very eagerness to help. On the other hand, he could discount their problem by defining it as a need for education in child management, and by suggesting they go on a parenting course.[2]

David's task as a counsellor is to pay close attention to the content and the process of Una's and Vincent's dialogue. He attends to

- what they are saying – *content*
- how they are relating to each other, alongside their words – *process*
- how their words are affecting each other – *process*

Any hypothesis David draws from his observations will be very tentative at this stage. As the session progresses, he will be looking for evidence to strengthen his hypotheses, or to modify or discard them. There is a wealth of lively interaction in Una's and Vincent's mode of relating (their process) for David to pay attention to. He notices that even though they are in unhappy conflict, each of them continues to reach out, making emotional contact with the other; and thus

- there is a vigour in their attacking and defending,
- each wants the other to change behaviour so that harmony can come into their home, and each feels blamed.

In their chronic complaints, there seems to be little entrenched bitterness, and it may be of positive significance that Una refers to

[2]An education course could teach Vincent and Una some useful parenting skills as a couple. When they have resolved their marriage conflict, and are relating to their children as a dyadic team, such skills may enhance their parenting. But these are not a substitute for counselling.

Vincent as Vince, and he calls her darling. Though endearments can also be used as manipulative ploys, there's no need to suspect that these are such. So David can make a reasonable hypothesis that both Vincent and Una have much invested in resolving their conflict.

We will return to this couple later, and move now to the scene of another first interview for David.

Tim and Sally

When David's churchwarden Tim and his wife Sally come for their first interview, David observes a different pattern of marital communication. Tim opens by going in to bat immediately.

Tim: 'Rector, we need help. I've brought Sally because I can't get through to her any more. She lets the house get in a frightful mess, and the children really don't know how to behave. When I point things out strongly enough, she improves for a while and then it's back to the old mess. It's dreadful coming home to squalling children and unmade beds. I've tried everything, Rector. I've been patient with her, I've even shouted at her – and I don't like myself for that, either as a husband or a Christian. And there's still chaos at home.

'And money, she spends it like water. Any money I give her just disappears, and she needs more. When I asked her what she did with this week's amount, she said food costs a lot more now; as if that's an answer. And she doesn't want to make love. She'll do anything to avoid it. I'm a loving man and I want us to make love, but even when she agrees, she doesn't enjoy it and that spoils it for me too.'

David's Observations

David notices that Tim directs his words to him without reference to Sally's presence. He notices also that Sally doesn't interrupt Tim, and he observes the expression that comes on Sally's face in response to Tim's blaming words. So while it is Tim who speaks, David is aware that both partners in the marriage are with him, and he is paying attention to a pattern of relating (perhaps not their only or habitual pattern) being played out in front of him.

As well as observing the couple's process, David is listening carefully to what Tim says – to the content of his words. He doesn't assess Tim as a chauvinistic male or as a hard-done-by husband; any assessment would be premature at this point and therefore unprofessional. ('Really?' responds the fuming reader incredulously. 'Not see Tim for what he is? What's premature about that?' Of course all of us do have personal responses to Tim. These may vary from fury to perhaps even sympathy, depending on our own frustrating experiences with – or as – a Tim or a Sally. However, a prerequisite ability for a counsellor is to move past personal feelings about a client's unproductive behaviour, for the very reason that such feelings in a counsellor are unproductive for the goal of client change.)

There is another reason why David avoids judgments and premature assessments. They pre-empt a counsellor's later attempts to *help a couple to define their problem in a way that will contribute to problem-solving.* Such an attempt must come later, after the counsellor has joined[3] with the spouses: after they can each trust that he accepts and understands their shared plight.

Having heard Tim, David decides to ask Sally an open-ended question.

David: 'Sally, how do you see these things?'

David will observe how Sally replies. She may speak confidently because she has been asked respectfully for her perception. She may speak tentatively with frequent glances at Tim. She may shift all blame for her plight onto Tim. In her response – and this will be very significant for David to notice – she may ignore the content of what Tim has said: the content of her words of response may have no

[3]In joining with the couple the counsellor succeeds in communicating to them that he is understanding the thoughts and feelings of each of them.

linking point with Tim's words. In fact, Sally's reply fits a different pattern again.

Sally: 'Well, he's right in a way. The house isn't as tidy as I would like it to be, and the children are difficult by the time he gets home. But Tim has no idea of the pressures on me through the day, and how hard I try to have everything tidy for him. The children are so demanding. I'm tired by late afternoon. Tim's no help, coming in growling and criticizing. He makes me feel even more helpless. He's much better at blaming than helping. He leaves his clothes lying around in the morning, he comes home expecting to be waited on, and he expects not to be pestered by the children.'

Tim: 'My working day's a hard one. I need to wind down when I come home. I need time to be quiet, and the children are not under control.'

Sally: 'You've had a hard day! What sort of day do you think I've had? I don't get a chance to unwind until the children are asleep for the night. And then there's ironing to be done, and you object if I watch television while I do it.'

Tim: 'You shouldn't be doing the ironing then. We should be spending that time together. I don't think you realize how it hurts when you show you're more interested in the ironing and the television than you are in me.'

David's Reflections

David uses the skills he has learned in pastoral care courses, of listening and empathy. He understands the importance of helping parishioners to talk about their own behaviour and feelings. He knows that a commonsense, reasoning response does not often reach the *feeling* interaction of a couple in a useful way.

David also understands that there are many complex levels to the interaction of any couple, and many motivations and meanings to their feelings, their assumptions and their behaviour. Some of these will remain outside of their conscious awareness always, and they do not need to be explored in order to help a couple to achieve conflict-resolution. Consequently, much of what David might speculate about Sally's and Tim's unconscious motivations he leaves aside, in order to attend to them and meet them in their present unhappiness.

His immediate task is to help the couple to resolve the area of conflict that they present. If they can accept and use his help, the resolution of this area of conflict may lessen their conflict in other areas. It may also give them the courage to become conscious of some of their underlying feelings and assumptions, and of motivations and meanings which at this stage are outside of their awareness.

David is faced with two people who seem very much bound up with each other, even though negatively bound. An important part of David's task is this:

- to help Tim and Sally each to 'own' their own feelings and behaviour;
- to insist even that they do so;
- and then, to begin helping them perceive how one provokes the other's response, and how that one then responds to the response.

So David is concerned with

- what Tim is feeling and doing,
- what Sally is feeling and doing, and
- how each is perceiving the other's behaviour and responding to it.

David: 'So, Tim, you're wanting some peace, and you're wanting Sally to have things under control. And Sally, you're wanting some respite and you're not getting it.'

Sally: 'Yes. He doesn't help. He criticizes instead of helping. He should be a real father and pay attention to the children and show he loves them. Then I could get on with the evening meal.'

Tim: 'I do love the children, but they're in such a state when I get home that I can't stand it. You really have to get your act together, Sally, and manage the children.'

Sally: 'There you go, criticizing me again instead of taking your responsibility as a father. You think you're God Almighty – oh, sorry, Rector – and you expect everything to be just right for you.'

David: 'So you each feel pretty desperate. Sally, you see Tim as critical, and Tim, you see Sally as letting you down.'

David has made two responses. Each of them is dyadic in form – that is, he refers to both partners in the one response – so as to emphasize the interactional nature of their behaviour.

Circular Interaction

As the process continues, David helps Sally and Tim to express more about their interaction: what they say, do and think as they relate to each other in the conflict. He decides it could be useful for them at this stage if he diagrammed the pattern he is beginning to observe. He has large sheets of paper and card that he can use for purposes such as this, but he decides to stand up and use the whiteboard attached to the wall.[4]

He invites Tim and Sally to shift their chairs a little so they can watch him producing this diagram.[5]

---

[4] As ministers are well aware, visual aids enable people to understand new ideas. Not all people 'audit' readily in the sense of understanding ideas primarily through hearing them. Apart from 'visualizers' who are helped by 'seeing' ideas, there are people who are primarily kinetic: their ability to handle abstract ideas is enhanced when they literally grasp them; for this reason a therapist may use movement, modelling in clay and similar kinetic aids.

[5] Counsellors who stand up and move occasionally (and appropriately) and invite clients to do the same, enliven their sessions by encouraging energy to flow. Energy can become 'stuck' when clients and counsellors simply sit and talk throughout a session.

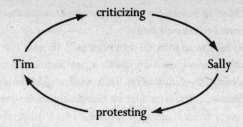

As he does this, David knows he is taking a risk. He is committing himself by articulating a process that he is still tentative about. However, he can do it acceptably by owning it as his perception.

David: 'This is how I see it. Tim, would you want to use a word other than "criticizing"? . . . Sally, is "criticizing" the word you would want there? . . . And Sally, is the word "protesting" about right for you? . . . And Tim, is it what you see Sally doing in this struggle?'

In David's experience couples usually agree to general words such as 'criticizing' and 'protesting'. (In Una's and Vincent's case, the words could well be 'correcting' and 'placating'.) David shows a readiness to accommodate to the couple's choice of alternative words, provided these are present participles and the couple agree on them together. It is vital that David keeps the couple to descriptions of their *behaviour* (criticizing, protesting), so they do not slide on to *motives* or the eventual *outcome*. Each may want to introduce words like 'hurt' and 'angry', or to explain an outcome, such as 'Then we each retreat into silence'.

When there is agreement about the behaviours, David can suggest the following pattern: Tim criticizes, then Sally protests, then Tim feels pressure to criticize more, then Sally protests more, and the repetitive behaviours are thus confirmed and reinforced.

David has given the couple a schema, and he has diagrammed it. It refers to their interactional behaviour. It is simple because it extrapolates one aspect of their conflict, but this does not mean that it is simplistic. The beauty of circular interaction schemata is that they give couples an opportunity to consider their conflict together. This shared considering can lead on later to conflict-resolution, which of its nature must be a shared thing.

Before seeing the schema David presents, Sally and Tim have each felt a rightness about their own position, and each has perceived the other as causing their difficulty. Thus each has been blaming the other. The schema, given visually by David as well as verbally, takes their focus away from blaming, and places it on a relatively objective and shared perception.

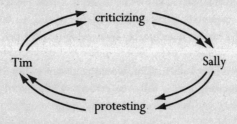

Tim and Sally can now grasp that each builds on the other's response and each gets into an extreme behaviour. The chronic process, which has seemed out of control, begins to make sense to them. They see that each contributes to it in turn, and neither of them is the one to blame. This brings a certain relief to them, a shared relief.

The relief that comes with objectifying the pattern of their conflict does not resolve it. It makes it more manageable for the couple. By this process, David has begun to change the definition of their problem into a form where changes can be made.[6] Thus he is beginning to define the problem for the couple in problem-solving terms – and in terms of observable behaviour. He will say that by protesting or criticizing, each of them has been really wanting to solve something, even though these behaviours have not worked for them.

We mentioned earlier that there are levels of motivation and meaning to Tim's and Sally's behaviour of which they are unaware. This is true of all of us. As their shared perception releases them to

[6]David starts with the particular conflict they present, and he knows that wider aspects of their relationship will come into focus as counselling proceeds.

begin problem-solving, each may gain insight about some of these other levels.

If Sally's resentment at Tim's criticisms has led her to act less competently than she is capable of doing, she may reach a point of awareness where she wants to say so. If Tim's habit of criticizing has been reinforced by his assumption that criticizing is the only way to feel strong (instead of helpless and out of control), he may reach some insight about what genuine strength consists of; and then he may want to disclose this verbally. However, such insights are very unlikely to emerge in a first interview.

It is not David's task to press for awareness of other levels of motivation. Such awareness may come as the couple engage mutually in problem-solving, but perhaps it will not come until long after their counselling sessions with David are over. And at this stage they are at the very beginning of their counselling.

David will bring the first interview with Sally and Tim to a close soon after he is satisfied that they have a shared perception of the circular nature of their behaviour. He will ascertain that both of them see criticizing and protesting as behaviours that they would like to modify, and he will take time to hear their relief and perhaps exhilaration at the possibility of finding a way out of this area of conflict – along with some doubts as well.

He will avoid taking up and expanding discussion on other aspects of their relationship, knowing that it is better for them to go away together with a shared theme and a clear focus. David will tell them that a number of counselling interviews will probably be needed to facilitate their task of changing the way they attempt to solve their problems.

Home Practice

David will also suggest to them some home practice: to catch themselves when they notice the negative behaviours that they have used in unsuccessful attempts to solve problems. Tim is to tell Sally when *he* catches himself criticizing her. Sally is to tell Tim when *she* catches herself protesting. It is a sound principle that home practice tasks are given only when they have already been practised in the safety of the interview, so David will encourage Tim and Sally to practise a little before the interview concludes.

This practice can be contrived with beneficial good humour, by encouraging each to give an exaggerated version of their negative interaction, beginning with Sally. David can coach them in this task. 'Come on Sally, tell him! "*You* try doing the washing and ironing and picking up dirty socks and attending to the children and ..." Tim, criticize her properly! Tell her she never cares about you enough, and she always forgets to have the children quiet enough. Right. Now Sally, begin to respond to Tim and then catch yourself. Tim, start answering her and catch yourself . . .'

David takes care that, as far as he can, he is enabling the couple to go away with some lightness and shared hope. (The strategy just described can be useful to that end for many couples, but not all.) However, if it cannot be achieved, he is content with simply affirming each partner comfortably as he negotiates with them the hour for their second appointment.

After the Interview

There are questions David asks himself as he reviews a first joint interview when the couple have left. Here they are:

- Do I think that each of the partners felt listened to adequately by me, and did each gain a new understanding of what they have been trying to do in their relationship?

- Is this a case within my competence, or is it better if I consider a referral to a more highly trained marriage counsellor?

- Are there any points which, on reflection, I recognize that I missed, or glossed over, or didn't know how to handle?

David then makes extensive notes of the interview, recording as much as possible the actual words and phrases the couple have used to describe their situation and their meanings in the struggle. He notes their presenting problem, along with his understanding and theirs of the underlying, circular pattern of relating. He notes also where he did well in the interview and where he thinks he missed some of the process, so that he can review the session with his supervisor.

5

SECOND JOINT INTERVIEW

Before Tim and Sally entered the previous chapter we introduced Una and Vincent and said that we would return to them later. We will focus on them in this chapter to demonstrate how a second joint interview might proceed. It will be an account of one experienced counsellor's specific interventions with a particular husband and wife, each of whom is a unique personality. It will also include our explanations and comments on David's use of theory and practice.

In a second interview with Tim and Sally, David's specific interventions would be very different, because he would be working with their unique personalities and their unique marriage. He would, however, be offering them a continuance of the structure provided by the circular interaction diagram, and encouraging each to take responsibility for their own part in the interaction. He would be making the same distinctions between *feelings* and *states* (and using them in relation to *behaviour* and *thinking*) that he will make in the session he is about to have with Una and Vincent. With Tim and Sally there would be similarities in the overall process on the diagram, but the particularities would be different.

All of this is part of the counselling *model* he uses. His *goal* with all couples is consistent: increased freedom (under God and goodness[1])

---

[1] Since all goodness and all truth comes from God, the goal of counselling is a consistent one, whoever the clients are. However, we are not implying that marriage counselling with couples who do not claim to be Christian is evangelism. While the prophetic and the caring tasks are present in helping people, by counselling, to know the truth, the role of the counsellor is not one of evangelist.

for the partners to receive and give love, and to face the sometimes painful truths that attend maturity in a marriage.

Therefore, what David would say to Tim and Sally, how he would say it, and the pace and timing of his interventions, would follow a different sequence and pattern from the counselling he will do with Una and Vincent. Attuned to them and flowing with them, he will counsel in a unique way, but still with the disciplines his calling requires of him.

We hope that ministers will benefit from the following account of David's counselling with Una and Vincent, not because it can offer a 'how to' of the exact words of response at any point. It can't. Its purpose is to help ministers gain familiarity with a model, and to see how the competent and effective use of this model is undergirded by a broad and deep understanding of theory and practice.

Una and Vincent

Una and Vincent had felt buoyant as they left their first session with David. They had taken with them a large sheet of paper on which with David's help and their own choice of present participles, they had diagrammed their interaction concerning their chronic conflict.

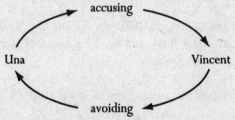

The couple have returned, and are waiting comfortably and thoughtfully for David to open their second session. He wants to link them back to their first session. He also wants them to begin with where they are right now. But Una and Vincent are politely deferring to David.

David: 'Where do you want to start?'

Vincent: 'Well, it's been an interesting week.'

Una: 'Yes, it has.'

David: 'How did you use our session during this past week?'

Una: 'We found it helpful. We actually had some fun catching ourselves. On the first night, I stopped what I was saying, and told Vince I was accusing; and he laughed and said he was avoiding. And it was true! We managed to catch ourselves several times during the week.'

Vincent: 'It was harder for me to catch myself avoiding than to see when you were accusing.'

Una: 'Yes, for me too. I'd be launched into accusing, and then think "What's going on? Vince must be avoiding and I haven't noticed, I'm so busy trying to get him to help me with the children." It's been interesting to notice what we do together in this circular way. But it hasn't changed anything; Vince still doesn't stop the children from fighting.'

Vincent: 'Oh yes, I did once. Don't you remember that time I shouted at them?'

Una: 'So you did.'

David: 'You shouted at them, Vincent? I thought that you were supposed to be the reasonable, placating one.'

Vincent: 'Yes, I surprised myself. Somehow the atmosphere was different.'

David: 'The atmosphere was different? For you too, Una?'

Una: 'Mm, it was a little, and he did shout once. But that's not enough to fix our problem.'

David has received indications from the couple that

- they have engaged mutually in their home practice;

- they have both become aware that a passive behaviour (Vincent's avoiding)[2] is harder to identify than an active behaviour (Una's accusing);

[2] Other passive behaviours, as we use the term here (it has another and specific theoretical meaning which we describe in chapter 12 pp. 143f) include being silent, placating, and changing the subject to a neutral one. These behaviours can go

- they have changed their behaviour at home a little;
- for Una at least, what they have done as a result of their counselling is not enough.

Gains at this stage are likely to be small. David would be sceptical if
the couple announced great changes. They are experiencing some
relief now that they have a method to start making sense of their
conflict, and this relief is likely to release some energy for positive
change in their relationship. David will reinforce their changes,
however small, with positive comments.

(At a second interview, a more resentful couple might report
negative changes: perhaps increased irritability with each other, or
lack of enthusiasm by one partner for home practice. David recognizes that new learning is not always easy to come to terms with and
integrate; and that a suggestion regarding new behaviour may be
threatening. He will tell such a couple that their negative reaction is
understandable. He will spend time empathizing and reviewing with
them while they establish with him a working system that they find
comfortable. David will not proceed further until *each partner experiences him as being on his or her side*,[3] and he will start by demonstrating
that he is taking seriously their sense of being threatened or uncomfortable.)

In the case of Una and Vincent, they have succeeded in doing
home practice, and in this present session they have reflected on that
practice sufficiently for David to further explore with them their
interaction.

David: 'Let's put your diagram on the whiteboard.'

unnoticed for a long time by both partners because their very passivity makes them
hard to pick up quickly and identify. The other partner tends to respond by
becoming bewildered, and with anxious over-activity tries to fill the gap. There is a
temptation for counsellors, too, to work with the active behaviour of one partner
and ignore the influence of the other's passive behaviour. It is easier to do so, but it
unbalances the counselling and makes it less productive.

[3] We do not consider a counsellor to be a neutral third party, an umpire or an
arbiter, but one who empathizes with each partner and, in that sense, is on the side
of each of them.

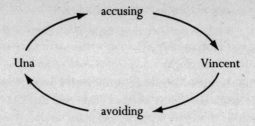

David: 'Una, just before you accuse Vincent each time, what are you feeling?'

Una: 'Angry!'

David: 'And just before you're angry, what do you feel?'[4]

Una: 'Oh, I feel let down. It's "here we go again".'

David: 'What's the feeling that goes with being let down?'

Una: 'Well maybe I'm scared. Things are getting out of control, so I feel scared.'

David: 'So just before you get angry and accuse Vincent, you feel scared.'

Una: 'I think so. Yes, of course I'm scared. I'm often anxious about our situation.'

At this stage, David writes the word *scared* across the arrow that goes from 'Una' to 'accusing' on the diagram. David glances at Vincent, who is looking thoughtful and attentive.

David: 'Vincent, Una does the accusing, and you do the avoiding. What are you feeling just before you avoid?'

Vincent: 'I don't know that I feel anything. I just see the situation getting more and more difficult, and whatever I do to stop her doesn't work. I mean, whatever I do to stop *it*, not *her*.'

David: 'So you're thinking to yourself "Whatever I do doesn't work."'

[4]David assesses that Una's anger is, for her, an attempted problem-solving response rather than her basic feeling. Anger is often used to rouse one's energy to action. David thinks that the problem for Una resides in what precedes this energy-arousing feeling of anger.

Vincent: 'I suppose I feel stumped. A bit desperate.'

David: 'So you're in a state of stumped-ness. Mildly desperate. Suppose you're in another situation, where you're in a state of *big* desperation. Your dinghy's caught in a current, and whatever you do to stop it doesn't work. Or imagine the bank is foreclosing your mortgage, and you can do nothing to stop it. You're really in a state about it. What are you feeling?'[5]

Vincent: 'You won't buy "desperate"?'

David: 'My word I will! But in my terms that's the state you're in. Along with your desperate state there's what I call a basic feeling, and I limit basic feelings to four: anger, sadness, joy and fear. If you accept this definition, what's your basic feeling when you're in a state of great desperation?'

Vincent: 'Certainly not joy! Panic. Scared.'

David: 'That makes sense. You're scared in a big desperation. And with Una, when you're a bit desperate with her accusing, what's your feeling nearest to — anger, joy, sadness or fear?'[6]

Vincent: 'Well, I get a bit sad, thinking about the situation, but that's in retrospect. I don't feel exactly angry. I find "scared" an extreme word, but I guess it's a little scare for a little state of desperation, in your terms. I can accept that.'

David: 'I'll buy "scared"!'[7]

Vincent: 'I can accept that if Una's scared when she starts accusing me, scared is what I am when I start avoiding her.'

David: 'Say more about your scare.'

---

[5]When he invites Vincent to escalate the state of desperation by considering an imagined plight, David is hoping that Vincent will use this experience to come into touch with a basic feeling strongly enough to identify it.

[6]David brings Vincent back to the ordinary reality of conflict with Una.

[7]It can be objected that David elicits the word 'scared' from Vincent in a contrived way, and that this is the only word he will accept. There is validity in the objection. However, it can also be said that the thought-form of any system of counselling (or of theology for that matter) requires certain formulae or descriptions of reality as a starting point. This is the way human beings and their thought-forms are. David's thought-form, based in understanding how human nature works, assumes that any defensive behaviour is preceded by a basic vulnerable feeling. He would accept 'sad' as such a feeling.

Vincent: 'I don't know what's going to happen when she accuses. Yes, I do! We're going to have a battle, with Una attacking me, on and on. I don't like it. It's not going to get anywhere, I guess. I'm scared. Yes, I'm scared.'

Una: 'You don't look scared to me when I accuse.'

Vincent: 'Neither do you to me! But I am scared, and I'm realizing that you are scared too. It stands to reason, doesn't it?'

David writes *scared* across the arrow that goes from 'Vincent' to 'avoiding' on the diagram, so that the diagram now looks like this.

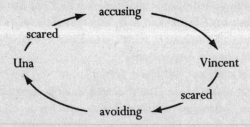

David has been coaxing and coaching Una and Vincent to track the process of their shared conflict. As with many women he counsels, David has found it relatively easy to elicit from Una what she feels while in the process of the conflict. She has been ready to say that she felt angry, and also ready to get in touch with the fear she feels in her state of let-down-ness.

David notes that, unlike Una, Vincent doesn't find it easy to identify and connect with his basic feelings. In common with many males, his conditioning has taught him to avoid conflict in his intimate relationships. Furthermore, on the sportsfield and as a boy enjoying working holidays with a very tough uncle, Vincent learnt to keep going and ignore his body reactions of pain and weariness: *he knows how not to feel what he feels*, in many different situations.

Using reason excessively, avoiding emotional conflicts, and not being in touch with body reactions during times of physical stress have been valuable habits for him to learn, and to use still in situations where they are appropriate. However, these habits have had their limiting effect on his emotional expressiveness.

Our basic feelings have physiological aspects. They are located in our bodies: we feel them physically. Vincent has been conditioned to distance himself from these feelings. Una's conditioning has encouraged her to connect to the physical aspect of her emotions.[8] David hopes that as a committed couple whose goal is the best marriage they can have, Una and Vincent will now be coming to the task of respecting and valuing the differences in each other, sharing them and even rejoicing in them.

In counselling this couple, David is helping them toward a change in perception. Una and Vincent were both initially surprised when Una discovered that fear, before anger, was her primary basic feeling. Observing Una's thoughtful struggle to understand her own process, Vincent was encouraged to struggle to connect with his fear. One of David's tasks now is to draw them into further shared consideration of their interaction, using their slightly increased vulnerability to each other. He may suggest to them the concept of *defensive behaviours* and see how far each resonates to it.

David: 'My hunch, Una, is that your accusing has had a very good purpose. Maybe you've been wanting to protect yourself from this very strong husband of yours.'

Vincent: 'Strong? She's the strong one, not me. Why should she want to protect herself?'

David: 'Hang on, Vince. That's how it seems to you, for sure, but keep it on hold for a while. Let's both just have a go at understanding from inside ourselves how it feels to Una.

I'm wondering, Una, if your accusing is a way of protecting yourself from powerful Vincent.'

Una: 'When you said maybe I protect myself from his strength, I thought "In one way I see him as very weak, and it's hard to respect him for that". But yes, in a way I see him like a powerful lump of . . . This may sound silly, but I've got a picture in my

---

[8]It is not social conditioning alone that effects male-female differences of the kind being discussed here. Genetic and body structure are likely to have their effect. For instance, the female corpus callosum (the white mass linking the right and left hemispheres of the brain) is larger and more richly endowed with neuronal pathways than the male.

mind of being a little girl again in South Australia on my parents' farm. And there's this great bale of wool that sits on the woolshed floor and does nothing. It's strong and powerful, and I can't possibly move it. But if I push and push, maybe I can rock it a little or swing it a tiny bit to a different position. How can you protect yourself from a great immovable strength that saps your own, if you don't accuse and attack?'⁹ (As she asks David her question there are tears in Una's eyes.)

David: 'Tell Vince "I'm so weak, and you're so strong and immovable, I have to accuse you and accuse you to protect me from your power".'

Una: 'Well, you are strong, Vince. Powerful. You eat up all my energy if I don't protect myself and accuse and attack.' (Una begins to weep. Vincent looks stunned.)

David: 'Vincent, Una's telling you she's feeling the overpowering strength of your passiveness as something that's scary. It saps her strength, she says, and all she can do to protect herself from it is accuse and attack.'

Vincent: 'But I'm not overpowering.' (He is shocked) 'She shouldn't feel like that.'

David: 'You don't feel strong and overpowering with her; and she doesn't feel strong with you.'

This discussion highlights the way David can work with an affectionate and mutually trusting couple. He may not be able to work with many couples so quickly and incisively: and we emphasize that though the discussion above may read as slow, even turgid, David has in fact engaged them in this work quickly. Whatever a counsellor says and does in this kind of session must come from continually supporting each partner; staying close to each and assessing how ready each is to accept painful truths that are to be faced. We have used the counselling of Vincent and Una to demonstrate, among

---

⁹A recurring mental image may be symbolic of more complexities in her situation than Una is aware of. Her counsellor will respect the significance the image holds for her that she has chosen to present, rather than exploring (out of his own interest) more of its symbolism.

other things, that *the assumptions held and the feelings experienced (and therefore the behaviour entered into) by spouses have separate meanings for each.* When unshared, they can stop couples meeting each other in their need. When shared, they facilitate the appreciation each can have of the other's desire to correct the marriage.

Later, David is able to help Vincent to connect to his painful feelings. Vincent has already been with Una in her similar experience, so he is a little more ready for his own process.

David: 'Una, let's have a go at really getting hold of what it's like for Vincent. It seems, Vincent, that feeling scared by this terribly strong wife of yours, you protect yourself from her by avoiding.'

Vincent: 'Well, yes, I do. But when she cried about my strength eating up hers, I could see how tough it is for her. She's not feeling strong when she accuses and attacks me.'

David: 'Stay with having to protect yourself from her when she comes across strong and accusing. Tell her about that.'

Vincent: 'I can see now you're not feeling strong when you attack me, but what else can I do but protect myself?'

David: '"What else can I do when I'm so scared"?'

Vincent: 'Yes, I'm so – I'm scared, Una.'

David lets the ensuing silence continue for a moment. He is aware that he is with two people whose painful spot in their relationship has been highlighted almost unbearably, so that they are extremely vulnerable. He can sense that Vincent's vulnerability is a great comfort to Una in her chronic pain around their conflict: here for once Vincent is not protecting himself by avoiding. David is concerned for Vincent, who just now has given much more ground to painful awareness than Una – who is more attuned to her feelings – has had to give. The sudden new vulnerability in Vincent is to be respected. David is thankful that Una, a straight-forward woman, is likely to avoid disempowering Vincent by manipulative put-downs later. David speaks slowly and caringly.

David: 'I wonder what would happen if scared Una could talk freely with scared Vincent? And vice versa?'[10]

Una: 'I wish I could. I think that I feel so let down that I would get angry.'

Vincent: 'And I'd get self-protective if I tried. I'm so wary.'

David: 'Let me lead you both. Una, will you say to Vincent "I'm very scared when I attack and accuse you, Vince."'

Una: 'Vince, when I'm accusing you, I'm actually scared.'

Vincent: 'It doesn't seem like that when you are in full cry.'

David: 'It may be hard for you to take on board Una's fear, but let yourself feel it, Vince. Don't avoid the pain of Una's fear.' (Pause)

Vincent: 'It's terrible to feel how scared you are of me. I believe you are scared. It's just such a strange thought to me. You seem so strong.'

Una: 'I guess I do seem strong, I'm so angry. But underneath I'm scared.'

David: 'Will you tell Vincent you're angry because you're scared?'

Una: 'I get angry with you because it is all too scary for me.'

David: 'True. Let me lead you, now, Vincent. Will you tell Una "I'm scared, really scared, when I avoid and placate you."'

Vincent: 'Una, I run away into placating and reasoning because I am scared.'

Una: 'You don't seem scared; you just seem superior and not there for me.'

David: 'Una, let yourself feel Vincent's fear.' (Pause)

Una: 'Yes, I know you're really scared. I'm cross with myself for attacking you just then about superiority. It's such a relief to hear you letting yourself be scared and saying so, that I guess I wanted to kick you! But that's not helping you to stay scared instead of avoiding.'

David: 'That's good reasoning.'

Vincent: 'You're taking over my job, Una!'

David: 'Well, reasoning is a great gift to practise, as long as we don't

---

[10]David is here using the notion of need-meeting in marriage (Genesis 2:18) and is suggesting that the needy parts of each might communicate directly for the benefit of resolving the conflict.

overuse it. And the same goes for feeling. So you may well let Vincent do some of the feeling in this marriage, Una. And value him when he tells you he's scared.'

David's counselling of Vincent and Una has aimed at addressing the needy part of their interaction and the chronic distortions in their requests (demands) of each other. Without getting into the aetiology of these distortions, the childhood origins, David has worked so that each partner has the opportunity to

- own his or her internal process,
- express a need in a way that helps the other to meet it rather than defend against it.

By counselling them in a joint interview, David has enabled them to practise their new behaviours and work toward these goals:

- Each partner can become increasingly aware of the other's process, and the other's fear.
- In future conflicts, when Una sees Vincent avoiding, she can think 'He is afraid of my accusing'.
- When Vincent feels attacked by Una's accusing, he can feel some empathy and say to himself 'She is angry, and before she's angry she is scared of my avoiding; same as I am afraid of her accusing'.
- Each partner can exercise some choice in responding, other than in a chronic, fear-driven way.

For home practice, Vincent and Una now have the task of practising this discipline. They will monitor their dysfunctional behaviour, own it, and own also the feeling (fear) that triggers it. When they catch themselves in their defensive behaviour, they will add to their statement or action 'and I'm scared'. It is very important that each partner respects the other sufficiently to avoid scoring points. Mind-reading the other is a common point-scoring technique;[11] it is a

[11]For a discussion of mind-reading see chapter 10, p. 115.

destructive habit, and it can be a trap not just for marriage partners who have learnt a little about psychology in human relationship courses and similar enterprises, but also for people who take training in counselling.

When a husband or a wife are struggling together to let go chronic conflict, mutual healing can be facilitated when each identifies the other's feeling. But identifying the other's feeling must be done creatively and sensitively. There is a creative way of adding 'and you're scared' to a statement made while trying to let go conflict. But there are ways of saying 'and you're scared', ways of using this potentially healing comment, that are manipulative and destructive and demeaning to the other: this is part of the mind-reading trap.

In counselling Una and Vincent, David's aim is to help them make sense of their interaction, so that they see

- its circular and cumulative nature;
- its predicability (its 'here-we-go-again' aspect); and
- how they confuse their need-meeting requests by distortion.

In seeing these things, they are encouraged to find ways of

- owning their defensive behaviours, and
- asking undistortedly for their needs to be met.

Enhancing Understanding

The essential skill of such a counselling process is to enable the couple to grasp, at a level of deep understanding rather than a mere cognitive one, what they are feeling and doing. And this takes time, not a counsellor's *telling*, to accomplish.

Rather than being a process of didactic telling, the task of counselling is to draw out from a husband and a wife their experience of their own inner processes in such a way that they are becoming aware of added dimensions of meanings to their actions and reactions with each other. This understanding then becomes something they can think clearly about, and as a result they can choose to put their wills into practising new responses to each other.

The more you are already in touch with your emotional self and have already integrated it with your cognition and your will, the easier you will find it to translate your self-understanding into circular interaction terms. In doing this you will enhance the meaningful use you can make with couples of the concept of circular interaction.

Some couples in counselling are more concrete in their thinking than others. They do not conceptualize easily and subtle concepts evade their grasp. With such couples, you may, for instance, never make distinctions for them between states and feeling. But with your own internalized understanding of these concepts, you will still be tracking their circular interaction, though perhaps making your interventions in a different way.

6

CONTEXT AND CASE MANAGEMENT

In the preceding two chapters our account of a marriage counsellor's work with two couples had a limited and specific purpose. That purpose was to demonstrate one aspect, a very basic one, of marriage counselling; it concerned the necessity for a counsellor to have

- a keen awareness of the circular nature of a couple's interaction;

- a method that helps couples recognize and own the way they use automatic, well-practised defensive behaviours to maintain their negative pattern of interaction;

- a way to encourage couples to feel positive about themselves and about their ability to take some control of their interactive process. (Then couples can begin to free themselves – out of their get-nowhere interactions, into productive ways of relating.)

Those three necessities were highlighted in the preceding chapters by the case examples we used. However, in doing so we had to narrow the focus of marriage counselling considerably. Broadening the focus is our next step.

We said that knowing a couple as parishioners gave David 'a context' in which to place them. *An awareness of the couple's context as well as an awareness of their interactions inform the counsellor's responses and her overall management of a marriage counselling case.* So in this chapter we focus on Emma's attention to her clients' context.

Context

A couple's context can mean their home and family and occupations and income, their families of origin, their place and community of worship, their culture and their class. It can include anything that impinges on them, affecting who they are, what they do, and what they expect in relation to each other and in relation to other people. Their context may strongly affect what they expect from their marriage counsellor, too.

A counsellor becomes aware of as many aspects of a couple's context as she can manage. She can't be aware of every aspect – the mind boggles at the possibility – and in her counselling she can't use all that she is aware of concerning the couple's context. But she learns to view them as two people who

- interact with each other in a circular way, and also
- belong to a setting, or rather a number of settings, upon which they act and which act upon them.

Each of us who counsels is a person-in-context, just as every client is. Stop for a moment and consider the context in which you have your being. The richness and diversity of its aspects may surprise you. You are impinged on and acted on by your context, and you act upon it as well.[1]

Counsellor in Context

Emma's style of counselling reflects her particular training as well as her unique personality. Prior to starting a bachelor of theology degree course she took a degree in behavioural science, and then a diploma in counselling with in-service training in a church agency for marriage counselling.

[1] There is an old prayer which addresses God 'in whom we live and move and have our being' (quoting Acts 17:28). It gives us an awareness of our Context – the Creator – in an awesome way: that Context is one we cannot change, whereas we may be able to modify the rest of our context, which like us is part of creation.

Now she is one of three ministers who share in the team ministry of a church and are mutually accountable. This church sees counselling as an important part of pastoral care; in appointing Emma it has specified that her ministry is to be largely in this particular area of pastoral care. She can be fairly flexible in the number of sessions she has with the people she sees, both those who belong to the church and those who come for counselling from outside the church. She is supervised by a professional social worker who is not connected with her denomination.

Emma is accountable to the minister appointed by the church as a team leader. The church members support her work with prayer, pay her stipend and attend to her insurance cover. It is clearly understood in the church that Emma's accountability includes her protecting clients' confidentiality. She does not reveal to anyone in the church, including the other ministers in the team, information about clients. (Some clients choose to disclose information themselves.)

At regular intervals Emma supplies the team leader with a record of the number of counselling sessions she has had, categorizing them broadly in terms like 'individual' 'sole parent family' and 'marital'. She reports on her management of the fee-setting. (The people she counsels pay according to a scale that takes account of their financial and other personal circumstances; their contributions offset a little of the cost to the church in providing the counselling service.)

The foregoing details describe one part of Emma's context. Her family of origin, her marriage and her children are other parts. Emma's context influences who she is as a counsellor, and who it is that a couple meet when they enter her study or counselling room.

Paul and Rachel

In her initial interview with any couple, Emma seeks their answers to four basic questions:

• What is wrong?

- When did your problem start?
- What have you done about it?
- What is good about your marriage?

The first three questions seek *the presenting problem as the couple experience it*. This is their stuck spot: the area of distress or conflict to which they return time and again, and which is uncomfortable for them.[2] Often there is more than one presenting problem for either or both partners.

In the case of Rachel and Paul, Rachel has chosen this counselling service because she has heard that Emma is a real Christian. She and Paul come from a church unconnected with Emma's. In their initial session, after Emma has made sure that they are comfortable, she asks the couple to go through her Information Sheet with her and give her some facts she requires for her records. (This sheet appears on page 65.)

With her encouragement Paul and Rachel make their replies to the questions together, until they come to 'Presenting Problem'. At this point Emma asks them to take their time as they think about the last three questions on the sheet, (those under the heading Presenting Problem), and to decide on their replies separately and without discussion.[3] Later she will insert their answers on the Information Sheet.

She adds that sharing their responses to these three questions will come a little later. After Rachel and Paul are ready, Emma invites them to tell her why they have come to see her. Rachel takes the lead articulately and with some intensity. She describes their problem as a spiritual one.

Emma: 'So, Rachel, you see the marriage problem you and Paul have as a spiritual one. Is that your view, Paul?'

[2]'Stuck spot' is a colloquialism for 'impasse'. Many couples respond to its use because they feel the force of its reality as a descriptive term.
[3]There is a benefit in this structured, initial procedure. It enables clients to settle quickly with a focus: first, the shared task of providing simple factual material about their context; then the more complex task of thinking about how each perceives their problem.

Paul: 'Well yes, I suppose it is. Rachel gets upset because I'm not open to the spiritual blessings that she has. But I'm a very different person from her.'

Rachel: 'But we should be one in Christ in all ways, and we're not. A husband and wife should be able to share spiritually in a deep and meaningful way. If we both love the Lord we should be so alive for him that other people see us as two Spirit-filled Christians and then we could be used together in wonderful ways.'

Emma: 'And you're yearning for you and Paul to be more alike in the way you experience your faith. When did this start to be a problem for you in your marriage?'

Rachel: 'It's always been there but for a few years it's really troubled me and I feel we've got to do something about it. Paul doesn't seem to even know what he's missing. I would love him to know the joy of the Lord in the way I do. And —'

Emma: 'And you want him to: for his sake, for yours, for other people, and for God too.'

Rachel: 'Yes, but I'd put God first in that list, of course.'

Emma is wanting to understand Rachel's urgent yearning *in Rachel's terms*. At the same time she thinks Rachel is wanting to bring into being a particular stereotype of a Christian couple, and suspects that in this counselling case she may have a wife who is hoping a Christian counsellor will help make over her husband to fit the stereotype. But Emma's primary task at this stage is to acknowledge and understand Rachel's longing.

On the other hand, Emma doesn't want to reinforce the intensity of Rachel's yearning, and so far Rachel isn't demonstrating flexibility in her thinking. She seems to be swamped with her own longing to the exclusion of taking an objective look at that longing, but *it would be premature to suggest this to her*.

Emma: 'Paul, you've said you're a different person from Rachel. You're unique, as she is. When did this difference become a marriage problem for you?'

Paul: 'Well it's been getting to us a lot since last year, but we've always been different.'

Emma: 'Let me ask you something else. Will you tell me about the ways you and she are one, even though you're a different person from her? And Rachel, will you think about that too, while Paul's telling us?'

By shifting the focus to something related, but positive, Emma is giving Rachel and Paul a chance to change gear, and also giving herself an opportunity to understand them in their context.

Paul: 'Well, as far as our faith goes, we were both keen to join the church we belong to. That was seven years ago . . .'

Paul goes on to describe how he and Rachel were attracted by the liveliness of their present church. (Rachel, taking her cue from Emma's request to think about it while Paul speaks, listens without interruption.) Paul says that in the face of their families' disappointment, they had left their parents' church which had also been Rachel's grandparents' church. They felt very much at one in deciding to do so, and as parents they felt close too, since they were offering their children a fresh and enlivening church experience. He adds that he and Rachel appreciate the freer form of worship they have now, and that Sunday services are a very real pleasure for him as well as for Rachel.

With Emma's encouragement, Rachel adds to Paul's narrative now. She emphasizes the sense of oneness they had on joining their present church. She refers to their move as a continuing disappointment in their families-of-origin, and expresses her sadness that she has less in common now with her parents, to whom she was previously very close. She expresses a wish that they and Paul's parents and all their wider family could be at one in the way they were previously.

When Emma explores this wish empathically, Rachel says she no longer expects that the families of origin will join Paul's and her church: this doesn't seem to be within God's purposes, and she has come to terms with her disappointment. She adds that although her parents are believing Christians, they don't understand the Spirit-filling joy she has in her faith and worship and she is sad about that.

Paul says he is more philosophical than Rachel about their families-of-origin. It has been harder on Rachel than on him. His own parents, though initially disappointed, were always more ready to accept that his and Rachel's spiritual journey was different from theirs, and it has never mattered to his brothers and sister that he and Rachel changed church affiliations.

Emma's request to Paul and her accompanying request to Rachel have led to their joining in a description of the families' reactions to their change in church affiliations. They are feeling at one as they describe a way in which they *are* at one, and Emma is seeing a different side to them – to Rachel especially – from their initial presentation.

The Counsellor's Focus

While Emma listens to Paul and Rachel she is attending carefully to them. They are speaking in terms of their religious or faith experience. Her attention is empathic; it is also objective.

Regarding the differences between the couple's previous church and the one they belong to now, Emma will have personal views. She may accept the doctrinal assumptions of one church as against the other's. She may prefer one style of worship over the other. But she sets her personal views aside because her task with Rachel and Paul is not one of making judgments on doctrinal matters or matters of faith expression. However, she takes these matters into account in so far as their change in church allegiance, for instance, is part of their context, and in so far as it is related to their ways of interacting with each other.

Emma may wonder about the level of Paul's personal commitment to Jesus Christ, or she may have concerns about Rachel's use of terms like 'Spirit-filling'. But the couple's particular expression of their Christian faith is not personally important to her. It is important to her in understanding how each uses their religion to reinforce their third system drives to have the marriage the way each wants it.

Emma's task is to take serious account of the needs and hopes and expectations that each partner has for self, for other and for the relationship. As her understanding of these things increases, she may be able to help them identify and attend to aspects of their past and present experiences that contribute to their current conflict. With their own recognition and acceptance of their needs and fears and expectations, and some modification of these, they may then be able to meet each other in a different way. The meeting will be in, and through and in spite of their differences.

With successive interviews, Emma gains many details about her clients' families of origin. These enable her, at an appropriate stage in the ongoing counselling, to encourage Rachel and Paul to draw up a genogram, and to assist them as they do so. (See Appendix B.) Genograms have been popular in recent years in marriage and family counselling. They have potential as an aid to a couple's understanding of the generational patterns they have been given, and thus an understanding of their own needs and fears and expectations.[4]

Using Case Records: a Task for the Reader

The subject of this chapter has so far been the clients' context and how a counsellor becomes aware and stays aware of context for the benefit of the clients. Case records are an important part of the counsellor's management of a case, and this chapter will conclude with a section on the making of records.

Using case records is both a challenge and an interesting task. We invite you to consider the material about Rachel and Paul that is found in the Information Sheet, in Appendix A and Appendix B. Use these records to make a number of hypotheses. The hypotheses will

---

[4] The risk is that counsellors introduce genograms to clients prematurely, or in a cognitive way, encouraging clients to make of them an interesting intellectual exercise or sometimes a destructive analysis of their families of origin.

consist of connections that you think may exist between the couple's context and their presenting problem.

A useful approach is to think in terms of chronology. Look for connections between Paul's and Rachel's current situation and events in their past: not only past events, but time factors such as the present ages and life stages of people who are significant to the couple.

Note what the Information Sheet tells about what is happening now, and what may be expected to happen within the next few years. (Timing of events, perhaps even more than the events themselves, may affect very strongly the relationship between a couple or between them and their children.) The life stage of Paul's and Rachel's parents may be connected with the yearning Rachel expresses. Or Paul may be grieving over the change (or loss) of relationship with his brother-in-law, and unused to expressing grief. These suggested connections may prove to be wrong, but they could be very important, and only the counsellor's later follow-up in counselling can test possible connections.

Go ahead and exercise your detective potential. Later, you may like to compare your connections with those suggested in Appendix C.

The Making of Records: an Exercise in Objectivity

Counsellors have their preferred and very individual methods of keeping case records. After recording the first interview fully, some make only brief notes on subsequent sessions, and find these sufficient to keep them on track with a case. There are two aspects to the making of records. One is the orderly *process* of recording, which can facilitate an orderly process in managing a case. The other is the factual *content* of the statements recorded, which can facilitate the making of sound hypotheses: these are an essential part of case management.

Regarding the content, there is a marked difference between the style of comments made by counsellors whose model is similar to

INFORMATION SHEET

Marriage Case No. 46   22nd August

Age and Occupation?
H 44 Sales Manager   W 45 Home duties, p.t. Secretary

How long married? 21 years
Previous marriages and/or relationships? Nil

Children? B19   G17   B12

Household members? H, W and the 3 children. (H says B19 plans to move to student accommodation after Christmas.)

Health? All in good health, except B12 has food intolerances.

Church affiliations? Independent charismatic church. H, W and B12 closely involved; B19 and G17 some links.

How did you come to this counselling service? Self-referred, i.e. W knew of counsellor through church friends, H agreed to come with her.

Presenting Problem
How do you see the problem?
W We are not able to share spiritually as deeply as we should.
H We are very different people.

How long has it been a concern to you?
W Many years, more so last few years.
H Approximately one year.

How would your partner describe the problem?
W Spiritual problem
H Personality differences

H and W were seen today in a joint session. They plan to have 5 more sessions a week apart and then a review at the end of October.

Emma's and by those who mingle statements of fact with their own opinions, biases and conclusions. But every one of us can revere our own intuitions so much that we are certain our impressions are accurately checked facts. In case conferences, for example, statements of this flavour may be heard.[5]

'She had a very unhappy childhood and was never affirmed by her mother.'

'His sister was the family favourite and he was always made the scapegoat.'

'Her upbringing was totally devoid of love and affection.'[6]

'While he can't remember instances, there is every indication that he is a survivor of sexual abuse from his uncle.'[7]

Clients make statements about their deprived and unhappy childhoods believing them to be the truth, the whole truth and nothing but the truth. Their words and their statements are to be accepted and respected as the way they are currently experiencing their earlier lives. The more we as counsellors have this understanding, the more we are likely to help people eventually let go pain from the past that is affecting their relationships now (including the way they feel about and therefore relate to themselves).

The words and statements of such a client make a useful contribution to case records when they are reported and quoted as part of an account of *what the client said*. But unqualified statements and words like 'never', 'always' and 'totally' rarely fit appropriately into our repertoire when we are writing or narrating a client's history.

[5]Case conferences are also a situation where the counsellor presenting a case for discussion may be helped by gentle, insistent queries: 'What's your evidence for believing that?' and 'How have you arrived at that opinion?' and 'Will you say more about your basis for that conclusion?'

[6]To conjure up a picture of child-raising *totally* devoid of love and affection is a challenge to the imagination.

[7]A verbal or written statement of this kind is an unsubstantiated guess. Like the previous examples, it attributes behaviour to someone in the client's childhood who hasn't the possibility of defending against or correcting the attribution. The client's narrative needs to be recorded in ways that give legal and moral respect to everyone concerned. It is part of a counsellor's professional discipline to do so.

Emma's records reflect her training in accuracy. For example, while accepting her clients' veracity, she qualifies her statements with 'W says', 'H says', 'According to' and 'Both partners report'. (See Appendix A.) Thus she avoids mixing into her clients' account of their history her own judgments and hypotheses. These she will record later under the heading 'Counsellor's Assessment', again with qualifications but related now to her judgments: 'He seems', 'Their responses are likely to be affected by' and 'She appears to'.

After each subsequent session, Emma adds a few notes to her records, with the date. They include a short account of what the couple (and she too) found significant in the session, and perhaps ideas for the following session. She also makes a note about any activity that the couple have contracted in the session to do in the interim – their home practice. This note ensures reference to the activity in the following session. Unaccustomed or spontaneous activity is also noted, e.g. 'Family picnic on Saturday – their first for two years, they say'.

In measuring changes in a couple's patterns of behaviour and relating, case notes tend to be more accurate than a counsellor's memory. So Emma, as well as looking at her notes on the previous session when Paul and Rachel are due, has another form of self-supervision. She re-reads her entire case records occasionally to keep herself on track with her counselling process and to remind herself of aspects of the clients' context that she may be overlooking: particularly their initial reason for coming, their presenting problem. And thus Emma's case management is enhanced, to the benefit of Rachel and Paul.

Addendum

You're thinking that Emma's style of record making is not within your capacity, or your limits of time and case management? Your style of recording may be different, but it is important that your writing up of your initial sheets (information and history/context) and later your assessment sheet should be adequate and extensive, not scrappy. Above all, whatever your preferred method of recording your cases, it is your contextual and accurate reflections (of a kind that lies behind Emma's recording) that will give your style a precision that will serve your clients, your counselling and your case management well.

Appendix A

CASE No. 46   INITIAL INTERVIEW   22 August

According to both spouses, they grew up in their parents' church where W's maternal grandparents were also active members and in which H and W married 21 years ago when W24 and H23. They describe their relationship as 'developing through shared church activities . . . friendship turned to love'. Their parents (all still living) approved of their decision to marry, W's mother advising them to wait till each 'had a good bank balance', which they did. No information yet about their sexual relationship.

Family   Both say their three children's births and developmental history have been normal. W says H has given 'more time and attention to the children than the average father'. Both say they consider H head of the household. They say also that W takes more initiatives, e.g. in choice of children's schools, decisions about holidays, major household purchases. They agree that they expect their children, the first generation of either f-o-o[1] to aim for university education, will 'do well in life'.

Finances   According to both, H's job is relatively well-paid and secure though sometimes costly in stress and long hours. By mutual decision they tithe their income which consists of H's salary. W budgets carefully and the three children earn regular pocket money, e.g. child minding, serving petrol. H's and W's high priority is paying off their long-term home loan. They say they have no conflicts over use of money.

[1]Family of origin.

Conflict Resolution   H and W say that earlier in their marriage H objected to what he regarded as the excessive amount of time W and her mother spent together; severe conflict between H and W resulted. As a result of attending a study group on marriage, about ten years ago, W became convinced that she should be less dependent on her mother and more so on H. Both agree that W acted on her conviction, thus resolving their 'major conflict' and 'strengthening the marriage bond'. Later, each supported the other in the face of family disapproval when they changed church affiliations. This was about seven years ago. Since then they have been able to resolve marital conflicts by discussion – until their current presenting problem became a pressing one.

Religious Attitudes   H and W say they enjoy worshipping together at church, where W is high profile and H has rostered practical duties on Sunday and sometimes goes as a leader to church camps and hikes. He appreciates their church's free form of praise and worship and feels 'renewed for the week ahead' by church services. H says W is 'more intense in her spirituality' than he, adding 'and that's right for her'. At home he asks a blessing before the evening meal, but likes to be alone for his personal prayers. He believes the children's need at this stage is for 'a stable home rather than being organized into family prayers'. W says she would like H to be the one helping their children maintain their spiritual lives, especially now that the older son is at university and seems less interested in his church. She feels sad that H 'does not share spiritually in a deep and meaningful way' and says she longs 'for him to know the joy of the Lord' in the way she and her close friends at church do.

Significant Others   Both say their families of origin mean a lot to them. They visit their parents frequently and have family meals with them occasionally, and also with some of their siblings' families. H has good friends at work whom he values, but he does not often meet with them socially. W values her church friends highly. She says they do not often have people in for meals because their busy lives and their children's study take precedence over entertaining. . .

Appendix B

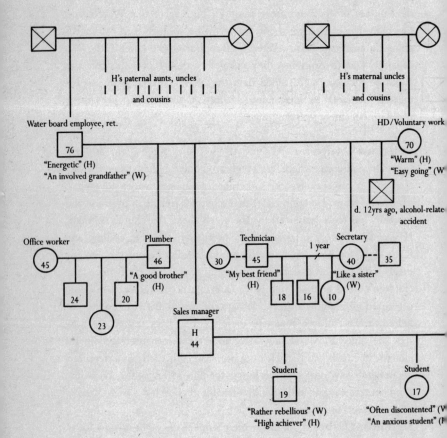

Water board employee, ret.

76
"Energetic" (H)
"An involved grandfather" (W)

HD/Voluntary work

70
"Warm" (H)
"Easy going" (W)

d. 12yrs ago, alcohol-related accident

Office worker
45

Plumber
46
"A good brother" (H)

Technician
45
"My best friend" (H)

30

1 year

Secretary
40
"Like a sister" (W)

35

24   20

18   16   10

23

Sales manager
H
44

Student
19
"Rather rebellious" (W)
"High achiever" (H)

Student
17
"Often discontented" (W)
"An anxious student" (H)

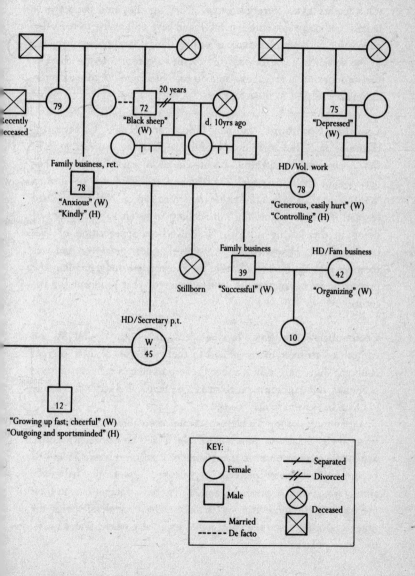

Recently
deceased

79

"Black sheep" (W)
72   20 years   d. 10yrs ago

Family business, ret.

HD/Vol. work
75   "Depressed" (W)

78   "Anxious" (W)
"Kindly" (H)

78   "Generous, easily hurt" (W)
"Controlling" (H)

Family business
39   "Successful" (W)

HD/Fam business
42   "Organizing" (W)

Stillborn

10

HD/Secretary p.t.
W
45

12

"Growing up fast; cheerful" (W)
"Outgoing and sportsminded" (H)

KEY:

◯ Female

▢ Male

—— Married

------ De facto

／ Separated

／／ Divorced

⊗ Deceased

▨ Deceased

Appendix C

COUNSELLOR'S ASSESSMENT   31 October

Following their fifth counselling session, H and W have contracted for a further five before Christmas. They say they find the sessions helpful, although sometimes painful, and have both come to trust the counsellor, although her 'way of seeing things' is not always theirs. In the sessions ahead they say they want to consolidate the changes they are making in their behaviour to each other, and to discuss some difficulties related to their children.

Couple's Comment   In their fifth session H and W reviewed their sessions. They identified helpful aspects of the counselling, e.g. the counsellor's respectful attentiveness to each of them, her concern for their marriage, her readiness to 'not judge us' and to 'hold us on track when one of us wanted to run on'. W said she had learned from the counsellor's modelling to listen to H 'instead of doing all the talking myself'. H showed his appreciation of W's comment and acknowledged he was feeling less pressured and was freer to express himself. H said he appreciated understanding the present in terms of the past and wondered what it meant for the future.

Counsellor's Review   It is evident that both H and W are committed to their marriage and to the resolution of their current conflict. They share values about the importance of religion, the use of money, and commitment to marriage, family and extended family – a firm base from which to start.

As their presenting problems indicate, the couple's conflict arises from their polarized positions along a self-containment/mutual dependency continuum. In their families of origin it seems H and W experienced different patterns of relating, W's family habitually aiming for mutual dependency and H's for self-containment. In their marriage each spouse has yet to learn how to feel safe with the other's position along the continuum, especially when, under pressure, they polarize strongly.

The goal of counselling is not to bring to conscious awareness the early roots of their (defensive) polarizing behaviours. It is rather to help H and W to find satisfying ways of dealing with their differences and to have a sense of security in each other's presence.

Counselling to date   Encouraged by the counsellor both partners have identified and disclosed a depth of feeling about significant events occurring at the onset of their current conflict. In particular they have gained some freedom to share the meaning for each of the unexpected marriage breakdown of H's brother and sister-in-law, the setting up of de facto relationships and the dividing of three children of that marriage between two new households. H and W are acknowledging together their grief and loss and the impact of the events on both families.

With the counsellor's support and encouragement, they have recognized together their current sense of anxious helplessness in the loss of family structure. As they increased their awareness of this sense, they began to understand their habitual patterns of response: H's attempt at problem-solving has been to support W and children by stoic reasoning and emotional containment; W's has been to urge for mutual dependency and the reassuring certainty of emotional closeness.

Thus each has sought to secure their image of marriage and family, and the form of their circular interaction has been to express their presenting problems to each other in these (unspoken) messages:

W: Let's make our relationship one of total closeness and not have emotional boundaries; then we'll be strong and safe.
H: Let's go on the way we've been, and not pay attention to our anxiety; then we'll be strong and safe.

In the safety of the counselling process, each partner is beginning to acknowledge and take responsibility for their safety-seeking responses to their anxiety and helplessness: W, for the urgency of her desire for one-ness (which H, afraid of enmeshment, tends to see as a threat) and H, for his self-protective containment (which W, afraid of disengagement, tends to see as a threat). With practice in the security of the counselling sessions, they are beginning to venture into some freedom to let the other be, and some freedom of mutual expression. They have contrasted the experience of this new behaviour with their habitual polarizing.

Working on the theory that life-stage changes can affect the stability of a couple's habitual mode of interaction, the counsellor introduced this concept to H and W and asked them to consider its relevance to their current conflict. W accepted the counsellor's intervention as permission to describe her anxieties about her mid-life years and menopause. In this session, H seemed safe enough to attend to the fears W was expressing about this aspect of their context, and to respond to them. He said he was relieved to discuss this as another likely source of their tension, and later expressed surprise and pleasure about the relaxed concern for W that he was feeling in her presence.

The counsellor has commented to the couple that natural events related to life stages, along with unexpected events related to significant people (as with H's brother and sister-in-law), can together disrupt a couple's familiar marriage structure drastically. This concept seems to have given the couple a structure to think together about their marriage conflict, and it may be possible for each of them to grow in appreciation of the different manner in which they experience a genuine faith in God.

Relationship   Over their five sessions W and H have referred to the strong religious content of their families of origin. This has given the counsellor opportunities to encourage their awareness of the patterns of their parents' marriages, so that they can identify ways in which their own unspoken messages reflect what they have learnt in their families of origin.

While encouraging the couple to recognize the positive aspects of their relationship, the counsellor is aware that a basic avoidance of intimacy beyond a particular point may be at the core of their current impasse. This avoidance may well be in both partners. For despite W's expressed desire for 'spiritual oneness' she, no less than

H, may feel unsafe in trusting an open relationship where neither partner controls the other nor invites control.

Future Counselling With their desire to consolidate the behaviour changes they are making, it may be useful for the couple to explore H's stress and long hours at work, and W's demanding hours of involvement with the Church's secretarial work and with members of her women's group. The meaning of these activities to each could be explored, and their impact on the amount of time and interaction that H and W have together.

H and W plan to discuss difficulties they have around their children. These difficulties are likely to be related to the children's lifestages, and possibly they are affected currently by H's and W's changing mode of behaving towards each other. Some family counselling sessions could be an option later. However, it could be more strengthening to the family for H and W, while consolidating their marital changes, to notice the effects of these changes on the behaviour of their children.

It is likely that in the continuing counselling, whatever particular aspects of the couple's relationship and their context are the focus, continuing themes will be those of distance and closeness, independence and dependency, helplessness and controlling; and also responses to changes in familiar structures.

7

THINKING AND FEELING

Some of us are strong on cognition and not so well-connected to our affect; others of us are comfortable with at least some of our feelings and can express these freely, but we are not so strong on thinking. In contemporary times there is a tendency to contrast the two, some people seeing a higher virtue in one than the other. If we incline to this perception, we will naturally favour models of counselling that fit with our perception, and these will influence how we work with clients.

Couples in counselling tend to feel more comfortable with a counsellor whose preference they share. But this does not mean that a couple who are feelers necessarily do better with a 'feeler' counsellor, while a couple who are thinkers do better with a 'thinker' counsellor. What clients need in a counsellor is encouragement to strengthen their less favoured and less practised mode, while having their favoured mode valued also.

Thinkers

There are spouses who are so quick to cognitize whatever you say and do in the counselling room that helping them stay with their emotional reactions is quite a challenge. They respond to ideas. Cognitively they gobble up what you present and do not digest it with the juices of their emotions. For these clients counselling sessions can become something from which they gain good ideas, not understanding that ideas *per se* are less nourishing than they think to the wholeness of their living, and that this wholeness involves integrating their ideas with their will, their affective side and their behaviour.

Cognition, then, has its risks for some clients. For their counsellor too, there is a risk. In a counselling session it is easy to enjoy intellectual discussion with another bright mind and thus move with one spouse away from a dyadic awareness of the couple. While you enjoy a little head trip with one partner, the other feels left behind and an imbalance begins to develop in your relationship with the couple.[1] You may redress the balance later, of course (excursions with each may be good for all) but the risk is there. Similarly, when counselling a couple where one spouse is a well-defended thinker, it may be easy to align with the more feeling spouse, and that is risky to dyadic process.

A cognitive couple may initially describe their situation and their feelings in a detached and matter-of-fact way. It is good for them if your responses are not only thoughtful but emotionally expressive as well. Join them on thinking and add feeling. A useful rule of thumb is to behave initially in a way that contrasts with the one-sided aspect of clients' self-presentation. This will immediately set the scene as one where you are offering your cognitizers a model of a thoughtful person whose feelings are free to flow. That's not to say you go over the top to display your own feelings (your cognitizers would probably cut and run if you did), but that you keep on responding to them in a way that lifts the level of emotional energy in the counselling room.

Cognitive couples may fear their emotions very much, and in consequence they may be using thoughts, ideas and rationality to guard against, even deny, their feelings. *Respect of all clients' defences is of great importance*, and the counsellor will offer this respect.

---

[1]Cognitive enjoyment shared with one or both partners may be concerned with a discussion of Scripture passages. But as a head trip this too has its risks.

Urging people to feel or trying to almost trick them into feeling is certainly not therapeutic.

Counselling can result in a thinker becoming comfortably in touch with a range of his or her own feelings, and then the thinking ability has an opportunity to take very good care of the person's more integrated self. The more usual outcome of marriage counselling, where there is a contrast between the two spouses, is that the thinker becomes comfortable enough with the feeler's emotional style to defend against it less, and also cognitively aware, at least, that thinkers are feeling people too.

Feelers

So you are a counsellor aware of the importance of being in contact with a range of emotions, and the importance of being emotionally available to others. You take care not to encourage a couple to go on head trips, and you don't join one or both in such a trip. And now a couple come for counselling who are very emotional, and it seems that before you have had time to establish a working relationship with them your counselling room is being swamped with their expressions of emotions. What do you do?

The rule of thumb mentioned above is a good one to keep in mind. Your task is to deal with *what is happening* in order to establish a working relationship. Furthermore, as their counsellor it is your responsibility to exercise enough authority to establish the direction of what you expect them to do in this session. Before choosing you as their counsellor, your couple may have had a series of would-be counsellors who have given them messages about feelings very different from those they need to hear from you. As we describe later, there is still a fixed assumption in many people that 'getting feelings out' is a virtue *per se*, and that somehow this activity solves something. Your clients may believe this and they may even think that the right thing to do in counselling is to behave as they are doing.

Relax and be still. Speak in a calm, even tone of voice. Ask questions and make statements connected to the content of what they are saying: questions and statements that require thinking responses from the couple. Avoid referring to or reflecting their feelings. Keep in mind that indignant voices and hurt tears and explosive reproaches are all reflecting, to some extent, the frightened or desperate 'child' in each spouse. Remember that little children need to know for their own safety that someone is in authority who is calm, not desperate, someone who is not afraid to give them a structure and a model for handling their emotional upheaval.

The emotional couple before you may function very well in many areas of their life, but here they seem to be taken over by their 'child' selves, and the feelings they are allowing to control them are likely to represent chronic reactions from the past. Later we will discuss the power of such reactions. (Berne's rather unpleasant word for them is 'rackets'.)

For the moment let's take the example of a client who breaks down, weeping and sobbing. It is too early for you to understand the extent to which her tears are a reaction to some current grief situation, how much they represent her unresolved (and therefore recycled) childhood misery, and how the past and present are connected for her. In any case, at this stage it isn't important. What is important is your response. She needs *your respect for her* to be expressed in a therapeutic way.

Often when a client begins to weep, her automatic response to her action is to say 'I'm sorry' and to go on weeping. Often the counsellor's automatic response is to say quickly and reassuringly 'That's all right!', to hurry forward with the tissues, and even to put an arm around the client. It all seems natural and right to the counsellor: something good must be happening because my client is crying, getting her feelings out.

With greater understanding the same counsellor will realize why such a client needs a different response from one of 'reassure – hurry with tissues – comfort and soothe'. It is therapeutic to sit quietly and wait. Attending respectfully to the client with an awareness of one's boundaries is important. So is setting aside a need to reassure or comfort oneself by comforting the client. Sitting quietly while someone is expressing grief over a recent loss is respectful, and it is usually the genuinely therapeutic response. Placing arms around them or otherwise responding with immediate physical touch is usually a reaction to *one's own* impulses. If the person is weeping over a long-past loss, the response of touching is very likely to reinforce the chronic nature of the sadness, by reinforcing the tearfulness.

If the weeping does not abate after a reasonable time, the counsellor will ask: 'Tell us what your tears are saying.' The tone of voice will indicate both interest and a confidence that the client can do what is asked. (It will be a gentle tone, but free from soupiness.) If the tears continue to flow, the counsellor will say in the same tone: 'You can talk and think and cry at the same time.'

Suppose a wife begins to weep, and her husband wants to hold her hand and cuddle her? Assuming that the working relationship with the couple is well established, the counsellor can ask the husband: 'Would you sit apart in your chair and let (Jane) do her own work of weeping? She can do it for herself.' The counsellor's respect for both partners and for the process will be apparent. Later the counsellor will ask the husband: 'While you were waiting apart, what were you thinking and feeling?' and then the husband's reactions – and his wife's reactions to his reactions – will become part of the process of counselling. It may be that the rescuer aspect of the husband and the victim aspect of the wife will come clearly into their awareness, but whether this happens or not the meaning, to each, of the weeping can be explored by them. When both partners are in a good spot, a position of mutual strength, probably at the end of the session, the counsellor will invite them to hug each other. This just might be an appropriate time for each to hug the counsellor too.

Thinking, Feeling and Doing

It is important that the counsellor attends to the *thinking*, the *feeling* and the *behaviour* of the couple, for each is influencing the others. The counsellor is continually asking herself questions related to the husband or wife. What are they doing? What is the feeling involved in that behaviour? When she perceives that *one* of these (thinking, feeling, doing) is dominant for the person(s), she needs to attend carefully to the other two.

Feelings and Make Feel

'Make Feel' is shorthand — or shortspeak — (taught by the late Dr Robert Goulding) for describing statements like 'S/he made me happy' or 'angry' or whatever. We give our marriage partner a great amount of power over our feelings. This is inevitable in the intimacy of the commitment of marriage, which is meant to be mutually need-meeting. However, in counselling and therapy it is wise to be aware of the way people use Make Feel as an abrogation of responsibility for feeling whatever they feel. Usually it reflects their assumption that what they feel depends entirely on someone or something outside themselves; and also that they are helpless to feel anything else as a response to a given situation.

John: '*She makes me furious* when she tells people my faults.'
Kathryn: 'Will you say to Jane, "Jane, when you talk to people about my faults, *I feel furious*"?'

For pastor Kathryn this is one part of the beginning of a counselling process, at the end of which she hopes John's response of anger to his wife Jane's behaviour will become an instrument of change for him and Jane. Indignation is appropriate, and his fury is understandable. However, his fury takes him over and seems to him the natural response. He needs to own it as *his* feeling that *he* generates; not as something that his wife Jane *makes him feel*. Kathryn's response to John's statement is inviting him to own his fury.

In counselling Keith and Kate, Julie is dealing with a more complex Make Feel.

Kate: 'When I think about my parents splitting up because of me when I was eight, *it always makes me terribly sad*.'

Julie: 'Will you tell Keith and me "When I think about my father leaving my mother when I was eight, *I feel very sad*"?'

Kate's Make Feel needs detailed consideration to understand its complexity. Kate is giving power over her feelings to two things: her parents' marriage breakdown when she was eight, and her thinking about it. As she expresses it, thinking about that event makes her sad, and the event itself (thirty years in the past) makes her sad.

For Kate's well-being, Julie needs a clear concept about what Kate does to herself with her feelings. Julie needs also a consistent way of working in consequence of her concept. When you first consider the concept, it may not make commonsense; but it certainly makes uncommon sense as a way of assisting Kate to let go her sense of helpless misery. This is the concept:

Kate makes herself sad by thinking about an unhappy life event that happened thirty years ago. She uses thinking about the there-and-then to feel sad now. Kate also uses the there-and-then (her parents' marriage breakdown when she was eight) to sadden herself in the present, in the here-and-now.

It is normal to feel terribly sad sometimes about a tragic event that brought a great loss, even so long ago. But Kate's chronic feeling is sadness. The whole tenor of her life in the here-and-now is tinged with sadness. When something – perhaps a television programme – triggers off memories of a loss from the past, it is natural for any of us to be sad for a few minutes. However well we resolved the grief of that loss long ago, we can still 'rubber-band' back to the grief momentarily. However, it is not natural for us to stay grieving about it. It is natural to rubber-band back again to the here-and-now, and feel whatever is appropriate in the present.

To explain this concept to Kate in a cool, matter-of-fact way would be useless, because she is used to having her feeling of sadness run her life. It would also be cruel, because it would seem to her that we were denying the reality of her sadness. So Julie goes about it in a different way. Julie's intervention ('Tell Keith and me. . .') gives Kate a slightly different message about her sadness from the message Kate runs in her head.

Kate's message to herself, well-practised over the years, is something like this: 'I am eight years old, and I have caused my parents' marriage breakdown' (this is Kate's magic thinking plight), 'and I will have to stay sad for ever' (this is Kate's *chronic feeling* plight).

Kate has given some evidence that she feels responsible for that marriage breakdown ('splitting up over me'). Julie decides that she is not going to focus on Kate's unrealistic sense of guilt at present. It is Kate's chronic sense of sadness that appears to be sapping her energy and Keith's.

Some people would hasten to assure Kate that she shouldn't feel guilty about her parents' marriage breakdown, working on the assumption that alleviating her guilt will release Kate from her sadness. This kind of rational, commonsense approach will not reach the little eight-year-old in Kate who has recycled sadness for thirty years. She may say 'I know I shouldn't feel guilty, but I do.' Julie recognizes that rather than her sense of guilt it is Kate's sadness that is more accessible at this point – and also more destructive to the buoyancy of her relationship with Keith.

Julie's task is to help her focus on the Make Feel with which Kate renders herself helpless. If Kate can revise her concept so that it is closer to the definition Julie is thinking and giving about her sadness, Kate can then begin to take charge of its all-pervasiveness. Julie's encouragement of Kate's revision of her concept and subsequent change of behaviour around her sadness will take place while she is working with Keith and Kate together.

As Kate's pastor, Julie knows some of Kate's strengths.

- Although Kate's circumstances as a child were tragic, and her sense of loss was very great in the there-and-then, Kate has survived to become in many ways a well-functioning woman in the here-and-now.

- She is married to a committed husband with whom she can frequently enjoy a constructive, loving relationship.

- She has the competence to gain and hold employment in the paid workforce.

- Her faith is firmly based. She believes in the grace and saving power of God in Jesus Christ. She understands that she is a sinner, but she doesn't wallow in guilt over her sinfulness, past or present. She believes Christ died for her, but she doesn't wallow in sadness because of his cruel death.

Therapeutic Interventions

Our most creative interventions in addressing someone's Make Feel comes from our inner freedom to own *our own feelings*. These interventions flow from experiences we had – perhaps in therapy – that enabled us to let go our own Make Feel. Julie's responses to Kate will be on that basis.

Kate: 'But, Julie, thinking about my childhood really does make me sad.'

Julie: 'What would you be thinking about if you didn't take your thoughts back thirty years?'

Kate: 'I guess I'd be thinking about going on a camping trip with Keith.'

Julie: 'And when you're thinking about the camping trip, what are you feeling?'

Kate: 'Excited.'

(In our formulation, 'excited' is actually the state in which Kate *feels happy* but this isn't the moment for Julie to fuss about exactitudes.)

Julie: 'Excited. Splendid! And feeling excited, what are you doing? Tell us as if it's happening right now: "I'm excited and happy about the camping trip and I'm . . ."'

Kate: 'I'm making a list of things to take, I'm packing enamel plates and the sleeping bags, I'm buying UV15 cream and – I'm doing a dozen things!'

Keith: 'And you're getting me to do another dozen!'

Julie: 'That's fine. Kate, you're happy and excited right now. You were sad a few minutes ago. How did you change your feeling?'

Kate: 'Oh, did I?'

Julie: 'Well, nobody else could change it – it's your feeling. How did you change feeling sad to feeling excited just now?'

Keith: 'And that's what she does at home sometimes, Julie, when she's not feeling miserable.'

Julie: 'Tell her, Keith. "Kate, when you. . ."'

Keith: 'Kate, when you stop being miserable at home and think about what's going on, you're really good fun to be around. You're energetic, you've got ideas, you do things with enjoyment.'

Julie: 'Kate, what do you say to Keith about that?'

Kate: 'He's right. I really am a pain when I'm sad –'

Julie: 'Hey, Kate, stay in the present! Tell Keith "Keith, I heard you say I'm really good fun . . ."'

After this interchange is completed, Julie comes back to asking Kate to reflect on her change.

Julie: 'Well, we had an interesting time with that – you really experienced that good feeling, but come back to how you changed your feeling from sad to excited.'

Kate: 'Well, . . . I started thinking about the camping trip and I started imagining the activity, and I started to feel excited.'

Julie: 'What happened to the sad feeling?'

Kate: 'It just disappeared.'

Julie: 'Will you say to Keith "When I stopped thinking about sad things back there, and started thinking about exciting things, *I changed my feelings* from sad to happy"?'

When Kate does this, Julie asks her to say it again to Keith, and then to explain to him more of the process of how she did it. In this way she is reinforcing the change and Kate's knowledge of how she changed, and therefore increases her ability to make that change in the future.

In working with a husband's or wife's Make Feel, your interventions will not be identical with Julie's. You are a different person from her. The couple you are counselling are different from Kate and Keith. The similarity between your work around someone's Make Feel will be in the management and the process of the counselling session, not in the specific interventions. In general, the principles for working with Make Feel are these:

- Have both partners present (if possible) when one is working on the Make Feel work of each.
- Rephrase their Make Feel statements, but without giving them correction in theoretical, cognitive terms.
- Invite the person to rephrase in similar fashion, and by implication, to own the feeling — as Kathryn did with John about his fury, and as Julie did with Kate about her sadness.
- Instead of confronting directly such statements as 'Thinking about X makes me sad', ask a question that implies the person has an alternative to thinking about X.
- Switch to using the present tense (the here-and-now) as the person begins to imagine an alternative. 'What are you feeling? . . . Tell us as if it's happening now. "I'm excited about . . ." '
- Support their alternative thought or feeling with enthusiasm.
- Identify the change as something the person has done, then invite their reflection on the fact that they had a choice about what they thought and felt, and they exercised that choice, and made the change.
- Use the partner's comments to reinforce the new behaviour.
- Finally, avoid asking a person in counselling 'How does that make you feel?'[2]

Clinical Depression

Kate's chronic sadness from the there-and-then thirty years ago was a contributing cause to the marriage problem she and Keith presented to Julie. Such a feeling is an automatic one in many well-functioning

---

[2]That question implies that people and events determine the client's feeling, or that the client is not responsible for the feeling.

people without its being classed as clinical depression.

It was pastor Julie's task – as it is for a marriage counsellor with every couple – to ascertain whether there are any health issues compounding the counselling agenda. Julie had the advantage as their pastor of seeing them at church gatherings, where Kate and Keith both presented as well-functioning people. She still had the responsibility of asking about their physical health and ascertaining as far as she could that their emotional health was normal.

The information Kate gave Julie did not seem to indicate clinical depression.

- Generally she slept well, and did not waken after a few hours' sleep and stay awake till morning. Her sleep pattern seemed normal.
- Though she thought sadly about her past (obsessing over it at times), she did not feel weighed down with depression.
- She did not feel chronically lethargic and exhausted, lying on a bed for hours feeling unable to move.
- She did not feel distanced from other people.
- She was often interested in having sexual intercourse with Keith.

Some people say 'I'm depressed' when they are just miserable. Some say 'No, I'm not depressed' when they really may be. The *use* of the word 'depressed' (which varies in meaning from person to person, and varies in frequency from group to group) is not a sure clue to depression. Julie's responsibility to those she counsels includes asking them to have a medical check-up if she sees health issues that clearly impinge on the counselling process.

With another couple, Julie thought that the husband Lionel might be clinically depressed. She could not discern strong signs of depression in him, but she noticed he sighed deeply at times and seemed to view life through grey-tinted spectacles. When she commented 'I rather think you believe you have to carry the burden of past sadness around with you for ever', he gave a sad smile and shook his head. Julie asked him to have a medical check-up, and also to tell his doctor (whom she knows) that she had asked him to do this.

If Lionel is diagnosed as somewhat clinically depressed, that does not mean that Julie stops counselling him and his wife. It is however a safeguard to have a medical practitioner supporting your counselling with a seriously depressed person, because it is the medical profession which our society designates to attend to those whose health lies outside the normal range. Some people have a strong physical and chemical component to their depressed feelings, and as a counsellor Julie takes account of this.

There are people like Lionel who have a general and constant damped-down feeling. There are others who have episodes of depression. There are people, too, whose depression lifts, disappears or is minimized through their being part of a therapeutic environment.

One such environment could be a series of marriage counselling sessions, with the pastor and the doctor having contact with each other. Another could be a church with plenty of healthy, well-balanced members. A third such environment is provided by various non-religious community groups and interest groups.

8

ANGER, JEALOUSY AND HURT

There still lingers a popular and false belief about feelings. It was popular in the 1950s, and remained so in some circles, though some sceptics soon dubbed it 'the hydraulic theory', and questioned its validity. 'Let out all your bad feelings and the good feelings will come flowing in.'

At a time when many disturbed children and adults suffered from extreme inhibition and excessive guilt, releasing tension by expressing feelings – screaming, yelling, flailing – could be a useful part of a treatment programme. It was not the final goal of treatment, and in itself it did not ensure emotional health. However, as with many strategies and procedures used occasionally by effective therapists and counsellors, the use of 'hydraulics' became a fad with enthusiasts.

In the 1970s despite the reservations and critiques of practitioners regarding its assumptions and its use as a method, enthusiasts took up 'Primal therapy' as the answer to life's problems. Inviting people into a drastically altered state of consciousness to relive early traumatic events may sometimes be part of an able therapist's treatment with someone committed to long-term therapy. Like belief in 'hydraulics', the efficacy of 'primalling' *per se* is ill-founded.

The popularity of encounter groups from the mid-twentieth century until the nineteen-eighties came from a similar belief. 'Getting out real feelings' was often an invitation for one participant to rage at another: the 'real' feeling was anger. Some encounter groups had their value, especially when their leaders were wise, benign people. Their use, misuse, and their limitations were high-lighted in the early 1970s. (For instance, well-documented research undertaken by psychologists such as Lieberman, Yalom, and Miles produced interesting and sobering findings.[1])

We are now at a different point of our social and psychological history. Rather than being a neurotic society in the sense of guilt-ridden, we are a disordered society in so far as we lack:

- a healthy ability to inhibit feeling;
- consistently taught and generally accepted concepts of right and wrong social behaviour;
- a stable social and personal will and conscience.

However, often the expression of feelings is still recommended uncritically as a virtue. More than that, two separate processes – *feeling a feeling* and *expressing that feeling* – are often not distinguished or discerned.[2]

In many situations, expression of anger reinforces anger. It does not release the resentful person from anger in a way that enables them to be closer to forgiving the one against whom their anger is held. For example, all of us have understandable reasons for feeling aggrieved that our mothers and fathers were at best very ordinary, limited bumbling people. (That's not a discount of anyone's parents, but a statement about human nature.) To deny this and to idealize our parents is not honouring to them or to God. But neither is nursing our wrath about their misdoings as parents. Most of our parents did plenty that was right; and perhaps much that we now see as wrong, or certainly less than ideal.

Owning our resentment, and then taking steps to let it go may be a lifelong task for some who suffered greatly as children. Those of us who work with survivors of childhood abuse of various kinds cannot

---

[1]See Lieberman, Morton A., Yalom, Irvin D., Miles B., *Encounter Groups: First Facts*, Basic Books, Inc. Publishers, New York, 1973, SBN 465-01968-4.
[2]Some counsellors say 'your feeling is valid' without making this distinction. See Empathy and Confrontation, chapter 10, p. 117f.

doubt that for some (not necessarily the worst abused, as far as we can assess it) the letting go of resentment and the task of beginning to forgive the parent (or at least to accept that the abuse belongs to the past) are painfully hard steps to take in their life journey. But that is what life calls us to do; that is part of the good news – beginning again and starting to forgive.

There are feelings and feelings

In marriage counselling, as in other people-helping endeavours, we need to have ways of discriminating between feelings. We need to work toward understanding how to own and use them rather than let them be in charge of our lives, manipulating us and those around us.

The most valuable conceptualizing about feelings that we have found comes from Transactional Analysis, a system developed by Eric Berne who died in 1970. Personally we owe much to teachers who were already able and creative therapists when they came to know and learn from Berne. One of these was the late Robert Goulding, another was his wife Mary. Of all our people-respecting teachers they most helped and inspired us by their training methods.

Transactional analysis is a full and rich system of theory, and to internalize it as a means of understanding oneself is not a quick and easy task. One of its benefits is that along with its theory it offers a method of therapy. The way any particular person uses a feeling will depend on their values and assumptions about life. Some criticisms of transactional analysis made by Christians have related much more to the philosophical assumptions that some transactional analysts appear to hold, than with the system of theory it presents. Others have related to slick, 'pop' TA.

There are some feelings that when attended to and felt and expressed, can lead to intra-psychic or inter-personal conflict-resolution.[3] (These include some forms of previously unexpressed grief over the

---

[3]See empty-chair work, chapter 11, pp. 130ff.

loss of a person, of a body-image, of a job, or of a personal identity.) There are other feelings that, when expressed, do not release the person.

In transactional analysis a distinction is drawn between *authentic* and *racket* feelings. In Berne's terms, racket feelings are chronic, stereotyped feelings that a person routinely feels in any situation of stress. That is, a person feels sad, angry, guilty, scared chronically and without discrimination. It is continually the same feeling whatever the situation. Expressing these feelings does not lead to conflict-resolution, either within the self or between self and other. These feelings are not to be dismissed as phoney and they certainly do not feel phoney to the person who is expressing them – the person is really feeling them. To view them as inauthentic is untherapeutic, too. But more about racket feelings in a moment.

'Authentic' Feelings

In transactional analysis terms, authentic feelings are those that can genuinely *serve* the person feeling them. They are an appropriate and specific response by the person to a particular situation. They are spontaneous and of limited duration. And they achieve something.

For example, at a meeting Beryl is patronized by a pastor who pats her cheek, smiles and asks "How are we today, my dear?" Beryl feels immediate anger, like a physical sensation in her chest. In a carefully calm voice she says: '*I* am not your dear, and how *you* are is patronizing. Will you *not* touch my face again.' As she sits down among the pastors with her coffee, her physical sensation of anger subsides. Her emotion of anger leaves her: that is to say, she lets it go, and quite quickly. The discomfort in the discounting male's face (an appropriate response) and the calm appreciation in the other pastors' faces (also an appropriate response) both help the process of her moving out of anger.

Beryl's anger and her expression of it serves a useful purpose. The offending pastor is given an opportunity to learn something about his need to respect women. Beryl gives herself a chance to practise a new response, rather than feel daunted by people of senior rank. The other pastors observe a model of a gentle woman expressing anger appropriately.

Anger, Joy, Grief and Fear. These are *authentic* feelings that can serve us well in given situations. We flow into these feelings and out of them again, according to need. We do not go on and on feeling them intensely after they have served their purpose. For example, anger, (as with Beryl above), joy at receiving a letter from an old friend, grief at some significant loss, fear when faced with a threatening situation.

'Racket' Feelings

If Beryl had remained in her daunted position with the senior pastor, her feeling may have been fear. This is the chronic stereotyped feeling she has when she faces an authority figure like her grandmother,[4] and probably the typical feeling that she has when she faces stress – her racket feeling. From that feeling (and the third belief system that goes with it) there is no way she can make a problem-solving response to the senior pastor. But she feels safe, in the sense that this is a *familiar habitual feeling* so that the world or life seems to be under control, even though unsatisfactory.

The racket feeling a person feels is usually a chronic one in the family. Beryl's mother was intimidated (scared) by Beryl's grandmother, and the grandmother, too, might have been scared in her own way. A racket feeling is modelled for or taught to this person by mother or father or both. It can often be traced back through the generations, and seems to be the right feeling to have in that family. In any situation, Beryl would have been taught to ignore angry or sad feelings and to feel scared instead. So this chronic bad feeling seems comfortable – the 'right' feeling to have.

The counsellor will be watchful for feelings that do not seem appropriate to the particular person in that particular situation. The counsellor might

[4]See p. 27, chapter 3.

ask 'What would happen if you felt X (the appropriate feeling) instead of Y (the chronic one)?' or 'If you weren't feeling Y what would you be feeling?' With each question, the counsellor is inviting the person to change the feeling, and to experiment with it and think about it.

Jane comes to counselling because her husband Karl is having an affair. As Otto works with her he notices that her dominant feeling is one of guilt. He thinks that guilt may be an appropriate part of her feelings, in so far as she is taking her share of the responsibility for the breakdown of the marriage – but guilt seems to be the only feeling she has, and it seems out of proportion. Otto plays a hunch:

Otto: 'How would you be different if you felt angry?'
Jane: 'But I'm not angry. I feel awful that Karl has gone off with someone else. I must have done so much wrong.'
Otto: 'Then will you feel angry at Karl for going off to this other woman?'
Jane: (non-plussed for a while, then) 'Oh, yes. How could he do that to me? What does he take me for? And he thinks that *I* should feel guilty! He thinks that he can do what he likes, and that it's all my fault.'

Otto notes that as she began to feel angry, her energy began to flow, and she now starts to think more constructively. She begins to see Karl's behaviour more clearly and to make realistic judgments about her situation. When she changes her feeling from guilt to anger (an appropriate feeling) she starts the process of problem-solving in her marriage.

Another approach that Otto might take is:

Otto: 'You seem to be beating yourself that Karl has gone off.'
Jane: 'I feel so bad about it, Otto. So guilty.'
Otto: 'I'm wondering . . . If you weren't feeling so bad, so guilty, what would you be feeling?'
Jane: 'Oh, I don't know. Oh, I suppose if I wasn't feeling so guilty . . . Yes, I'd feel angry . . . (pause). What a horrible sneaky thing

he has been doing. Seeing that woman all these months. Look Otto, I haven't been the perfect wife, but it hasn't been all my fault. He isn't all that wonderful.'

Otto notes that her energy is rising and she is starting to think differently, and is likely to make more realistic decisions about what she can do about her husband and her marriage. In each instance, Otto is working on the theory that the *chronic* stereotyped feeling is a well-learned substitute for the *authentic* feeling.[5] He uses these methods to move Jane to experience the authentic feeling from which she is likely to make more appropriate decisions about her marriage and her life.

Otto will need to help Jane to practise moving into her angry feeling and maintaining it enough to think clearly and well. He knows that it will be easy for her to slide back into her chronic guilt, and he will help her to think through how to move back into the angry feeling when she needs to. She needs to practise changing her feelings, and she will do this by

• thinking differently about her situation and so feeling different.
• behaving differently in her personal relationships as a result.

She will change what she does with Karl, and make more constructive demands on him.

This simple substitution of the authentic feeling for the chronic or racket feeling can work in many cases, and may be enough to help the person to change significant parts of their living. However, often the feeling system is too entrenched, and the person finds it extremely difficult to live outside that feeling for significant periods. This suggests that the decision to adopt that feeling was an *important survival decision* early in the person's family-of-origin, and that the new feeling was prohibited in that family. In this case, the person

---

[5]For a more extensive discussion of racket feelings and authentic feelings see *TA Today*, I. Stewart and V. Joines, Lifespace Publishing, Nottingham and Chapel Hill 1987, pp. 207-30.

may need to do more work around that childhood decision with a counsellor experienced in this field.

Jealousy and Hurt

When we who are ministers and counsellors recognize jealousy and hurt in our clients, we realize that these responses are more complicated than the chronic well-practised feelings of fear, anger and sadness. Both are self-protective and defensive reactions, like racket feelings; but both fit better with the definition of *feeling states* than of chronic simple feelings. A feeling state represents a constellation of feelings and thinking.

Like our clients, we might say 'I feel inferior' or 'inadequate' or 'destroyed' or 'abandoned'. We are describing our feeling state, a state that suggests a sense of helplessness, and is expressed from a victim position – often blaming someone, a perceived persecutor, for our situation. Even more than with these states, the feeling states of hurt and jealousy present a challenge as we seek to relate to others in a healthy, sturdy way and help clients do the same. Hurt and jealousy are early basic responses that we all know about from experience.

Jealousy

The first thing to be recognized about *jealousy* is that it is not synonymous with *envy*, though the two words are often used interchangeably in ordinary language. While jealousy concerns our wanting to keep something that belongs to us, envy is about wanting to have something that someone else possesses. Those who have been conditioned from childhood to experience themselves in constant competition with others tend to be chronically envious people. Often they are not recognized as envious people because of the assured confidence of their self-presentation to others. But competing is basic to their sense of identity: they must outdo others. In relation to status, power, money and other possessions, they automatically want to appropriate for themselves someone else's position of Topdog. If something is to be had, it must be had. This is not to say that all competitiveness is wrong; and certainly the pursuit of excellence is a virtue. It is the compulsive pursuit of what others have that is the essence of the deadly sin of envy.

It is interesting that in the concept of the seven deadly sins and their contrary virtues, *gentleness* is named as the contrary virtue to *envy* – a superbly subtle and perceptive piece of ancient wisdom, when we come to think carefully about it. Along with the other six contrary virtues (humility, temperance, chastity, patience, liberality and diligence) gentleness aligns with the fruits of the Holy Spirit.

And after that serendipity, back to *jealousy*.

Jealousy is a primitive response connected in our minds with the fear of non-survival. Someone seems to be taking something that belongs to us: a new sibling, for instance, deprives us of the mother's lap that we have always taken to be our exclusive possession and has kept our sense of being and identity safe. In normal adult life, from time to time we are threatened with the loss (to someone else) of a significant loved one, or status, or thing – of someone or something that we experience as part of us and rightly belonging to us, assuring us of who we are.

Our reaction of jealousy is sharply (or smoulderingly) painful. Among its complexity of elements, fear is primary; there is also a primitive, impotent desire to do away with the intrusive taker. We can admit perhaps to the fear of losing our loved object, and to the indignation that often overlies our fear. But usually we feel ashamed or guilty too, and perhaps frightened by the fierce strength of our desire to do away with the taker. We want to destroy the threat, and we feel helpless in the face of it. Little wonder, then, that the 'child' in us feels uncomfortable. For our 'child' knows that the behavioural manifestations that betray our jealous state are unacceptable to the loved ones around us on whom we depend for survival.

We are jealous, then, for the protection of something that is our possession. And our jealousy is made up of many elements: fear, which is overlaid with anger and a secret desire to destroy the threat, accompanied by a sense of helplessness. (There may be other elements, but these are common ones.) And what is so terrible about jealousy? Only this: it can take us over in the form of a chronic state of angry helplessness and possessiveness which is destructive to ourselves and spoils our relationships.

Jealousy at its best is a spontaneous and appropriate response by which we move into protection of ourselves in relation to someone or something that is, in a very real sense, ours. Remember Jahweh's message to his people through Moses? 'I the Lord your God am a jealous God.' What does God's jealousy mean? It means that he won't have the people who rightly belong to him whoring off after other gods. Filled with zeal and protective solicitude for his people, he will have them for himself.

Husbands and wives, too, are properly jealous of their exclusive relationship with each other. Many a spouse has become intimidated and uncertain in the face of the fashionable and falsely simplistic decree 'All jealousy comes from lack of love'. It doesn't.[6] It depends, for instance, on what a spouse is jealous of and jealous for, and it depends on the sense in which he or she is jealous.

In regard to working with couples in which jealousy is a factor, the best that can be said briefly is this:

Look for the fear and helplessness in the jealous person. Working with fear is the core of working with jealousy.

The response of wanting to do away with the intrusion on the marriage relationship can usefully be defined as understandable, when the counsellor is aware that it is the jealous person's defensive 'child' way (a 'magic thinking' way) of dealing with his or her fear.

The counsellor understands, and helps the jealous person to understand, that the early childhood situation of fear and helplessness is different from their current situation. The counsellor helps

---

[6]To decree that all jealousy comes from lack of love takes no account of the nature of commitment and trust. It has been used at times both to justify a disengaged attitude toward a spouse, and to belittle commitment by calling it 'merely symbiotic attachment'.

the jealous person differentiate between the reality fears they have in the present, where they also have many inner resources, and the 'child' fears that are affecting their sturdy, effective use of those resources.

If a spouse's jealousy is of a deeply unhealthy and all-pervasive nature, the counsellor will consult with a supervisor on appropriate procedures. But in normal situations, the counsellor will help the non-jealous spouse to explore the meaning of his or her apparent reasonableness and to take seriously what the jealousy is communicating. Here, as in other marriage counselling, the counsellor will conceptualize and counsel in terms of the couple's circular interaction.

Hurt

When we feel hurt, the paradigm (as with jealousy) is childhood experience. As little children, at times we come in confident trust toward a trusted carer and are rebuffed; an offering of ourselves is rejected; or an unexpected slap or sharp reproof cuts across our buoyancy. It seems as if our very being has been unfairly wounded. That's the way everyday life is: rough and tumble. Personal hurt is an inevitable part of it; and while it is good to avoid being hurtful to others, we cannot always avoid it, even as caring parents, any more than we can avoid feeling hurt by others from time to time.

In our adult life it is important to deal with our tendency to be hurt, and to do so as far as we can as each hurtful incident arises. Otherwise, feeling hurt can develop into a chronic and much-used state from which we manipulate and control others. In families where hurt is a favoured response, members learn to suffer reproachfully at each other.

The learned reaction to a powerfully used feeling state of hurt is a powerfully inhibiting shame or guilt. Spouses who engage in a circular interaction of hurt and guilt cannot offer their children a model of straightforward communication. Instead, they give a false model of relating 'lovingly', so that for family members love comes to mean 'never upsetting and never hurting others'.

In the family of the Church, congregations can be controlled by the hurtability of one or two powerful (usually long-term) members. These members may be generous and helpful within the church to the point of apparent indispensability; in which case it is even harder for ministers and other church leaders to risk 'upsetting' them. Thus unacknowledged collusions can arise, and hurt feelings are treated with reverence – for instance, when there is a suggestion that something in the church that is dear to the hearts of the hurtable ones might be changed.

Whether the minister feels manipulated by the hurtable ones, or whether he is touched by the expression of their wounded feelings and responds with a would-be compassion that comes from pastoral concern, the outcome for the family of the church is no more healthy than the outcome of hurtability is within the nuclear family. Instead of keeping his focus on *principles* – and principles include equal opportunity in decision-making for all church members – the minister becomes tangled with *personalities*, and then aligns with a faction in the *power politics* of the church.

The hurtable person sees him or herself as very sensitive. They can and do present as sensitive to another while in rescuer role to that other, for whom they feel they have much understanding. While their self-perception goes unchallenged, all seems well. But basically they are sensitive to their own feelings and their own situation.

In a Christian marriage, the hurtability of one spouse can mesh powerfully with the other spouse's fear of being an upsetting, hurtful person – all in the name of Christian love. In fact, often in the church sensitivity to feelings and not hurting other people are presented as basic Christian virtues, without specifying the kind of sensitivity and the kind of hurt that we're meaning.

When working with couples where the interactive meshing just described seems to be a strong factor, it is important not to confront the power of the hurtable spouse. It is also wise to be wary of upsetting the interactive balance early by giving subtle permission to the other spouse to 'upset bravely', as one minister termed it. That's a sure way to lose a client couple.

Keep in mind that hurtability is the known way that one spouse is using to control his or her environment; and instead of becoming indignant with that spouse for using a power play, recognize that in the 'child' mind of the spouse, survival depends on being able to control the environment. Keep in mind also the strength of the desire of the other spouse not to upset: that too is his or her way of keeping things in control.

Briefly, the counsellor's approach is this:

Recognize the fear underlying one partner's guilt about hurting, and the other partner's readiness to be hurt. Recognize that for both partners the basic issue is surviving well, together.

The counsellor understands that there are healthier (and safe) ways for couples to interact. The couple don't know this. If the counsellor gives them the message cognitively, neither partner will hear it except as an idea.[7] It is only after much practice of a new way of relating that any of us understand how it is safe and healthy.

Engaging with clients' underlying fears is a skilled and slow task. As the spouses join with the counsellor, each is sure to manifest their well-practised hurt and guilt in relation to him: the upset-avoiding spouse will try not to upset the counsellor, and at some stage the counsellor will refer to this as an issue. The hurtable spouse will be 'hurt' by the counsellor, and the counsellor will refer to this, also. In his direct and very gentle, sensitive responses to the ways in which the spouses relate to him, the counsellor will give each spouse opportunities to examine their interactions with him. The time and skill involved in the process is not to be underestimated.

---

[7] For instance, a well-meaning counsellor who said 'I believe God often hurts us but he never harms us' was expressing something that had tremendous meaning to him, but for spouses where hurt is an issue the statement would have no power to help them change their feelings and attitudes.

9

SHAME, GUILT
AND SELF-ESTEEM

We need an understanding, both theological and psychological, of shame, guilt and self-esteem. Christians (and others) often use these three terms in very muddled ways.

As Christian counsellors we need to consider carefully what theology and psychology have to teach us about these concepts, and to see how the similarities and differences in understanding fit with the reality of who God is and who we are in relation to God. It is easy for those with a leaning toward popular psychology to dismiss the Church (or Christian faith) as messing up people with shame, guilt and low self-esteem. And it is easy for some Christians to reject psychological counselling as giving people permission to do sinful things guilt-free.

When competent psychologists and competent theologians are thinking carefully from within their own frames of reference about the three concepts, there are not such radical differences between them as to prevent dialogue. The difficulties come from assumptions expressed in views like these:

'Psychology says it is wrong to feel guilty, and this encourages people to behave as they wish.'
'The Christian faith makes believers feel ashamed and encourages low self-esteem.'
'Psychology talks about self-esteem as if it were a virtue, and this encourages people to be proud and arrogant.'

'Christianity has improved as a religion recently, because it has
   started putting the focus on love, not guilt.'

Both Christian faith at its best and psychological thinking at its best
help to lessen the prevalence of such views. As counsellors,
including marriage counsellors, consider more carefully the concepts
of shame, guilt and self-esteem they are better equipped to understand how to think about them in relation to individuals or couples
they counsel.

Guilt

We begin with guilt because, though developmentally it comes later
than shame, it was one of the phenomena studied and emphasized in
early formal psychology. Originally and for many decades psychoanalytic treatment was aimed at alleviating neurotic conflicts, neuroses
being seen as the result of a harsh super-ego.[1] Given the understanding of the psyche at that time, that diagnosis fitted patients sufficiently.

   In psychology, as in theology, when any tide of either fresh or
recovered ideas is flowing strongly, some previously understood
truths tend to be lost temporarily. As the assumptions developed in
popular thinking that all guilt was pathological, and that emotional
problems disappeared as guilt disappeared, a grasp was lost on an
obvious reality. The reality is that it's a healthy response for us to be
able to feel guilty when we have acted in ways that are contrary to
what we understand to be right behaviour. Popular thinking was not
making this distinction.

   A healthy conscience that accompanies normal human development is one that can be offended when we behave, or fail to behave,
in certain ways. It develops as parents and parent-figures teach us by

[1]Super-ego is a psychoanalytic term that covers references to one's internalized standards of behaviour; these are linked to the rules we introjected from authority
figures early in life. However, the use of the concept super-ego doesn't clearly
distinguish between states or feelings of guilt and those of shame.

example and precept that it is right, for instance, to be honest, truthful and just in the way we treat people, and that it is right to be considerate of others and willing to put them before ourselves for the good of all. Learning (gradually) the ability to behave in accordance with these values is a mark of both normal human development and a healthy conscience.

Some forms of popular psychology and also some modes of counselling lost sight of the reality that we are emotionally healthy when we are capable of feeling guilt. They came to assume that all guilt is bad. In some cases, the assumption seemed to be not only that all feelings of guilt were pathological, but that a state of objective guilt did not exist.

In line with this belief the concept of 'value-free' counselling gained popularity in the 1960s. It is an erroneous concept. Whoever a counsellor is and whatever she says reflects her values in some ways, including the value of not imposing (or even offering) her ideas about what is right. More than a decade passed before some of the keener proponents of 'value-free' counselling recognized this, and the term is rarely used now.

There flourished, along with the term 'value-free', a belief about guilt that took firm enough root to continue to influence some forms of counselling. It was that people should be helped to free themselves from the cause of their guilty feelings and thus from all the feelings themselves. (This strong 'should' went hand in hand with counselling that aimed at being 'value-free'!) We can credit early counsellors with a motive of compassion for people heavily burdened by excessive guilt about many of their actions and thoughts; earlier in the twentieth century harsh super-egos were more common than now.

Crippling guilt results in guilty feelings that are not realistic and *not in proportion to the action* to which the guilt is a response. It results, for instance, in an automatic fear of authority figures and a severe inhibition in freedom of one's choices of behaviour.[2] These reactions are in marked contrast to the 'oops' response most of us

²See 'racket' feelings, pp. 93ff.

tend to have when, for example, we catch sight of a police car. Within a split-second we check our speedo and perhaps our speed, even if we habitually drive according to the road rules, and to (normal) super-ego or conscience.

There is an appropriate (authentic) guilt-response to our un-constructive behaviour.[3] It is to recognize that we have offended against our conscience, or against the statutes; to give ourselves a rebuke; stop the behaviour and make restitution where possible – a sincere apology, for instance – and then get on with living. When we have confessed, been forgiven and made what restitution we can, we are free to put it behind us and get on with the next thing; our freedom of choices of behaviour is not inhibited by continuing guilt.

Shame

'Shame is an emotion insufficiently studied, because in our civiliza-tion it is so early and easily absorbed by guilt' wrote Erik Erikson in 1950.[4] While guilt has been of psychological interest since Freud's time, it was only in the 1980s that counsellors began to attend care-fully to their clients' shame and to distinguish it from guilt in the following way. *Guilt has to do with our reactions and our limitations; shame has to do with who we are.*[5] When we have feelings of shame, when we feel shamed and ashamed, our personal identity is involved.

When we feel guilty, we are responding to our awareness of the aspects of our behaviour that we find unacceptable. When we feel shame, it is in response to others witnessing our unacceptable selves. (Blushing is an outward sign of shame as well as of other emotions.)

As counsellors we can increase our understanding of shame if we do some self-examination and face, admit and experience our feel-ings of shame. This *can* be done alone; it is usually more productive to do it with a trusted counsellor or confidant.

[3]See 'authentic' feelings pp. 92ff.
[4]Erikson, Erik H., *Childhood and Society*, Norton, NY 1950 (2nd Ed 1963) p. 252.
[5]This is the import of Erikson's thesis in *Childhood and Society* op.cit. pp. 251-8.

In your experience of *facing your shame*, you do not need an over-feeling response from the one who is listening. When clients are feeling into their shaming experience, that is not the response they need from you. The goal of the exercise is for the shamed one to gain release from some of the intensity of the experience, and a sentimentally sympathetic response does not facilitate the release. Nor does expressed indignation about the one who did the original shaming.

In exploring our memories of the dreadfulness of being shamed, we learn experientially to distinguish between guilt and shame. It is easier on the whole to deal with much of our guilt than to come to terms with our shame. In dealing with guilt, often we can use cognition to assess fairly realistically the extent of our responsibility, now or in early life, for something we did or failed to do. We can also take some considered action to deal with some of our guilt – both with the objective fact of our guilt and with our guilty feelings. Shame is not so easy to come to terms with. It is pervasive of our being and less open to cognition than guilt.

Some couples who come to a marriage counsellor feel ashamed because they need help with a marriage difficulty.[6] This is specially so for those Christian couples who assume that all good marriages are conflict-free. The identity of each, as a spouse, has been threatened by their difficulty; they may have denied that their marriage was in trouble as a way of defending against what seemed a threat to the very personhood of each. From their counsellor they need a keen respect and a very sensitive understanding of their shamed situation.

But the feeling of shame does not begin when a spouse's self-concept (as a marriage partner) takes a tumble. It begins early in life. Or, to describe it in another way, the shame felt from loss of self-concept as a marriage partner links on to an earlier sense of shame.

One spouse lives with seemingly inescapable shame because, fifty years before her birth, her great-grandfather committed suicide. Through the generations this sad event has been a painful family

---

[6] For a similar reason, some pastors and other counsellors may have difficulty in being open to assessment of their counselling.

secret. Another spouse goes through life striving for more and more financial and educational status, but still feeling shamed (as his family-of-origin felt) because his parents and grandparents lacked the standard of affluence and education of those around them. Yet another, who felt persistent shame from childhood, until he resolved it much later in life, had been the child of a broken marriage. His Christian mother had left his father when he was a little boy, and he carried her unspoken shame about herself as if it were his own.

In non-verbal and pre-verbal ways, family shame passes from one generation to the next. The events that led to the shame are not admitted, the shame itself is not owned and talked about feelingly and reasonably, and its strength is thus magnified and intensified. To the extent that we do not name our shame, we give it control over us; it is as if we *are* our sense of shame. Speaking about it lessens its power over us. *The experience of shame needs articulation.*

Dealing with Historical Shame

With couples who are sharing their historical pain with each other, the counsellor keeps the focus on admitting and describing the formerly unspeakable feelings of shame. The outcome of the couple's articulation may be vigorous assertions such as 'There wasn't anything wrong with me!' and 'What a lot of useless shame my family held on to, instead of feeling good about who we are!' The shamed person may, in the counselling room, want to sidetrack into blaming others who were involved in causing the shame, or become discursive and detailed in narrating incidents of being shamed. The counsellor keeps the focus on helping the spouse to just feel their past shame so that eventually there will be an expression of healthy new responses.

When you have become accustomed to articulating your sense of shame to your spouse and to hearing your spouse express theirs, you may choose to talk to your children about it. Though they may shrug off your disclosure and assure you that they do not feel a similar shame, it is still worth doing. Shame tends to affect people as if by osmosis, and naming yours could well have some freeing effect on them.

Similarly, in marriage counselling, when a couple are comfortable disclosing shamed feelings to each other, it may be appropriate with sensitive timing to encourage them to do the same for their children. Parents rarely do this, for the pain seems unspeakable and is very hard to acknowledge.

The messages you and your spouse or a couple in counselling give to the next generation will be somewhat equivalent to these: 'Isn't it sad? I'm the fourth generation to feel shamed because your great-great-grandfather committed suicide. Let's celebrate – I've stopped carrying the family shame.' 'Just because we wanted to keep up with the Joneses and couldn't, our family has felt ashamed for three generations. There's no way God ever meant us to be the Joneses, and it's time we valued ourselves for who we are.' 'When your nan and granddad split up I spoilt years of my life feeling ashamed. I wasn't to blame, but I felt I was.'

Early Shame

The source of the shame we have been describing lies in family history; let's call it *historical shame*. Another kind of shame we carry comes from being humiliated and embarrassed as children, for instance for answering a question wrongly or breaking wind. We can call it *early shame*. Both kinds of shame are connected by the fact that parents burdened with historical shame are likely to put their children down more harshly than they would if they felt good about themselves. Parents tend to see their children as extensions of themselves at times, and shaming them is a pitiable attempt to deal with their own shame.

Sometimes parental criticisms that shame relate to a child's appearance or attributes; more often they are responses to a child's behaviour in family or social occasions. It is easy to understand how a child's being is assailed by criticisms like 'You fat little toad!' or 'You clumsy clot!' Rebukes like 'Your behaviour in church was disgraceful, everyone was disgusted with you!' shame the child too; much more than correction, even a harsh correction, that is targeted at the specific unwanted behaviour.

This is not a contradiction of what we said earlier about guilt having to do with behaviour. In contrast to feeling shamed by the rebuke just instanced, a child would feel guilty in response to a reproof that specifically targeted the wrongness of the behaviour. 'It's not polite to talk during prayers and bang your feet loudly' reproves behaviour and does not shame the person. (Whether the child responds to such a reproof with excessive or normal feelings of guilt depends on many factors, a simple one being the severity of the reprover's voice.)

One child may be the recipient of parental shaming while another child in the same family avoids it and gains the identity of the 'good' family member by conforming to what the parents consider accept-able in their own being or behaviour. Unresolved shame, it seems, has to go somewhere. In marriage counselling we are sometimes dealing with a couple where one spouse is the recipient of the shame the other feels and thus takes a kind of scapegoat role – often the same role he or she had in their family-of-origin. Parents don't always scapegoat their own shame on to a family member: they may attempt to deal with it by being critical of people outside the family; and thus they give their children a model for disparaging others. The children, who still experience their parents' unacknowledged sense of shame as if by osmosis, are given a model of an unsuccessful attempt to deal with shame.

Marriage counsellors who are aware of the effects a sense of shame can have on couples – and through them, on their children – are in a position to respond therapeutically.

So far we have indicated that people receive in childhood a sense of historical family shame almost by osmosis; that it has a reinforcing effect when in early life they are personally humiliated, or given permission to disparage others as a way of displacing a sense of shame; and that in marriage one partner can continue to follow a childhood pattern of disparaging the other to avoid facing his or her own shame, while the other continues to accept the role of the recipient of that displaced shame.

Healthy Shame

Is there such a thing as healthy shame, in the same way as there is something we call healthy guilt? We believe there is, but it is of a very different order from the shame we have been describing.

In their socialization Western children learn the basic manners and customs that ensure their acceptability by their social group, and when their parents use reproof and shaming as one way to ensure their children's conformity it does not necessarily cause a damaging sense of shame. In fact children feel good about themselves when they demonstrate the social competence expected for their age, and avoid feeling ashamed of their behaviour. An example of healthy shame is instanced somewhere by Erik Erikson: When the little Eskimo child stepped on dangerous ice, tribal jeering for his action shamed him into learning quickly to distinguish where it was safe to step. His response of shame, being essential to his survival, was healthy shame.

When we feel ashamed of our nation because many of its members — including Christians, and maybe including us — are racist, it is a healthy shame that we experience: appropriate, responsible shame that motivates us to promote in ourselves and our group a change of attitude. When Ezra expressed distress before the Lord, tearing his garments and pulling out his hair because his people (though not Ezra himself) had been unfaithful to God, his sense of shame was healthy. And when in prayer we confess our personal sins, the shame we feel before our loving, forgiving Lord is a healthy response of feeling that strengthens our will to turn from wrongdoing.

Self-Esteem

'My problem is I have very low self-esteem.' Over and over again, the counsellor listens to this opening remark from clients in first interviews. 'What I am doing with this couple is working on their low self-esteem.' Over and over again, the supervisor hears this comment from counsellors in supervision.

As with shame and guilt, around the concept of self-esteem there is much muddled thinking. In popular usage the term 'low self-esteem' implies a serious condition in the form of a precise malady — something similar to having a problem with low blood pressure. However, 'low blood pressure' as a descriptive term is a clear medical entity and is a measurable thing, whereas 'low self-esteem' as a descriptive term is not useful because it is vague and inadequate. People can use it like the proverbial wooden leg, feeling bad about it, encouraging others to feel sad for them for having it, and the more they refer to it the less able they are to do anything positive about it.

When a counsellor identifies (and encourages the client to identify) their problem as having low self-esteem, what is the counsellor saying to himself about the client? It could be 'This poor person has a bad opinion of herself. She had an unhappy childhood and nobody loves her enough.' It could also be 'If only I can help her to feel good about herself then her basic problem will be cured.' If he thinks in these terms, the counsellor is perceiving the client as being only acted upon — as if she were a pawn and a victim.

Some Christian counsellors, unpractised in seeing a client as a complex person of ambiguities and contradictions and paradoxes, take up the concept of esteem with enthusiasm and they 'work on the low self-esteem' earnestly. They get nowhere that's genuinely therapeutic for the client, especially if they seek to engage the client's cognition and use a sympathetic tone. 'But you are a worthwhile person. God loves you, I love you too . . . You are special to him . . . You are a very special person.'[7] A common response from the client's 'child' is to resist the truth in such a response; and then the counsellor will try harder, and still fail to convince. Or the client will find the counsellor very kind and sympathetic and affirming, and go away feeling temporarily comforted. But in either event, the rescuer has once again failed (as rescuers do) to turn the victim into a genuinely self-valuing person.

When a more experienced counsellor responds to the concept of

[7] An attempt to sympathetically engage with such a client is, of course, kinder than responding in a rejecting way.

'low self-esteem', he may work with the client's thinking and feeling – even with her 'child' determination to stay feeling bad about herself – and he may eventually give her opportunity to accept some personal responsibility for feeling bad about herself. However, by accepting 'low self-esteem' as a diagnosis, his counselling runs the risk of leaving her in a self-referential position, but with her bad feelings now turned outward instead of inward. The counsellor in this case has taken her in the direction of feeling good about herself at the cost of feeling defensive toward those she perceives as wanting to put her down and being responsible for the lowering of her self-esteem. So the outcome can easily be that her new, higher regard for herself is at the expense of her perception of her detractors. Such 'heightened self-esteem' means she is alone, individual, and against the perceived oppressors. She is still seeing the power as outside herself, and she is pitting herself (even aggressively) against them, as a way of dealing with her self-definition.

Going with the concept of self-esteem as an absolute, a counsellor does not discern and take account of the client's hidden aggression, self-centredness and self-pity. If all along he helps her attend to these hidden aspects of herself, he will be working more therapeutically with her self-concept, for these hidden things are in fact reinforcing her bad feelings about herself and her victim position.

Behavioural Statements

For useful therapeutic interventions we start by encouraging the client to change the statement 'I have low self-esteem' into specific behavioural statements: 'I tell myself I am inferior when . . .', 'I feel bad about myself when . . .' Statements of this kind define the changes in behaviour she needs to make in order to draw the power back to herself and so regard herself differently and relate differently to others. (Other chapters indicate ways to proceed in counselling from a new definition.)

In counselling a couple, it is useful to encourage both husband and wife very early to regard the partner who says 'I have low self-esteem' in a different light. Unless this encouragement is given, a spouse often continues to do just what unpractised Christian counsellors tend to do, as in the example above. While a spouse reinforces the partner's victim ('low self-esteem') position with sympathetic rescuer responses, the couple's potential for growth together toward a mutual positive regard suffers a limitation.

Many counsellors have come to see the ancient theme of 'Deny yourself' as the basis, even the aetiology, of low self-esteem. Jesus Christ said 'Deny yourself': and he said more than just that. Working with clients who have been compulsive deniers of self, these counsellors have frequently reminded them that Jesus tells us to love ourselves; that when he reiterated the ancient law by saying 'You shall love your neighbour as yourself', he emphasized the necessity of a self-love that is equal to the love of others. And counsellors do well to give this reminder to many clients, as long as counsellors understand also the concept of self-denial.

For we are indeed called to deny ourselves – to die to self. But in order to truly do so, we first have to have a self and to own our self in all that self's complexity, and then we have to *value* our self. It is to the extent that we both own and love our self that we are free to deny self or die to self. Thus the call is to find and own our self, love our self, and deny our self. (Then dying to self becomes a life-affirming thing.) It is in obeying the call to do all three things that genuine self-esteem lies. Skilled counselling that facilitates our finding and owning of our self can also lead us to love our self in a sturdying way.

Feeling good about self

Marriage counsellors then, are dealing with the self/other love Jesus spoke of. They see that we reach toward the fullness of our humanity as we come to relate well to self, to our significant others, and to the context in which we live. So genuine self-esteem develops as we feel good about our self, about those we relate to closely, and about the wider community. Feeling 'good' does not mean a constant self-satisfaction, and it does not mean smugness; nor does it mean an uncritical acceptance of the behaviour and beliefs of others, or an acceptance of what is going on around us. Feeling 'good' implies a position of strength in affirming what is right, in identifying and standing against what is wrong and in seeking to correct wrongs.

Genuine self-esteem is very like genuine humility. It leads to a *realistic assessment* of our self, our limitations and abilities, and a realistic assessment of the quality of our relating with intimates and of our response to our context.

Genuine self-esteem in a counsellor includes the ability to take care of himself (e.g. by ensuring adequate rest as well as adequate preparation for his work). In this way he takes good care of his clients, being usefully available to them in counselling. He also shows them by his model that the self he is taking care of is not a wilful little kid who wants to be omnipotent, but a concerned person wanting to be available and responsive to others.

All this is a far cry from the commitment to some vague concept of 'self-esteem' that is so often referred to. As we who are pastors and counsellors seek to live out from within ourselves the attitudes to self that were discussed above, we will increasingly be of use to clients who feel bad about themselves and define their situation as suffering from low self-esteem.

10

EMPATHY AND CONFRONTATION

The use of empathy in counselling is much more complex than it first appears. While a novice counsellor will need to practise and practise empathy as taught by Geldard or Egan, the process of learning to empathize accurately and deeply will go on throughout her ministry.

Empathy demands profound respect by the counsellor as she seeks to enter the internal world of the client. She must remember that *this person's private world is holy ground*. So the counsellor is not *inquisitive* – does not seek information for her own curiosity or satisfaction, but only in so far as what the client has to tell is part of dealing with the issue.

The counsellor will curb her desire to *interpret* – she will go no further than the client has said. She will aim to say what she thinks the client has said or meant, so that she is perceived as being with the client in that moment.

The counsellor will avoid *psyching-out* – knowing more than the client about what he is feeling or thinking. There is a temptation for a counsellor to read the client's mind by responding 'What you're really saying is . . .' or 'What you're really feeling is . . .'[1] This counsellor may seem to be building on what the client has said, but is actually jumping ahead of the client in *deciding the meaning for the*

---

[1] Or a more sophisticated statement: 'I hear you saying . . .' followed by what the counsellor imputes to the client.

client, without checking with him. In so doing, she is disregarding or discounting what the client has said, for no one can know what another person is thinking or feeling unless the person tells her. An experienced and perceptive counsellor is able to make a shrewd guess, but does not *know* until the client confirms the guess.

Experienced counsellors find value in checking from time to time the quality of their listening and of their empathy. We found that a half-day workshop on listening skills was valuable to the staff of a marriage counselling agency, every few years. To get right back to basics was a valuable discipline for experienced counsellors, and a time of fun and mutual support amongst those who were carrying heavy case-loads.

Capacity for Empathy

Not everyone who aspires to be a counsellor has the capacity for the quality of empathy required for competent counselling. The capacity will depend partly on the person's experience of facing difficulties in living her own life and in the experience of struggling with relationships. People who seem to sail through life without problems have limited capacity for empathy: they find it almost impossible to understand *from the inside* the internal conflict of another person.

In her training a counsellor is required to identify her own *compulsive or routine unexamined ways of looking at the world*. Our defensive human responses are commonly described as fright, fight and flight. For some, a first response to danger or the unknown is to freeze and become immobile. Others respond by becoming angry and aggressive, while others will flee the scene either literally or metaphorically (physically or emotionally). These are almost automatic responses, habitual and well-practised – and they are used whatever the stimulus or trigger. They are not thought-out or evaluated. In spite of 'being there for the other', the counsellor tends to use her habitual mode, though perhaps in a more sophisticated and modulated way, when for any reason she feels defensive in the interview. In so doing, she limits her capacity to feel with the client at that moment.

Enthusiasm for a preconceived solution can undermine the quality of a counsellor's empathy. One who has an automatic problem-solving method which she uses compulsively with herself and others will often miss the core of what the client is saying to her.

Platitudes like 'forgive and forget' and 'look on the bright side' are likely to result in the client believing the counsellor does not understand what is real to him at the moment. 'Pray about it', 'Praise the Lord' and 'Let us lay hands on you and pray over you' may be helpful at some stage of counselling when the timing is right, but frequently seem to the client to be pious dismissals of the significance of their problem.

Discriminating Empathy

Counsellors must be discriminating in their empathy. Whether they realize it or not, counsellors are always choosing which part of the client's experience they will empathize with (for the client's person and experience are always more complex than any empathic statement we can make). At times, the counsellor will choose to empathize with the sad, angry or scared part of the client in encouraging the client to explore the destructive part of the self and seek ways of dealing with it. At other times, she will empathize with the rational decision-making aspects of the self, or with the aspects concerned with self-responsibility, values and caring. Growth in skill in the counsellor (including ever-increasing understanding of theory) will result in better choices of empathic responses.

The counsellor must beware of reinforcing a client's tendencies to self-destructive behaviour and attitudes. For example, she will not laugh with a client who laughs as he talks of killing himself or describes some non-constructive activity in an amusing way.

Some counsellors say: 'Whatever you feel is valid.' This kind of empathy is usually an attempt to express acceptance of the client's feeling. However, it seems to confuse two meanings of 'valid' when applied to feelings. A distinction must be drawn between these two meanings: a) This is the appropriate (valid) feeling because it is a natural get-somewhere response to the situation, or b) This is the feeling you actually feel (valid, in that sense) even if it does not motivate you to the kind of action that will help you to solve the problem. It may be the chronic well-practised familiar feeling response you have whatever the stimulus.[2] A counsellor who is making this distinction may choose to empathize with the latter (racket) feeling as a temporary measure (e.g. 'it seems important for you to feel X, for now') to enable the client to feel safe enough to review the feeling, and move towards the authentic feeling.

Through training and supervision a counsellor is encouraged to reflect on her experience in counselling and so expand her understanding of empathy – from *the ability to reflect accurately the words and feelings of the client.* With this consistent stance she responds authentically not only to *the inner world of the client,* but particularly to *that part of their inner world which is seeking to live well and relate well.*

Confrontation

Empathy is the ability to feel into where the other person is, while maintaining objectivity. It is basic to the way a counsellor uses herself, and that is why much time in counsellor training courses is spent on practising empathic responses to another person. Enhancing one's skills in empathy is an essential and continuing task for the counsellor.

Sometimes as we listen to counsellors speaking about empathy, we wonder if they believe that being truly empathic means one must never confront. They speak of 'unconditional positive regard' and 'acceptance' as if those terms are almost a synonym for counselling, and as if they preclude confrontation.

However, part of one's ability to be empathic is the ability to confront appropriately. If a counsellor regards a client or a couple in counselling highly, that regard will sometimes issue in confronting. Terms like 'prizing the client' surely mean valuing clients highly

[2] See 'authentic' and 'racket' feelings, chapter 8 pp. 92ff.

enough to query the wisdom or the rightness of what they say and do.

Sometimes the term '*tough love*' has been used in relation to therapeutic relationships. It can be a useful term — as long as it is never taken as permission to attack a person and cut them down, in the guise of caring. We are suggesting that using tough love genuinely with oneself is an essential part of self-care. Do we as counsellors use tough love on ourselves? Practice in doing so is a prerequisite to the ability to be an empathic counsellor whose empathy includes sensitive confronting.

Self-Confrontation in Repentance

One way we experience confronting as self-care is in considering our personal wrongdoing. In our own church we have an opportunity to do this at every service, in the silence that comes after the pronouncement of God's law — usually in the form of the two great commandments Jesus Christ gave us — and before we share as a congregation in the formal words of confession. When the silence comes (unless it is unfortunately shortened to a little pause) we can confront ourselves in more than a quick and fleeting way. Our self-confrontation may be the way we talk to God in this time.

We each have our own unique way of communicating with God. For some of us, it may be feasible to say silent words like these: 'Oh God, that was a rotten thought I had about someone I call my friend . . . What a beastly sharp tongue I used on my spouse . . . I guess I'll be back here, Lord, next Sunday, confessing the same habitual sins . . . I move so slowly in my journey with you . . . thank you for your patience . . . and I don't even want to admit that I let myself off a hook with that half-truth, but I did.'[3]

---

[3]Talking to God in this familiar way may not be feasible for Christians who *emotionally* do not relate to God as a merciful as well as just God. Their image does not necessarily come from any lack of genuine faith in God's love and redeeming power. With some people it comes from third-system experience with somebody akin to Beryl's stern grandmother (see chapter 3).

Confronting myself before God in the silence — daily, not just at Sunday services — is an exercise in empathy and positive regard for myself. If I haven't much ability to feel into where I am before God, while maintaining some objectivity, I am lacking in empathy for myself. It's in penitence (sometimes almost despairing) and in faith (accepting God's positive regard for me in my sinfulness) that I confront myself. Or, more accurately, that God and I confront each other.

Self-confrontation in Friendship

A second way we can experience confronting as self-care is to talk to a trusted friend or pastor at regular intervals about our habitual failings. Such a friend is one who wants the best for me, and has no personal investment in putting me right. As we sit and talk together a little and spend time in silent prayer together, I confess my sins before God in the presence of this friend. Then the friend makes comments which include loving confrontations. For any of us who have such a friend, this method gives us practice in receiving responses from someone who takes us seriously enough to offer us tough love, and who thus helps us in our self-confrontation. Supervision offers the same tough love about our professional practice.

Learning from the 'Child' Within

There is a third method of self-confrontation, and it is one that can aid discernment between *attack that comes from disregard* and *confrontation from positive regard*. This method involves something like empty-chair work, except that you can do it without moving if you wish.

The first step is to set aside a quiet time in a quiet place, and recall an incident earlier in your life when you said or did something that needed correction. Then recall the words and tone of someone confronting your behaviour, and open yourself to your own remembered response to that confrontation.

Perhaps the confronter shamed you. *'That was a silly way to behave . . . Everyone at church was shocked . . . You made a laughing stock of yourself.'* Hear the words that shamed⁴ you and open yourself to your inner 'child'. If you or I shame someone who has come to us for counselling, it is a misuse of our power and it damages further their inner 'child'.

As a reasoning adult you understand that the rebuke you received in that incident came from someone who felt responsible for, and thus embarrassed or shamed by, your behaviour – and who displaced their shame onto you. (The words of the rebuke tell you that.) As a child you felt the shame of being shamed. We counsellors can use more subtle and thus more powerful ways of shaming clients than the cross words you might recall from your incident.

Perhaps in an early incident of confrontation you were reproved. *'You can do better than that. It's not good enough.'* It is possible that your response to these words was a useful sense of guilt – but only if the tone of the reproof was encouraging and gentle, and the assessment contained in it was accurate. Hear the words that reproved you, and be aware of the 'child' within. Is it a harsh demanding confrontation at which you feel despair? To rouse in someone we counsel a despairing guilt is another misuse of counsellor power: it disables, instead of facilitating.

People come to counsellors in a dependent, needy position. Counsellors hold, therefore, great power over them. It is the 'child' in the client, unprotected by reasoning and self-care, who is likely to receive the brunt of the counsellor's confrontations. Later we will discuss the timing of confrontations. For the moment we want to re-iterate these things:

- However much or little formal training we have had in developing an understanding of what empathy entails, the three suggested methods of practising self-confrontation can sensitize us to how people we counsel may feel when we confront them.

⁴In retrospect, you can understand what the situation in early life entailed: shame was displaced onto you, rather than your behaviour being so terribly shameful. While this understanding may not be sufficient to heal the bruising, it can be a step toward such healing.

• When people in counselling begin to experience from us that they are accepted and positively regarded, their 'child' is likely to be joined by their more reasoning and more self-regarding self. This supports and protects the 'child' so that, when we confront, they are able to receive our confrontations — and if necessary, reject them. But in any confrontation we make, we still have gentle regard for the sensitivities of the 'child'.

Supportive Confrontation

In continuing the third exercise suggested, imagine yourself a child requiring correction, and sense how you might respond to the following confrontations when given by a benign, gentle corrector who wants to engage your own thinking and self-regard.

'I guess you have reasons for doing it like that. How would you do it so it's not hurting yourself and him?'

'Would you be willing to say that again, in a way that's softer and more tender to you both?'

'I don't understand how it seemed good for you to do that just now. Will you tell me?'

'How is it that X seems okay to you when Y is what you're wanting?'

As you imagine yourself to be a child receiving these confrontations, the chances are that you experience them as regardful, not bruising of you. That's because they are coming, not from the confronter's third system (as shaming and guilt-producing confrontations tend to) but from someone relatively whole.[5] None of us is Jesus Christ, none of us in this life can ever be whole in the sense that Jesus was, but our confrontations will be increasingly like those he made to bruised and failing people, as we learn what positive regard and tough love

[5] As a client, I may feel some genuine shame or guilt as a result of some intervention by the counsellor; but it will be because of how I confront myself with the intervention, and not because I feel shamed or accused of guiltiness by the counsellor.

are about. As we become more genuinely empathic with those we counsel, we are able to confront in ways that are healing to them.

It remains possible for some counsellors to believe that confrontation is always wrong, or to be so condoning that they never offer appropriate confrontation. A counsellor said to a client 'I'm shocked that your pastor has questioned your life style. Put him in the empty chair and tell him it's your decision how you live your life and he has no right to intrude! Shout at him! Tell him to get out of your life!' It is a moot point whether the pastor's questioning was shocking. It is very likely that the counsellor's invitation to the client was a strong response from his own third system.

Timing a Confrontation

There are contemporary workbooks on counsellor training that include sections on the skill of confronting.[6] We can consider effective confronting as depending on

- a trusting relationship that has built up between the person or couple being counselled and the counsellor, so that *communicated empathy* is experienced;

- the counsellor's clear thinking about and understanding of theory, through personal and professional experience; along with the counsellor's accurate perception of the other person's position;

- the readiness that the counsellor perceives in the client to receive the confrontation.

For the person being counselled, the moment of readiness is when they are *beginning to sense an incongruity* in their position or their behaviour: an incongruity between the good they are wanting and the way they have been going about getting it.

[6]For example Geldard, D., *Basic Personal Counselling*, Prentice Hall, Australia 2nd edition 1993 or Egan, G., *The Skilled Helper* 2 Ed. Brooks Cole, California 1982.

The following model, attributed to Talcott Parsons, is one we find useful in teaching counsellors the place of confrontation in a person's process of change.

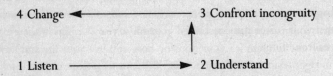

When we have presented this diagram at clergy courses, participants have expressed enlightenment in these terms.

'I was taught just to be empathic, and my counselling has remained on the bottom line. I've listened and empathized unfailingly – and haven't facilitated change in the person.'

'I guess I've tried to help people by correcting them, and my counselling has been on the diagonal. I've listened and confronted gently or abrasively – and they haven't achieved change as a result.'

The model above reminds us that for confrontation to be effective, it must make clear the incongruity of the person's position. In the best confrontation, *the counsellor confronts by pointing up an incongruity,* then *the person counselled confronts his or her own current behaviour.* 'How is it that X seems okay to you when Y is what you're wanting?' is an example of confronting by pointing up an incongruity.

The second best confrontation is when the counsellor is perceived as confronting *from on their side,* i.e. the counsellor has so identified with the person by understanding how life is for them (empathy) that the confrontation seems friendly and not attacking. He may comment 'You say you don't want to be talking about your difficulties, yet you're here' and so contrast the verbal defensiveness with the willingness to be present. Sometimes the incongruity can be brought into focus by the question 'Really?' or even by a puzzled look.

All counsellors make mistakes in confronting clients, and the diagram above provides a way of understanding how mistakes may be analysed and corrections made. If a person rejects a confrontation or is unable to understand the confrontation, the counsellor needs to think about the position on the diagram. He knows that he needs to backtrack one step on the model, and empathize with the client's resistance or confusion, until the client is ready to hear and use the confrontation.

The same strategy applies when the counsellor's empathic response seems to be missing the client (again, resistance or confusion is involved). He then knows that his correction is to go back to listening carefully, and he may say 'I seem to have misunderstood what you said; will you tell me again, so I can pick up where I missed you?' In these ways the counsellor demonstrates a quality of respect: respect for the person by demonstrating that he, the counsellor, needs to be corrected so that he can be sure he is meeting the client accurately and usefully.

The Talcott Parsons model can be a useful concept in preparing sermons. We who are members of a congregation need to feel that the preacher hears and understands our predicament (empathy). Then we are more likely to hear the confrontation (prophetic word) as edifying. 'Edifying' means 'building up', and the real building up that sermons provide is something that enables us to change our behaviour.

11

WORKING ON
COMMUNICATION

The idea of 'lack of communication' is still dying a lingering death. In the third quarter of the twentieth century it was a popular term to describe an inability of a husband and wife to talk through their conflicts. At one stage it was dubbed the most common difficulty bringing couples to counselling, but it was as vague a description of marital dysfunction as 'incompatibility' — vague and therefore useless.

Filling in their required record and statistics sheets, many counsellors would tick 'lack of communication' or 'breakdown of communication' for their cases that did not fit into easily definable categories like 'financial problems' and 'adultery'. The categories provided were not mutually exclusive in any case, and they were never as simple as the ticks placed in the statistics boxes suggested.

Communication difficulties were involved in all the categories. Yet between all couples, communication goes on continuously: the turn of a shoulder, a facial expression, a flicker of the eyes or of a smile are all part of what is being communicated. Spouses in their home who are not speaking much to each other may be communicating a variety of messages:

- I am comfortable just being with you, and I understand you are comfortable just being with me.

- I don't like you much at the moment.

- Talking to you has a low priority with me.

- I'm waiting for you to apologize so I can forgive you.

When they are apart, and make few phone calls or write seldom, the communication in this behaviour may communicate one of two very different messages:
- I don't want to communicate with you.
- You and I trust and love each other, and constant contacts are unnecessary.

Let's look at other, more complex messages being communicated at home. Is a spouse silent? What is the silence saying? It may be one or more of these messages.
- I'm afraid you will cut me down if I respond to you.

- I'm afraid whatever I do or say won't be right for you.

- I have strong feelings about what you have said, but I won't try to express them: I can't or dare not.

- You have such strong feelings that I cannot match them. I just feel helpless.

- I'm depressed.

- I just can't bear to think about and respond to what you are saying.

- I'm not interested in making contact with you.

- You and your feelings and your demands are not worth responding to.

- I'm hostile to you, and I'm letting you know by my silence.[1]

- I've given up on you.

[1] This may not be apparent when a couple seem to have good relationships with others. A minister and spouse each gave the other hostile messages by 'lack' of communication. In their home and at church, they each made warm and positive contact with others. It was only after much familiarity with them that the church people noticed their lack of positive regard for and open communication with each other. Their reaching out to others deflected the awareness of others from the couple's mutual hostility. Church roles, persons and relationships can allow couples

Is one spouse a ready and frequent talker — perhaps talking with increasing intensity? The over-talking may be a communication of some of these messages:

- I'm afraid if I don't keep talking you will not be there for me.

- I'm afraid however I try to be, it will not be right in your eyes.

- You are so strongly self-contained I can't reach you.

- I'm sad, and talking stops me feeling my sadness.

- I just can't bear to stop talking and think about what your silence is saying.

- My every thought, wish and feeling are important and I have to speak them.

- I'm hostile to you, and I'm letting you know by my words.

- By keeping on talking, I'll keep myself disengaged from you.[2]

Messages Outside Awareness

So in both silences and over-talking, messages are given to one's marriage partner; and those suggested above do not form a complete list.[3] The content of these messages is usually outside of the awareness of the giver, to some extent, and *more so* outside of the receiver's awareness.

This does not mean that such a message is not really being given and received. It is given, and it is received, and it affects greatly what happens between the couple. In fact, it is so powerful that it determines to a large extent the relationship of the husband and wife. The

---

— not only ministers and spouses — to continue with their negative communication unnoticed. However, the dysfunction is debilitating to them and to others around them, whether noticed or not.

[2]Two people can remain disengaged by both over-talking to each other about all kinds of trivial and seemingly important matters — avoiding matters that would involve engagement with each other, i.e. a taking of each other seriously.

[3]The silent spouse may be either husband or wife; the talkative spouse likewise.

giving and the receiving of the message are powerful because of the very fact that the message is given and received *outside* much of the couple's awareness.

An important aspect of counselling is to give each spouse freedom to become more clearly aware of their hidden messages. The less skilled counsellor might say 'I have a hunch that you don't talk to your husband because you don't think his feelings are worth responding to.' Or 'I suspect you keep talking because you want to keep disengaged from your wife.' This is intrusive mind-reading. To tell clients what I (the counsellor) think, is imposing my interpretation instead of helping them identify their secret messages.

Ideally, the wise counsellor gives the couple not just time to test and trust her, but also the respect of always letting *them* find, test and trust their own hidden messages. As they do this, she continues to help each feel safe in becoming aware of the power of their secret messages.

Action Modes for Changing Faulty Communication

This title is a shorthand way of referring to something the *counsellor* does that allows the *couple* to do something. It is not meant to conjure up a picture of a counsellor whose actions are *changing* a couple. People are not puppets worked by someone's actions.

It is the counsellor who provides the action modes in the counselling room – the techniques, the therapeutic methods, the suggestions of practising new behaviour, right there. It is the couple who, facilitated by what the counsellor provides, do the practice and the actual changing of their communication. It is only they who can change aspects of their communication and their relationship patterns.

Using the Empty Chair

In providing action modes, the counsellor can make various uses of two-chair or empty-chair work. The goal of these uses is to clarify messages: messages given by self to self, and messages given between self and others. By using two chairs as hosts for the speakers and listeners in a dialogue, messages are differentiated.

In counselling Tim and Sally,[4] David notes that they continue to play out in a session their circular pattern of criticizing and protesting. He asks Sally and Tim to turn their chairs directly toward each other. Then he asks Sally to move from her chair and observe from a corner of the room. He then invites Tim to criticize the Sally whom he 'sees' sitting in the chair opposite – to criticize (his perception of) Sally.

David: 'Tell her what she's doing wrong.'

Tim: 'She knows what she's doing wrong. It's just that she won't do anything about it.'

David: 'Speak to Sally-in-the-chair, and tell her she knows what she is doing wrong and she won't do anything about it.'

Tim: 'All right. I'll try, but don't expect me to do it well.'

David: 'Fine! Just have a go.'

Tim: 'Well, Sally, you know what you do wrong. The real trouble is you don't want to do anything about it.'

David: 'Fine. Tell her more.'

Tim: 'If only you did your work in the proper order, and at the proper time, things would be good.'

David: 'Step it up. Really criticize her!'

Tim: 'You'd think you would want to do your home duties well, but you mess around all day. Then you expect me to fix up the mess when I come home from work. I need some care and you just put demands on me. Why don't you organize your day better, and then welcome me when I come home?'

David has the option now to ask Tim to go over to Sally's chair and, as Sally-in-the-chair, reply to Tim-in-the-chair. However, David chooses to stay with Tim's side of the pattern, helping him to say aloud the sequence of words he habitually says in his head.

[4] See chapter 4.

David: 'Tim, will you tell Sally-in-the-chair what you really want when you come home.'

Tim: 'Well, Sally, I want you to take me seriously, instead of complaining. I'd like a warm welcome.'

David: 'Tell her more of what you want.'

Tim: 'I want to be important to you. I don't want to be ignored and have a job dumped on me. I want a kiss and a hug and a chance to wind down.'

David: '"I want to be important to you."'

Tim: 'Yes. I *need* you to see me as important to you.'

Tim is moving from criticisms of Sally to expressing his needs in a vulnerable way. Invited by David to step up the criticisms, he says 'Why don't you . . . welcome me?' and it is this David picks up on. 'Tell her what you really want.' Thus, however uncomfortable it is for Sally to observe Tim's *criticisms*, she is soon watching him express *needs*.

David chooses this moment to bring Sally back to her chair. Since she has observed the criticisms from a little distance, rather than being their actual recipient, David expects that she will be less defensive and protesting; more free to respond usefully to Tim's statement of his needs.[5]

But what if Sally comes to her chair defensive and protesting? This would indicate that David has been premature in inviting Sally back to her chair. Choosing the moment well comes with David's awareness of Sally's inherent goodwill to Tim and desire for better communication with him. It also comes with David's development of empathic awareness in the plights of many Sallys and Tims. Every counsellor who uses two-chair well has learnt to do so by reflecting on experience with many couples' communication patterns.

David: 'Sally, from over there you heard Tim criticize his perception

[5]David is adding a dimension to the two-chair technique, by bringing in the other partner to receive the newly considered message: the message that her husband has worked out in his two-chair exercise. David adds to this a communication exercise by bringing Sally to the chair to respond to Tim.

of you. And then you heard him speaking out his need. Will you respond to that?'

Sally: 'Look, I'd love to give him a hug and a kiss when he comes in. But I know the house is a mess and he's going to be upset . . .'

David: 'Will you speak to Tim, respond to what he said?'

Sally: 'Um, I'll give you a hug and a kiss when you come in, if you don't criticize me.'

David: 'Would you be willing to tell him "I'll give you a hug and a kiss even if you criticize me"?'

Sally: (laughing) 'That's asking a lot!'[6]

David: 'Here's a bit more! "I'll give you a hug and a kiss even if I want to protest against your criticism."'

Sally: 'Well, yes, Tim, I suppose I could do that. But I would want you to do something about the criticizing.'

Tim: 'I'd like that, Sally. I really don't want to criticize you. Look, if I got a welcome like that, I'd really pay attention to *you* instead of the mess.'

Sally: 'So are we making a bargain? Am I supposed to give you a hug and a kiss while I'm resentful, and are you supposed to stop criticizing?'

Tim: 'It seems a bit like that. I just think it would be great if we could find a better way.'

David: 'I guess nobody's saying you're *supposed* to hug and kiss him, Sally, or you're *supposed* to stop criticizing her, Tim, when you're both resentful. But do you think a sort of bargain between you would work for you both?'

Tim and Sally are taking a step in a continuing process. There is more for them to do in the counselling room. However, David sees that Tim has used the chair work to move beyond his criticizing to express a need; and he has expressed it in a way that enables Sally to move toward, rather than away from him or against him.

---

[6] David is certainly asking a lot. He believes that, in Sally's obvious goodwill to Tim, she can take the step. He has already worked with her so that she has identified her protesting as a defensive behaviour.

Sally's Work

David uses the empty chair later, to work more directly with Sally. He recognizes that Sally is mainly in a passive responsive position rather than in an active initiating position. He invites Tim to vacate his chair and, like Sally earlier, to observe from a little distance. He asks Sally to move from her own chair and, as if she were Tim, criticize Sally-in-the-empty-chair. He asks her to sit in Tim's chair, assuming Tim's posture and manner of speaking.

Sally: 'You're no good as a wife. You're always in a mess. You don't take proper notice of me. You do your jobs at the wrong time. You're just trying to avoid me. You're avoiding loving me.'

David: 'Go over to the empty chair and be yourself responding to Tim.'

Sally: 'Tim, you have no idea how hard it is to keep the house tidy when there's so much to be done and the children are so demanding.'

David: 'Protest more, Sally.'

Sally: 'It's all very well for you. You can be a real somebody at work. You can have interesting conversations. I'm stuck with the children and I know we planned all that when we married, but I'm bored. Often I'm bored. And in you come expecting me to wait on you!'

David: 'Go over and be Tim, and respond to that.'

Sally: (**as Tim**) 'There you go making excuses, expecting special treatment, wanting me to do your duties after my day's work.'

David invites Sally with a gesture to move back to her own chair.

Sally: 'Well, what else can I do? I'm doing the best I can, and you think it's not good enough.'

Here, David helps Sally to say out aloud the sequence of words and dialogue she hears in her head. She is relating not only to the actual Tim, but also to the Tim she carries in her head. David helps her to play it out *as she understands it*. He does not question or correct her understanding, but rather asks her to heighten her protesting to the criticisms she voices as Tim. Now he moves the scene away from the marriage.

David: 'If it were not Tim in the chair, who would it be?'

Sally: 'Not Tim?'

David: 'Whose criticisms would you be protesting to, if they were not Tim's?'

Sally: 'Oh, I see what you mean. It would be Father's, of course. I could never do it right for Father.'

David: 'Come to this chair and be Father saying you can't do it right.'

Sally: (**as Father in Tim's chair**) 'You really could do better, Sally. Your mother and I know it. You're not trying hard enough.'

David: 'Come over and be Sally who's about seven years old.'

Sally: 'I do try hard, Dad. I wish my marks for spelling were better, but I really did try.'

David motions Sally to the other chair.

Sally: (**as Father**) 'Well it's not good enough. We're both very disappointed in you. And your room isn't tidy and that makes work for Mummy.'

David motions her to the Sally chair.

Sally: 'Well I wanted it tidy and I tried, and Mummy didn't like the way I tidied it.'

Sally: (**as Father**) 'You're always making excuses. It's not good enough to do that. Please stop making excuses, Sally.'

The parallel is clear – between Sally's perception of her interaction with Tim and her perception of little Sally's interaction with Father. David seeks to heighten the emotion in the exchange between little Sally and Father, watching for a change in Sally's attitude. So far there has been none. David changes tack to facilitate this.

David: 'Tell Dad "If I don't make excuses, then . . ."'

Sally: 'Dad, if I don't make excuses . . . What do you mean, David?'

David: 'Finish this sentence to Dad. "I *have* to make excuses, Dad, because if I don't, then . . ."'

Sally: 'If I didn't make excuses, Dad, then you wouldn't take any notice of me at all. You wouldn't notice what I do.'

David: 'Try this. "When I make excuses, Dad, you know I'm around, and I know I'm around."'

Sally: 'Yes, Dad, you do notice me when I make excuses.'

David: 'Will you tell Dad "I'm a bright little seven-year-old, and I've got a way of getting you to notice me."'

Sally: (Smiling) 'Yes, I am. I mean I was. Whether my room was reasonably tidy or very untidy, I was great with my excuses. And Dad always jumped to respond when I made excuses. He would beg me not to.'

David: 'Sally, tell Tim over there about this bright little girl.'

Sally: 'Yes, Tim, that bright little girl really made her father take notice of her.'

David: 'Tell Tim "I'm the bright little girl who . . ."'

Sally: 'Tim, I'm the bright little girl who makes my father take notice of me with my excuses. And I get you to take notice of me too, but I don't like the kind of attention I get.'

David: 'What would you like from Tim? Tell him.'

Sally: 'Yes, Tim, I'd like you to pay attention to me positively. I want us to stop this criticizing, protesting stuff. I'd like to give you a hug and a kiss when you come home and I'd like you to do the same. I'd like to take you up on that bargain we talked about earlier.'

David: 'How would you need to be different to do that, Sally?'

Sally: 'Well I know that Tim isn't my father, and he thinks I do a number of things well. I need to know that he knows I'm tired and I have tried to keep the house well. I want him to show me he loves me even if the house is in a mess. But then I know that anyhow. It's just that we haven't been good at letting each other know it – we've been criticizing and protesting instead.'

David: 'So how will you be different?'

Sally: 'I'll welcome him and give him a hug even if I'm tired.'

David: 'And what do you want from Tim? Tim, come back into your chair.'

Sally: 'Tim, I'd like us to let each other know we love each other when you come home, without the criticism and excuses.'

Tim: 'I'd like that too.'

David has helped Sally to reconsider her childhood decision about how to survive in life. He has helped Sally to affirm the decision of the little girl to get the attention she needed when she had very limited options. In affirming that decision then, Sally is more free to re-decide how to get the attention she needs in her marriage, where she has more options. She will need to practise her new decision frequently, and David will help her to monitor her progress. He will remind her that it is easy to slip into the old habits, but that she now knows how to move to this more constructive position.

Use of Empty Chair

David uses the empty-chair technique in two different ways. Its use with Tim helps Tim identify the *aim* behind this critical pattern of relating to Sally: the aim of getting Sally's attention. David's different use of the empty chair with Sally helps her to become aware of her protesting pattern, the aim of which is to hold Tim's attention.

Both uses of the technique are designed to let an habitual and inter-active pattern come to a new level of conscious awareness. Sally and Tim have each been running silently in the mind something like a scene from the past. (In the counselling described, Tim's third system dialogue has not been explicated and spelled out as Sally's has. Nevertheless it can be imagined and its power in the present appreciated.)

The needs that they have not communicated clearly ('Please notice me and attend to me') come into sharper focus for both when they

- speak them out instead of running related but un-assessed dialogues in the mind;

- gain distance and therefore a different perspective, through physically separating out the aspects and meanings of their internal dialogues.

As David helps them hear their criticising/protesting conflict in a new way, Tim and Sally begin to evaluate its (*magical*) meaning more accurately and to make this available to their experiments in changing their communication.

As David tracks Tim and Sally in their empty-chair work, he is free to move with them, enhancing the range of their responses. He does this by encouragement, by inviting them to emphasize and exaggerate, and by coaching them to experiment with varied responses. Thus he invites them to change their current communication, which in their neediness at the end of their day's work is driven by criticisms and protests that belong to their third systems.

Effective use of two-chair techniques requires much more skill than is immediately apparent. A common use is where a counsellor is wanting to help a person consider the messages being communicated by one part of themselves, Topdog, to another intimidated part, Underdog. The person's stuck spot comes from the Underdog part's inability to refuse to obey the Topdog. In Perlsian Gestalt terms, this stuck spot is called an impasse. Too often counsellors' work is ineffective in their attempt to resolve the impasse with two chairs. They encourage the client to replay the internal dialogue without helping them review it or resolve it.

Ineffective use of this kind results in the client feeling increasingly helpless and angry as the Underdog, seeing the Topdog as a resented parent-figure from the past rather than a fearful and inhibiting part of themselves. Effective use requires sensitivity to the client's process. Counsellors best equipped to use the technique are those who, in training groups, have experienced it both as clients and as a counsellor working under supervision.

Issues in Two-Chair Work

In considering the use of this technique, the counsellor holds some principles in mind.

- 'Hear' some of the client's *internal dialogue* before initiating a two-chair way of externalizing it.

- The first task after this 'hearing' is to encourage *externalizing the dialogue*, i.e. having the client speak it out to acknowledge both sides of the dialogue which determines their behaviour. They can then, in a new way, pay attention to it as an internal communication of their own.

- Encourage the client to *increase the intensity of the dialogue*: to increase the submission, anger, fear or helpless sadness to calamitous proportions.

- Then *look for changes in the client*: changes in the words or tone of the dialogue, changes in posture or intent. If need be, invite the client to experiment with your own suggested changes, encouraging her to try them out and so experience new possibilities in communication with the other.

- Encourage the client to *practise the new behaviour* and to feel its power; to imagine the responses from the other to what this new behaviour is communicating; and in turn to think about how to respond to these responses, from this new position.

- Have the person come back to their own chair (their 'child' chair) at the conclusion of the exercise, and affirm them in that chair. *It is essential that the person concludes in this chair* – i.e. the chair from which they began their dialogue and in which they experience their 'self'.

- Be aware that this – like any technique – will not always work for the particular person. When it falls flat, have ways to simply affirm the person regarding the accomplishments they have made to this point. Affirming the accomplishments to date might take this form: 'So talking to your Topdog isn't yet achieving the very real freedom you're wanting. Maybe it's a little too early. I guess somewhere inside you there are good reasons to be letting your Topdog hold that power for the moment.'

As counsellors, we pay attention to communication at many levels:

- the verbal and non-verbal between the marriage partners;
- the internal dialogue within each client;
- the verbal and non-verbal between client and counsellor.

In doing so the counsellor's task is to help them identify, clarify and enhance their communication.

12

VIOLENCE IN MARRIAGE

Physical violence in marriage is a frequent or constant theme in the media. A few male judges were under fire in the early 1990s for seeming to say that a certain amount of sexual roughness in marriage was acceptable. Those responsible for women's refuges see a pervading culture of male violence toward women and children and call for drastic action.

Various studies indicate that the marriages of church members are certainly not exempt from violence, nor are clergy marriages. 'Violence' and 'violate' both relate to injury and outrage: to violate is 'to treat profanely or with disrespect'. Those who work professionally with violence as a community and family problem discriminate between its various forms, and also between different kinds of male abusers.

Forms and Modes of Violence

It is not pleasant to focus on the subject of domestic violence. It is easy to become anxious or disgusted, instead of staying attuned to both the husband and the wife who as church members need their minister's pastoral care in their miserable situation. In thinking about violence, concepts are useful to us. We can use a variety of concepts as alternative approaches.

One of our concepts relates to observable behaviour by which forms of violence are identifiable.[1]

1. Physical violence – pushing, punching, squeezing, and other body damage; at its worst, homicide.

2. Verbal violence – shouting, criticizing, talking down to the other person in an intimidating way, and degrading name-calling.

3. Contextual violence – restricting the partner to the home, withholding resources such as money to buy food, and excluding from decision-making.

4. Intimidating postures – standing over the partner or otherwise assuming a threatening attitude.

Verbal, contextual and postural violence, as we define them, may not seem to be of the same order as physical violence. However, all these forms of behaviour that we are calling violence involve the violation of personal rights, threats, and intimidation of another (the marriage partner) through inappropriate use of power. For some women in abusive marriages the forms of violence they find most debilitating are the latter three of the four listed: it is the non-physical forms that they experience as the most destructive to them. To identify verbal, contextual and postural behaviour as violence in one's own mind helps the counsellor or the minister to plan appropriate interventions with the couple in pastoral care or counselling.

Another concept of ours distinguishes two modes of physical violence. As experienced from within the perpetrator[2] it relates to the internal, subjective processes of such a person.

---

[1]These forms and modes of violence relate to behaviour from parents toward children, as well as from men to women (and sometimes women to men). We focus here on their relation to behaviour from husbands to wives.

[2]Refer to previous footnote.

1. Violence that is acceptable to the perpetrator. In his mind, and by his values, it seems to this physically violent man that using force is the right thing to do.

2. Violence that a perpetrator commits at the end of a process in which he has been trying not to lash out physically. Sometimes he has been trying desperately not to resort to it. His action is followed by remorse and shame, though these may be hidden and the violence denied.

The counsellor's or minister's interventions are likely to be more useful to the husband if she can distinguish his response to (or his belief about) his own physical abusive actions. Does he think the behaviour he has just committed was a right action, morally justified? Does he think it was a wrong action, morally unjustified?

'Righteous-Self' Violence

We are calling '*righteous-self*' violence abusive behaviour that is acceptable to the perpetrator. In his family of origin or subculture, it is likely that the pattern of physical abuse practised was accompanied by statements like 'There! You got just what you deserve.' This attitude has a flavour of guilt-free justification about it. The husband who responds to a marital conflict with modelled righteous violence does so with unfeeling, authoritarian power to make his wife conform. He will say or imply 'She deserved it'.

A church member who uses modelled righteous violence has a belief about his role as a husband which is contrary to all that the Christian Gospel is about. His violence is not *ego-dystonic*: it is *not out of harmony with what he thinks is goodness and right behaviour*. The minister's task is to confront the husband's belief system in the light of Christian faith, yet to accept him as a person of worth and someone precious in the sight of God.

It is not always easy to feel accepting of such a man, and it is not easy to get him to examine his belief system. It is however, very easy to put such people in the Too Hard basket of pastoral care. If they are going to change their behaviour, they have to get to the point of believing it is wrong. Thus their care is a challenge to their minister.

Counselling an abusive husband, whether individually, with his wife, or in a group of men with a similar problem, is long-term and skilled work. It is better for ministers to refer such church members to the best source of specialized counselling help available. However, the minister still has a pastoral task with such a husband.

'Helpless-Self' Violence

The kind of behaviour in the second mode of violence described above can be called '*helpless-self*' *violence*. For the husband whose behaviour is of this mode, it is useful to understand a common process identified by J. Schiff et al.[3] There are four distinct steps to this passive behaviour process.

1. **Doing Nothing**   In the ordinary demands of living in a marriage, this husband does not actively engage in issues that need addressing. He works on assumptions that come from a childlike state, and are not based in reasoning and predicting consequences. One of these assumptions is that if he does nothing, the problem will disappear. Another is that it will solve itself. In Schiffian terms, he discounts. He discounts the existence of the problem, or its importance, or its solvability; or he discounts his ability to engage with the problem, or in useful discussion about it. The problem gets larger, yet he still does nothing.

2. **Over-adaptation**   This is, in Schiffian terms, a more intense version of the first step. Inside his head, the wheels are spinning; he is not connecting to the obvious need not to be passive. Externally, his wife is nagging more, or complaining more, and he is trying desperately to calm her down – but without engaging himself with the problem.

[3] See 'Passive Behaviours', in Stewart, I., & Joines, V., *TA Today*, Lifespace Publishing, Nottingham & Chapel Hill 1987, pp. 175-7.

3. **Agitation**   There are physical accompaniments to the internal wheel-spinning, such as foot-tapping, fist-clenching and jaw-tensing. These behaviours take the place of engaging in problem-solving. He uses them as a substitute for thinking about the problem.

4. **Incapacitation or Violence**   He becomes immobilized, perhaps shaking all over. He implodes. Or he may erupt into violence. The violence comes out of a sense of extreme helplessness (incapacitation) and not from a position of feeling strong. While such a man may be physically strong and healthy, he is in fact feeling weak and oppressed.

His situation feels to him like one where he is a small child over whom an oppressive and threatening big person is bending, controlling him. As he becomes increasingly still and passive, the big person presses and pressures him more and more intensely. A small person in this plight feels increasingly helpless, almost suffocated. He has no option but to lash out, with arms and legs and all his strength against the pressures. It is a survival necessity to do so.

The husband is a grown-up strong man, not a small person who really has no option but to lash out. Yet, because he has not learnt how to engage actively in personal encounters with intimates, and to feel strong with them, his behaviour is that of a child frightened by life into passivity.

Michael and Lisa

Michael aged twenty-four and Lisa twenty-eight made an attractive couple. They were carefully dressed. They seemed somewhat shy and very pleasant people. Both were in full-time employment and as yet they had no children, though they planned to have a family later on. Their presenting problem when they came to their first interview was persistent quarrelling through much of their three-year marriage.

The last quarrel had ended with Michael leaving home abruptly, saying the marriage was over. He had stayed with a friend for four weeks, rejecting Lisa's pleading for him to return. (The friend had wisely kept out of their crisis except for providing a room for Michael.) Suddenly Michael had returned home and there had been a tearful reunion. In the year prior to this separation, Michael had rejected Lisa's request that they go together to a marriage counsellor. Now he agreed to do so.

When the counsellor asked them to discuss together how a typical or a specific quarrel of theirs began, continued and ended, both seemed unable to be specific. Their descriptions were vague. They found it hard to focus on the details of their quarrels. Michael said with a smile: 'They seem to be about nothing. Afterwards I don't even know what we've been fighting about. I'm not one to hold grudges.'

They said they quarrelled about money, about Lisa's preoccupation with her patchwork quilting, and about the amount of time Michael spent with his two friends at spectator sports. When the counsellor asked whether their quarrels ever reached the point of throwing things or hitting each other, Lisa said: 'Not really.' Michael added quickly that if Lisa didn't nag him and attack him with harsh words, their marriage would be very happy.

Lisa agreed that she 'harangued' Michael, but she thought she had reason to do so. He helped very little in the house, her job was stressful and she managed all their finances. She wanted him to spend less time watching football and more relaxing with her at home. That was why she criticized him.

Noticing their evasive reactions to her earlier question, the counsellor thought violence might be involved. If so, they were not ready to trust her enough to admit it – though Lisa's reference to 'haranguing' could represent some admission of verbal violence. The counsellor continued to track for details in a less direct manner, giving them time and opportunity to join with her comfortably.

Lisa and Michael continued to move to generalities, away from particularities of their mode of relating to each other. Lisa's *affect* (expression of feeling) seemed flat, while Michael seemed shy and uneasy as he continued to respond very politely to the counsellor and to Lisa. He, like Lisa, was still finding it hard to express himself frankly and directly, even though the counsellor gave him many opportunities to be specific about particulars.

It was not until their third session that the beginnings of an open exchange took place between the couple. Lisa reproached Michael sharply for failing to meet her at an appointed time and place to travel together to this session. Eventually she had come on alone, and Michael had arrived later. (The counsellor had thought it wise to wait for Michael's arrival rather than start with only Lisa present, so this session began half of the hour late.)

When Lisa reproached Michael, he said nothing except to repeat that he had been delayed at work. Lisa continued her reproaches, saying she had been anxious coming late and without him, and was embarrassed that he had kept the counsellor waiting so long. She added that she knew he didn't want to have counselling with her — he had told her so that morning — and she feared he would do nothing to fix their problem, and instead, leave it all to her.

Michael's reply was given in a tone of long-suffering reasonableness, but with an overtone of anxiety. 'Of course I'm coming to counselling. I'm here, aren't I? I couldn't help being delayed today. You don't ever let up, Lisa. You keep on and on about trivial things.' To the counsellor he added: 'Lisa doesn't seem to understand she just *makes* trouble when she goes on and on attacking me. She gets upset and nags about everything. I've got enough pressures without her rocking the boat. I wish she'd understand that.'

The counsellor commented to Michael that in begging Lisa not to rock the boat he seemed very concerned to pour oil on troubled waters. Michael replied that he just wanted them to be happy; he was a very happy person himself, at work and with friends, and Lisa and he could be happy together too, if she wasn't so critical of him.

The next session started on time. Michael was dressed even more carefully than usual. While he was very courteous and pleasant to the counsellor, she sensed in his demeanour an underlying uneasiness. After a while Lisa spoke: 'I have to say this even if it is rocking the boat. The night after last week's talk here, Michael hit me and hit me' – she indicated bruising on her arm – 'and it's happened before, quite a few times. Sometimes he smashes things too.'

Confronting and Joining

Michael showed acute embarrassment. He told the counsellor with some distress that he knew it was wrong to hit Lisa, but she drove him to it. The counsellor's main task in the rest of that session was to attend to Michael, and if possible to get through to him that while she in no way condoned the violence, she was not rejecting him. Joining with such a client requires great skill in being very sensitive to his state of helplessness and fear, yet not implying a condoning of the violence.

Using violent words, smashing domestic items in anger and hitting a person (one's spouse) are abhorrent actions. Whether Michael was admitting this to himself or not, the counsellor could not tell. Perhaps he felt more shamed than guilty about his actions. She saw that so far he had not been taking responsibility for his behaviour. He had been shifting all blame for the conflict onto Lisa ('she *makes* trouble'), saying in effect that she had to take responsibility for the resolution of their conflict ('I just want us to be happy together, and we could be if she wasn't critical').

Michael was reacting to the normal stuff of everyday adult life like a frantic little child. That little child experienced 'being happy' as being disengaged from whatever unpleasant or challenging things were happening. He was denying that he was part of what was going on. Like a child blissfully detached from the stresses attendant on grown-up living in relationship, Michael just wanted to be happy, as he could be with his friends watching a football match.

Michael had lashed out at Lisa like a frantic child reacting to pressures. But it was from a man's powerful body that the lashing came. Though she felt repulsed at the thought of his attack on Lisa, the counsellor could stay with Michael empathically. One reason was she was well aware that the seeds of violence are in every person. Like most of us, she was able to *limit* the expression of her violent impulses, and her *mode* of expression was different. She had some-times used a violent tongue, but not fists; and she had felt like punching and kicking objects, though she had never yet hit a human being or an animal.

Before the session concluded, the counsellor spoke firmly and gravely. 'Michael, it is important that you do not hit Lisa again. You should move out to ensure her safety. Lisa, you must not be in a position where there is a chance of further bodily harm to you. Michael, you have to be the one to decide where you must go for Lisa's safety. You can discuss it together, but you, Michael, must ensure Lisa doesn't get hit again. Where could you go?'[4]

By these words the counsellor was doing what was ethically required to ensure as far as she could the safety of Lisa. She added that she hoped the safety measure of separation would be only temporary, while Michael and Lisa were changing their way of relating. In this way she indicated that in counselling about the issue of Michael's physical violence, Lisa would be expected to consider alternatives to haranguing Michael.

Although Michael and Lisa were sobered by the counsellor's gravity, both were unwilling to accept her direction that Michael should plan and carry out her proposed safety measure. He said it was unnecessary: he was certain he would not hit Lisa again, and as he was going to continue seeing the counsellor, he felt it was better for them not to separate. Lisa was equally unwilling for Michael or for her to move temporarily, and for the same reasons as Michael's.

[4] 'Must' and 'should' are words rarely used by counsellors with clients, because they are likely to be heard as external parental words of authority. Counselling aims at encouraging clients to 'grow themselves up' and develop an internal 'parent' of their own which they can use to make healthy decisions. For that reason, counsel-lors tend to use words like 'It would be better for you if . . .'. Suggestions rather than commands facilitate growth. Even suggestions are infrequently given where clients are used to thinking clearly and predicting consequences accurately. However, in a few situations, as with a couple like Lisa and Michael, an authorita-tive, directing word like 'must' is necessary.

Causes of Violence

Lisa's haranguing was not the *cause* of Michael's violence, and the counsellor would make that clear. The causes had to be seen by him as located within himself. For Michael to stop his violent behaviour, he had to see its cause as located within

- himself;
- his expectations of himself and of other people;
- his assumption that he had no alternative to violence when stressed.

If Lisa was not the cause of Michael's violence, was Michael then not the cause of Lisa's haranguing? Lisa's reaction to Michael was understandable: he wouldn't take a fair share of the housework; he would go off to football instead of giving Lisa his company at home. No wonder she became angry and harangued him.

In everyday language you might say Michael *made* Lisa angry by his behaviour,[5] and thus Michael *made* Lisa harangue him. However, this would be a get-nowhere diagnosis. There is nowhere to go with it, as a means of helping the couple have a satisfying relationship. (It would be even more useless to say Michael's two friends caused the conflict because they kept taking him off to football, away from Lisa.) Describing a linear process of cause-and-effect is different from noting the process of circular interaction.[6] The circular process is where Michael's helplessness *follows* Lisa's haranguing, which in turn *follows* his doing nothing, and so on, and on. If Michael and Lisa can understand this, they will begin to see the meaning of each other's behaviour.

Lisa's anger and haranguing came from her third system. She did it on the basis of her assumption that this was the way to get Michael to conform to her wishes — as her parents had done with her. All parents scold irritably at times. When they do it they are feeling

[5] See 'Make Feel' chapter 7, pp. 81–4.
[6] See chapters 4 and 5.

particularly frustrated or helpless, and they stop thinking in a confident, level way about the best method of getting a child's co-operation.

Lisa's parents harangued angrily very often. In the face of their
little girl's stubborn strength, they felt rather helpless, but they
knew how to attack verbally until she gave in and did what she was
told. Lisa had learned the process well. She didn't behave like this in
more formal, social environments, where she was very lovable. But
in the intimacy and intensity of her most significant relationship —
her marriage — angry scolding seemed the automatic way to react.

Although Lisa knew that her criticisms of Michael became very
nasty at times, she would not have looked on them as verbal
violence. (Unlike physical attacks, the verbal kind doesn't have an
objective measure). But Michael experienced Lisa's angry words as
violent, and felt heavily attacked by them.

For Lisa to stop her automatic response, she would need the counsellor's help to understand its cause as being located within

• herself;

• her expectations of herself and other people;

• her assumption that she had no alternative to haranguing when
  stressed.

The Family of the Church

We have spelt out in great detail what this couple's conflict meant as
a marriage counselling case. Let's consider now the meaning it had
for the members of Michael's and Lisa's congregation.

We call our congregation or parish 'a family', but when crises like
this couple's become known, our church family tends to react like a
very messy family indeed. Physical abuse by a Christian husband —
one of our members — is repugnant to us, as it was to Michael's and
Lisa's counsellor. But unlike their counsellor, we don't want to
recognize that the seeds of violence are in every one of us; and that

to some extent we experienced those seeds in our families-of-origin.

So we tend to feel very threatened – pastor and people alike. Some members of a church in these circumstances can become as chaotic as ants when someone steps on their anthill. They scurry around in all directions, confused and disordered. And in Michael's and Lisa's church family, some members went into scurry when Michael's behaviour became known.

Instead of being reticent, instead of thinking in a restrained and level-headed way, they generated drama among themselves. They expressed shock and horror, and talked piously to each other. They named the couple, especially Michael, in their share-and-prayer group. It was the minister who took firm steps to establish order, and to foster a spirit of restraint and genuine concern in the place of officious excitability.

Continuing the Counselling

After the fourth session the counsellor's plan was to refer Michael to a colleague who ran therapy groups for physically abusive men. Such groups when run by counsellors who are specially trained for this role can be most effective with men who are well-motivated to change. They are valuable also for those whose motivation needs to be strengthened: they provide a model of men (participants) who are practising a different way of being: of living without keeping violence at the ready.

However, the colleague who led groups for violent men was unable to take Michael immediately. The counsellor began a long, slow process of counselling Michael and Lisa separately, in individual sessions. At one of his sessions, Michael began to entertain the idea of seeking separate accommodation to ensure Lisa's safety from his violence. He changed his mind when Lisa asked him not to go. She said she was sure Michael would not hit her again, and anyway she hated the thought of their being apart because she loved him.

The counsellor was getting indications from Lisa that she was using denial as a defence against facing the reality of her domestic situation. This denial was intermittent; sometimes now, Lisa was very ready to let people know Michael had hit her. But when she used denial, it seemed to be Lisa's way of keeping herself and Michael a unit against the world. She often played down (discounted) the significance of his hitting, saying that though it had happened, it was now in the past and they were getting on with their life together.

In his individual sessions, Michael showed considerable ambivalence. At times he seemed willing to take genuine responsibility for his behaviour in the marital conflict, instead of projecting blame onto Lisa. However, at times like Lisa he discounted the significance of his hitting, and wanted to believe that it was now in the past and that he and Lisa were facing the future together as a loving husband and wife.

Michael hit Lisa again. Lisa still resisted going to a safer place, despite the pressing invitation of a church member to come and stay as long as she needed. As this church member was full of righteous indignation against Michael and protectiveness toward Lisa, the counsellor was glad Lisa didn't accept the invitation. But Lisa could have gone elsewhere and she chose not to. In her childlike thinking it seemed to her that, as she and Michael loved each other, she had no need to go.

Michael and Lisa were isolated from their families-of-origin. Their church and their faith meant a lot to them, and so did their minister. They asked their counsellor if he could ring her, and gave both counsellor and minister permission to discuss their situation. The result of this collaboration has been positive. As the counsellor continues now in her *counselling* role, the minister is continuing in his *pastoral* role.

What is the Minster's Pastoral Role?

Through contact with the counsellor, the minister's awareness has been sharpened so that he understands that

- Michael and Lisa are in a symbiotic marriage where Michael is sometimes physically violent;

- Michael, in so far as he still projects onto Lisa responsibility for his hitting, continues to fit the 'helpless-self' category of violent husband;

- Lisa harangues Michael, and also colludes with him in denying the reality of his violence;

- Their pattern is firmly entrenched even though Michael does not hit Lisa frequently.

The minister was already of the opinion that Lisa and Michael required specialist help. He is thankful that it is available to them. At a simple practical level, he is thankful that they are in a financial position to afford such counselling. He knows that even with this specialized help, Michael and Lisa will take slow steps forward and also some steps back.

The minster's role in relation to Michael and Lisa is not to *counsel* the couple, but to *understand* what their situation consists of. The greater his understanding the better able he is to minister to them.

The church people need his ministry too, in relation to the couple's situation that they are aware of and are reacting to. We said earlier that the minister took steps to foster a spirit of restraint and genuine care among a group of excited people in the church. One of his steps was to exercise his prophetic role. He preached two sermons, one on James 3, another on James 1:19-20. We leave you to imagine how he did it without discounting the sensitivities of the people.

We leave you to consider some questions, too. If you were in that minister's place, *how would you minister to the family of the church at this time?* He guesses that Michael's and Lisa's counselling will continue for a long time. He realizes that the outcome is still uncertain, and so is the future of their marriage. In his place, *how would you minister to Michael and Lisa?*

13

MORE ON VIOLENCE

As we discuss violence in marriage, we are aware that the ideal counselling circumstances are not readily available in all regions.

Our example of a case of marital violence is a relatively simple one – as it must be in order to spell out something of what violence entails, and how counselling is used in the best of current circumstances. There are of course many cases of much more extreme and destructive violence than Michael's and Lisa's case. Their case is one where specialist counselling is appropriate. How much more is specialist counselling needed in more extreme cases.

And yet, over and over again, simply because specialist referral and consultation are not available, counsellors and pastors have to settle for good-enough counselling – their own. This is a fact of life, just as it is a fact that violence is endemic to our human condition: violence that is usually based in both chronic anger and a chronic sense of helplessness, or fear of helplessness.

God's specific grace to those who seek daily to serve him works in remarkable ways. God's common grace at work in the world is also remarkable. Some ministers are used in marital situations that seem beyond their capacities. They become channels for God's grace because continually they seek spiritual maturity and emotional maturity, and have, as a result, wisdom and understanding about how human nature works.

Some marriage counsellors who do not claim to be Christians are used in a similar way: they are channels for God's common grace to people. They are ready to seek out the healthy aspects in a couple's commitment and love, and respect these aspects. They work with optimism, seeing beyond the destructive aspects in the relationship. And thus these destructive aspects are touched and ameliorated — because through ordinary, persistent counselling the couple's healthy aspects are being strengthened. Destructive verbal violence and even more dramatic forms of violence can be touched by good enough[1] counselling. Those who exhibit the fruits of the Holy Spirit in their own lives provide a powerful model of non-violence for people they counsel.

What we have just said is not intended to give anyone a mandate to sit lightly in a situation of violence. It is vital that the couple be directed to the best source of counselling available. We are, however, pointing up some realities that can make a difference to those who have no option but to do their own best when counselling in such situations.[2]

We believe there are two principles to be followed by all counsellors, regardless of their professional skills and limitations, which are essential to authentic counselling because they are true to the way life is and the way goodness is:

- We must never condone and never appear to condone personal violence in those we counsel.

- Each of us, counsellor or client, must be held responsible for our own violent attitudes and actions.[3]

In the matter of marital violence, there are two *doctrinaire* positions

---

[1]For the concept of 'good enough', first posited by Winnicott in the 1950s, see chapter 16, p. 196.
[2]Even in the absence of referral possibilities because distance precludes it for the couple, the counsellor can have consultations by telephone with practitioners experienced in the counselling of violent people.
[3]In these two principles concerning violence, we include the four forms of violence identified in chapter 12 p. 141, e.g. the inappropriate use of power by intimidatory postures. Such abusive anger can easily appear to be condoned in the counselling room unless the counsellor is consciously living out the principles in his or her life.

that we question. One involves a ready perception of violence, especially physical violence, as having a demonic cause. Some people who are accepted as spiritual counsellors identify the cause of the problem as 'a spirit of violence'. Then they set out to deliver the perpetrator from the spirit or demon, in the belief that the marriage (or the perpetrator) will be healed as a result.

In this kind of approach, the evil seems to be put onto a category of beings – demons – and the attack is made on the evil. This approach seems to be (and is easily seen by perpetrators to be) shifting responsibility onto an evil outside themselves. And so it diminishes personal human responsibility; and this diminishes the Gospel.

The Gospel is about Saving Grace, about God changing us through grace, through which we repent. And repentance involves our acceptance of responsibility for sin – even sin we don't know how to stop. Repentance is a sobering inward change: not emotional declarations about being a sinner, though the latter is sometimes more impressive to observers than the former.

The other doctrinaire position we question strongly is one that involves identifying males as the source and cause of the phenomenon of violence. It sets out to free women by attacking men, in the belief that thereby a social evil can be dealt with. This approach seems to put the evil out onto the male half of the human race. As with the other position described, it too diminishes the personal, human responsibility we each have for dealing with the anger and violence within our own attitudes.

The Limitations of All Parents

Violence, as we have said, is endemic to our human condition. Chronic anger, as against 'authentic' anger[4] is a form of violence. Do we see others as violent and not ourselves? Do we believe the seeds of violence are not in all of us, and that they do not have their subtle and not-so-subtle ways of flourishing in us?

[4] See chapter on 'racket' and 'authentic' feelings, chapter 8, pp. 92ff.

In our role as care-givers to children, all parents and other adults are abusive at times, in the sense that none of us can avoid sometimes abusing our power and modelling violence. We do it because we are all flawed people. The best of good enough parenting gives some model of abusiveness.

Effective parenting involves loving our children enough to stop them sometimes from doing what they want to do, and to insist sometimes that they do what they don't want to do.[5] The motive is not primarily the satisfaction of our own compulsive desires, or even our own understandable and real needs. It is the well-being of the children that motivates us in effective parenting.

We never do this *authoritative* kind of parenting perfectly; but we do it. And it is different from what we do when we become *authoritarian* with our children. Authoritarian actions and reactions put us in persecutor role. They are usually generated by our sense of helplessness or our fear of helplessness, and at their most invidious they come from our lust for power. They result in expressions of abusive anger.

When our persecutor role distresses us, we want to move out of it and avoid it. But where do we move to? We find it hard to move to a genuinely authoritative and a caring position: first, because we are already well into a child-state of helpless and angry feeling; and second, because with contemporary confusion between authority and authoritarianism, we find it more socially acceptable and personally satisfying to move into a sentimental attempt to be unconditionally accepting. Such an attempt, which involves taking the role of rescuer[6] in relation to the children for whom we have care-giving responsibility, is not sturdy-making for them.

So, because we are flawed people, we are always going to care for our children in such a way that the seeds of violence within us will

<hr />

[5]Sometimes we adults have this done to us, appropriately, and we do it with other adults for whose well-being we have responsibility. Those who in current times are including all such actions in their definition of violence seem to be taking a doctrinaire position that does not accord with the reality of healthy community and relationship living.

[6]See discussion of the related roles of Persecutor, Rescuer and Victim. Stewart, I., and Joines, V., op. cit. p. 236ff.

affect them. However good enough our caring is, however limited our perpetrations of abuse, we are sometimes doers of violence; and thus we are models of violence as well as non-violence.

The Counsellor's Role

As counsellors, we are working with some who are expressing violence, often verbal, sometimes physical. Like us and all those to whom we have been care-givers, they have been raised by care-givers carrying violence within. They need from us, as their counsellors, strong insistent care that does not move into anger against them.

How can we give this kind of care to perpetrators of violence? As Christians we can be very aware that God's saving justice — righteousness — is not served by the chronic anger within us; that this anger is never a means of achieving God's goodness. Chronic anger cannot heal anyone's violence, though it may check it temporarily. Nor is God's saving justice served by a compulsion to do things for people that diminishes their sense of responsibility. Such activity gives the one who is in the role of rescuer a sense of power and a conviction of being loving and kind — as with a child with whom we don't want to be angry.

When we give this care from a position of principled authority — which is a position of (sometimes very tough) love — we are sturdy-making to others. The more we have functioned under that same kind of authority, the more ready we are to identify our own abusive behaviour as violence. And the more we do this, the more ready we are to own it as wrong and feel remorseful about it.

Having done this, we are freer to empathize without condoning: we are holding mercy and justice together for the perpetrator.

14

SEXUAL COUNSELLING
IN PASTORAL CARE

Early in his ministry John became aware of the value of counselling skills. As minister in charge of a church, he believed his calling was to pastoral care, and that while pastoral care involved much more than counselling, his natural aptitude for counselling enhanced his ministry. Wanting to expand and shape this aptitude, John had availed himself of an opportunity to undertake an extended course in marriage counselling.

During the course he noticed that married couples in his church were using his ministry increasingly and in a more intentioned way. He realized too that he was strengthening his ability to respond to their deeper issues. This pattern continued when, having completed his course, he went on with regular supervision of cases within his pastoral care.

A Couple Ask for Sexual Counselling

Thirty-three-year-old Fiona was discussing with John the Bible study she co-led with her husband Bill, when she said quietly that they both wanted to see him about a marriage problem. John was a little surprised. He considered theirs a very good marriage. They were an affectionate couple with an obvious and shared energy between them, and their partnership generated positive energy around the church.

160 For Better, for Worse

Bill rang John to confirm the suggested appointment time, and in the course of the phone call he mentioned that the problem was a sexual one. Ministers of congregations, including John, don't have many spouses from their churches asking for sexual counselling, which is hardly surprising. By the very nature of pastoral ministry, and often enough by personality as well, the church minister doesn't come to many couples' minds as a source of help for a sexual difficulty.[1] Too often, no-one comes to a couple's mind, and they go unhelped. (While it's usually a healthy inhibition that checks couples from ready and open discussion with outsiders about the details of their sexual behaviour, shyness can unfortunately prevent couples from approaching a potentially useful source of help.)

However, it is their minister whom Bill and Fiona choose as their counsellor. What does John think about as he prepares for his first interview with them? While gratified by their regard for him and the trust they are demonstrating, John has doubts about the wisdom of counselling them. Any counselling of parishioners runs the risk of blurring and muddying a minister's other roles in relation to them. An attempt at sexual counselling will hold additional risks.

John's training has taught him that all counsellors walk a fine line as they encourage spouses to be sufficiently specific about a sexual problem and thus enable them to move toward some resolution of their difficulty. On the one hand, there is the risk of a real or apparent clinical detachment which two people with a common human problem find insensitive. On the other hand, a counsellor may seem to indulge in a kind of voyeurism which is titillated by receiving intimate information.

As he prepares to see Fiona and Bill, John considers also the limitations of his counselling skills. Does he have the capacity to help them with their difficulty? It could involve one or more of the following matters:

- Demands from one spouse for sexual pleasuring and intercourse that the other spouse finds too frequent or too intense

[1] Some spouses will go to a medical practitioner, but (like most ministers) general practitioners do not usually have skills in sexual counselling.

- Occasional or chronic inability to sustain an erection
- Impotence
- Timing of ejaculation
- Absence of orgasm
- Painful intercourse

The issue may involve also a fear of pregnancy or a lack of fertility. Or it may be a problem of old resentments being remembered and recycled while sexual lovemaking is taking place.

Bill and Fiona

At the beginning of the first interview, as Bill and Fiona sit with him in his office, John waits quietly for them to speak, respecting their inhibition. His own sense of ease helps him to be content for them to take their time as they try to express themselves safely to him. It also frees him to be sensitive to them rather than over-conscious of himself and his role.

Comfortable with the continuing silence, John is aware of some embarrassment in the couple, and he decides to break it. He could say 'You've mentioned that you have a sexual problem.' Instead he chooses to reflect on the immediate situation.

John: 'I guess it's hard for you both to start talking about your sexual difficulty.'

Fiona: 'Yes. It's difficult. I'm afraid I'm not a good wife for Bill. I don't seem to want to make love as often as he does. I do try to be loving, but it doesn't work. I just wish I could be better for him.'

Bill: 'But I don't want you to push yourself. I want it to be natural for you to want to make love. When I hug and kiss you and you don't enjoy it, I feel a failure. You don't seem to get excited about me, like I do about you. I've tried all sorts of things, but it seems you don't want me.'

Fiona: 'But I do want you. I know I don't get excited like you want
me to. I want you, but not like you want me to want you. Then I
feel a failure. Sometimes I give up and stop, sometimes I tell you
to go ahead. Then I usually enjoy it, but not the way you want me
to, and so I know I've let you down, and I feel I've let myself
down too.'

John notes that Fiona begins by blaming herself for not satisfying
Bill: satisfying him would be having the sort of sexual excitement
in intercourse that he thinks she should have. She implies that
because she can't reach this level of excitement, she's a failure. John
also notes that Bill seems gentle and sensitive; at the same time
he seems to expect (to Fiona it seems a demand) that Fiona
should be 'natural' and get sexual excitement and satisfaction of the
order he expects for himself, or imagines should be the norm for
Fiona.[2]

John is not the kind of counsellor who might define this marital
difficulty as one which will be resolved by sexual techniques to
ensure arousal and orgasm for Fiona when the couple have intercourse. Nor will he decree that they should have intercourse only
when Fiona wants it enough to initiate it. Even less is he likely
to suggest that Fiona should pray to be accepting, submissive, or
'naturally' orgasmic.

However, from the time they arranged the appointment, John has
kept in mind the possibility of suggesting gently that they seek help
from someone else. He knows that his competence in sexual counselling is limited, and he is prepared to refer difficult cases to an
experienced marriage counsellor whom he trusts.

In this case, he makes a preliminary hypothesis that the couple's
difficulty is not primarily a complex sexual problem. He is choosing
at this stage to define the problem as one where *needs and desires are
not being expressed adequately; and therefore they are not being examined*

[2]There is another difficulty here. Bill is assuming that a high level of arousal is
'natural'. In fact, there is a wide range of sexual arousal: high arousal may be natural
for some, but is routinely out of reach of many. There is also variability in level of
arousal for the same person at different times; this is especially so for women.

and responded to usefully. John also thinks that Fiona and Bill lack some information: that when one partner expects the other to be 'natural' and 'spontaneous', the very pressure created by this expectation stymies naturalness and spontaneity.

The value of this preliminary hypothesis is two-fold:

- It gives John a framework for testing any new information they give him: does it fit his hypothesis or does he need to modify that hypothesis?

- It starts to describe the problem (or part of the problem) in potentially problem-solving terms.

If it addresses some part of the problem, and describes the problem in a way that can lead the couple to resolve this part of their difficulty, then it is a useful definition.

John is aware that useless definitions are often made of personal and marital problems. 'Lack of communication', 'low self-esteem' and 'incompatibility' are examples. These are jargon words and catch phrases that may impress, but they are dead-enders as definitions. If John tells himself that *Fiona and Bill are not expressing their desires adequately*, and that *consequently they are not examining and responding to their desires*, he has a way in which to proceed with them.

In any case (and even if he plans to refer them), he will need to stay with Bill and Fiona as they talk of their difficulty.

John; 'So each of you is wanting to be good for the other, but somehow you miss, and each of you finishes up feeling a failure.'[3]

Bill: 'Yes, we do love each other and get on really well in so many ways, but we are very disappointed in our lovemaking. I wish Fiona could be more enthusiastic, and when she isn't, I feel rejected and irrelevant. Then I am disappointed and don't want to try.'

John: 'You feel a failure and you think it's Fiona's fault.'

Bill: 'Yes . . . er, No! I want her to have a good time. I've read some

[3] Note that John includes both of them (the dyad) in his response.

books and I know how important orgasm is for her, but I don't seem to be good enough for her to have it. I should be able to satisfy her and I can't.'

Fiona: 'You shouldn't blame yourself. You try very hard, almost too hard for me. I don't know why I don't feel what you want me to feel. Well, I do sometimes and it is great, but usually I don't and I know you're disappointed.'

John: 'So sometimes you enjoy an orgasm with Bill, and usually you feel pushed by Bill to be right for him?'

Fiona: 'Yes. It seems that he expects so much of me. He doesn't realize how tired I get, with a job and a home and weekly netball. It's just too much.'

John: 'It seems like just one more load.'

Bill: 'I don't mean it to be. I don't want it to be. I want it to be a joyous thing. I want there to be joy in our one-flesh, as the Bible says.'

John: 'So you want something really good and biblical for Fiona. But for you, Fiona, it often seems like another burden, a further demand.'

Underlying Issues

John has been developing the interview by making empathic responses first to Bill and then to Fiona, and now he makes a dyadic response, addressing each of them in the same response to emphasize the interaction. As he considers the burden for Fiona and the disappointment for Bill, he has some ideas about underlying issues in their marriage. John does not spell out these ideas to the couple, but they will guide the way he responds to what Bill and Fiona say.

- He thinks they need to clarify their confused responses and emotions, their conscious beliefs and their magical messages about sexuality.

- He believes they don't realize that it is right for them to ask their partner for what they want, and for the partner to be free to agree, disagree, compromise or negotiate.

- He suspects that Fiona and Bill have not acknowledged the extent of their disappointment and resentment in their experience of their perceived sexual failure.

When John attends to this third point, his approach will be something like this: He will ask Fiona to tell Bill how burdened she feels and how that inhibits her responses to him. She may then tell Bill she resents his expectation that she perform for his satisfaction, even when she is tired. John will encourage Bill to tell Fiona how hurt he is when she turns away from him and rejects him: how he feels unloved and unlovable, and how she should put more effort into caring for their marriage.[*] Very likely each of them will respond with initial defensiveness as they hear the other speak so plainly. But John expects that by sharing their hurts in the safety and vulnerability which he has generated in the interview, they will begin to hear each other in a new way and gain strength and comfort from the process.

The careful opening up of their communication makes possible some new beginnings.

- Bill can begin to understand and monitor the demands he is placing on Fiona.

- Fiona can begin to understand how her giving up seems like rejection to Bill.

- By expressing their hurts in a more open and less defensive way to each other, together they can begin to realize the possibility of developing more creative ways of asking and receiving.

While Fiona and Bill practise, in the counselling room, their new ways of asking and responding, John encourages them to enjoy communicating directly and clearly. He also watches for ways by which they tend to block themselves as they seek to make positive

[*]There is a risk in this process: it can allow strongly negative feelings to emerge. Many an inexperienced counsellor, having taken the risk, has then not known how to help the couple handle their feelings. We suggest that a counsellor should have enough role-play practice in training sessions to be sure of his own sensitivity and skills, before attempting such a process with real clients on any issue.

changes. Giving up ingrained habits is not easy; John encourages Bill and Fiona to identify for themselves how they lock themselves into self-protective positions and into the magical thinking by which they sustain those positions.[5]

As John encourages each partner to ask for what they want, he also invites the other partner to consider and try out a range of responses. Later, in the intimacy of their home, when Bill says to Fiona 'I would really like to make love', Fiona may feel free and good about herself as she replies 'I don't want intercourse just now, but I would like us to hold each other and have one of our really good kisses'. Both partners can enjoy the love and mutual respect they share in this situation.

Let's be clear that not every sexual difficulty of the kind Bill and Fiona present can be resolved easily and by simply following the line John takes. Nevertheless, his approach is a useful one. He encourages the couple to gain some healthy freedom from the confused, magical thinking by which they exacerbate their own distress.[6] He also encourages their liberty to negotiate around what each wants from, as well as for, the other – and to do this with open, frank communication.

The increased freedom that John's counselling facilitates may also enable deeper difficulties in Bill's and Fiona's marriage to surface. Their practice of a new style of communication may bring into focus for them some underlying sexual issue that they have. As he works with this couple, John keeps in mind this possibility.

---

[5] Some of the magical messages we habitually give ourselves are these: 'I shouldn't have to ask for what I want.' 'It should all happen naturally.' 'I'm never going to get what I want.' 'I must never hurt people's feelings.' When we identify these and bring them into our awareness, we can see their self-defeating nature and confront them with reality.

[6] Magical thinking is evident when Fiona says 'I'm not a good wife. I've let you down' and 'He expects so much of me. It's just too much'; and also in Bill's statements 'I should be able to satisfy her' and 'I feel rejected and irrelevant'. Note the distortions: each partner takes exaggerated responsibility for the other and also blames the other. See other chapters for further comments on magical thinking.

Respectful Compromise

Assuming a deeper difficulty doesn't emerge, John's task will be to reinforce Fiona's and Bill's practice of respectful compromise. In this way their sense of being mutually loved will have an opportunity to strengthen. John might also help them to consider other options, other ways of communicating about their sexual loving.

In the intimacy of their home, Bill could take another kind of initiative, telling Fiona that while he would like to have intercourse he knows she hasn't the energy, and suggesting 'So let's make love by kissing and caressing'. Or Fiona could initiate: 'I'm not up to super lovemaking, but I want us to be close, so let's have intercourse that's mild for me'. In this way she would indicate her awareness of his needs and hers, let him know she's satisfied not to have an orgasm this time, and cooperate in taking care of them both, in a way that neither violates her nor rejects him.

The Minister's Resources

What are the resources that John brings to his method of working with this couple? There is of course his capacity to assess Bill's and Fiona's situation and to time his interventions appropriately. For example, in encouraging them to set up the kind of communication described, he is guided by the extent of their readiness to talk about their sexual responses: he judges the moment when they are free to articulate their needs more directly than they have done so far. But as well as his counselling skills, John brings other resources to his work.

First, *John's primary resource is himself*. He has a comfortable appreciation of himself as a sexual man and of others as sexual men and women. His understanding of who God has called him to be and his disciplined practice of this call translate into the respectful way he relates to people. So he is free to give Fiona and Bill friendly, easygoing encouragement with warm interest – even enthusiasm – and with a quiet confidence in himself and in what he is doing.

Second, *John's ability to call on his own marital experience appropriately*[7] is a resource for him. All marriages are in some ways alike, and while his marriage is in specific ways unlike that of his clients, John and his wife have had to learn the common marital task of negotiating around their individual sexual responsiveness. They have learnt to use a range of responses to both their own wishes and their partner's; and over the years their sexual loving has included taking account of each other's tiredness, stress levels and occasional illnesses.

Third, a real resource for John is *his awareness of the false and destructive portrayal by contemporary society of what a sexual relationship and acts of sexual intercourse are about.* The image of free floating sex as the apex and the norm seems to have blunted the sensibilities of many people, both Christians and others, to the meaning of sexual loving. This meaning has long been the heritage – as an ideal at least – of many, both within the Church and in wider society. Sexual loving is intrinsic to the lifelong relationship of a committed married couple. While its expression in marriage may have a wide and varying range, its inherence is something that develops and strengthens throughout a marriage.

A superb part of marital loving, sexual intercourse is meant to be nourishing and enlivening for the love relationship of a wife and husband. And this is so when it's wildly exciting and when it's ordinary – and the latter is more often the case. ('Wildly exciting' means unusually intense emotions and erotic feelings, and it may include multiple orgasms for the wife. 'Ordinary' doesn't necessarily mean that the wife doesn't reach orgasm, but for some couples often it may mean this.) John's understanding of this is a resource for him as he considers realistically the sexual relationship of the couple he is working with.

Bill seems somewhat unaware of the value of *the ordinary* as against *the special* in sexual loving. 'Special' is, by definition, unusual and not ordinary. Contrary to false media images – which tend to depict sexual intercourse as activity that is free from the constraints of

---

[7] 'Appropriately' precludes giving details of matters that are intimate to his wife and himself.

marital or any other everyday structures – real people live much of their lives at the ordinary level of good-enough relating. For husbands and wives the *ordinary* is the real in their sexual relationship, and the special (while real too) is *special*. An awareness of this is a resource that John brings to counselling, and it will help Bill as his understanding of sexual loving matures.

Ongoing Change

Fiona and Bill have been missing each other in their attempts to negotiate their sexual relationship. By his careful listening to the hurts they experience when they miss each other, and to the meanings they take from these hurts, John is helping them to listen better to each other, and to understand the meaning for the other of particular acts. In this new understanding, he helps them express their wishes to each other in such a way that encourages (or at least doesn't discourage) their partner to respond usefully. He affirms them when they cooperate in this way, and helps them express their appreciation to each other of their achievements in need-meeting.

New behaviours are not easy to maintain. John will work with the couple when their new practice breaks down – when each wants to come to a loving compromise but doesn't achieve it. Bill may ask in the old way, or Fiona may hear his request as if he has asked in the old way. John helps them to catch themselves and each other in this distortion, and arrange for ways of correcting it. For instance, when Bill asks Fiona 'You wouldn't want to make love now, would you?' (the form of the question expects a negative answer), and Fiona can reply with affection, 'If you're asking me whether I would *like* to make love, the answer is . . .' John encourages them to maintain the new clarity of communication they have achieved, and to correct themselves when they lapse into old patterns, so that mutual need-meeting is enhanced, and their sense of being loved and loving grows. He helps them to see that they don't have to stay stuck with a mistake when they make one, but can move to the new behaviour again.

Emergence of a More Complex Issue

In counselling Bill and Fiona, John has kept in mind the possibility that a further sexual problem could emerge as they practise their new freedom to communicate about their sexuality. We're now going to suppose that Fiona feels free to say that she never really wants to initiate sexually loving behaviour, is never inclined to have sexual intercourse, and has never had an orgasm during intercourse. In this case, John will be empathically affirming of both partners for having shared and accepted this new issue as an important one for them both. He will encourage in Fiona and Bill an optimism that sexual non-responsiveness can often be ameliorated. On the other hand, he will not give false hope that it can be resolved easily and completely.

As he raises with them the appropriateness of referral to a specialist for this problem,[8] he will also encourage them to talk about it together at home, in an atmosphere of intimacy and shared tenderness. John will help this committed couple to go on viewing the problem as a joint concern: one to which they can bring all their own resources of mutual love and not as a defect which defines Fiona.

John may encourage the couple to explore in their discussions at home some questions which will be relevant when they reach the specialist help they decide to seek. These questions are inviting them to keep an open mind about the aetiology of Fiona's lack of erotic and genital responsiveness, which may possibly be organic, or emotional and psychological, or a mixture of these components.

- When was Fiona first aware of her lack of orgasmic response?

- Could it have a physiological cause, or one related to some chronic, long-term health problem?

[8]Even if John has the adequate and specific skills, it will not be appropriate for him to enter into long-term therapy with Fiona and Bill. Apart from the likely time involved, his close links with them preclude this possibility. He has known them as friends and colleagues for some time and this aspect of their contact will continue. However, he may see Bill for an occasional individual session, if Bill feels the need because he has got into an anxious or resentful position.

- Might it be based in pervasive but hidden guilt which Fiona has yet to take into her conscious awareness?

- Could her genital responsiveness be traumatized because of early experiences?

John's expectation is that this couple's discussion of their shared concern will draw them closer and prepare them to make good use of specialist help. He will not, however, enter into their discussion on these questions, because as their pastor it is not appropriate for him to do so. What is appropriate and very necessary is that he consult with counselling colleagues and with sensitive medical colleagues so that an appropriate referral can be made.

As with many counsellors, the challenge to John is to see that Fiona and Bill are referred to someone who is skilled in diagnosing (and then treating) physiological components of the problem; who has a respectful approach to its shared and marital nature; who can sensitively and skilfully explore the possibility of guilt, early trauma and excessive sexual inhibition; and who is prepared to refer to, or work in conjunction with, an experienced and able counsellor in the field of marital and sex therapy. These qualities are found only in a rare and very special person. Ideally Fiona and Bill need someone who is a medical specialist and much more beside.[9]

So John takes advice and help from his counselling and medical colleagues. He also discusses referral possibilities very carefully with Fiona and Bill, so that when they begin their visits to the specialist, they have an informed confidence in the person they are choosing to see, as well as realistic expectations of that person.

---

[9]In marriage difficulties that involve an early traumatizing experience suffered by one partner our strong preference is for both partners to be involved in the therapy. While it is sometimes distressing for a husband or a wife to be present during sessions where the focus is on their spouse's early traumas, it is potentially very healing for both. Still, when and how to involve the supporting spouse calls for delicate decisions, and of course the final decision is with the couple.

Donald and Heather

When Heather rang to make an appointment for Donald and herself about a sexual problem, John began to wonder whether word had got around that he was a good counsellor about marriage and sex. While inwardly he groaned a little, he felt pleasure at this possible acknowledgement of his counselling skills, and prepared to see this couple with some degree of confidence.

Heather begins the interview by saying she and Donald are having difficulties in their sex life because Donald 'comes too soon', and it isn't at all satisfactory. She is usually disappointed and frustrated, and wishes that Donald would do something about it. Donald says that he tries to delay his climax, but it seems that the more he tries to delay, the quicker he comes.

Alongside his skills of empathy and joining with each of them, John is already forming a number of questions he will consider in his attempt to understand and define the issues in the marriage.

- Is Donald's premature ejaculation sometimes or always?

- Did it start recently, or has it been through all or most of their marriage?

- Could his problem have medical reasons?[10]

- What exactly do they mean by 'too soon': does he manage intromission, and if so, for how long before ejaculation?

- What are the feelings that Donald has at various stages of their lovemaking, and what is his internal dialogue in this?

- Has he had traumatic sexual experiences in childhood?

John has a number of unspoken questions about Heather too.

- How disappointed is she and what does she do about her disappointment?

[10]For example, impotence and premature ejaculation can be a problem for men who are on particular medications prescribed for certain physical ailments.

- What does she do about her physiological arousal as well as her emotional arousal? Or has she reached the place where she deliberately avoids getting aroused because Donald is not going to satisfy her?

- What does she do about her resentment – how does she express it and to whom?

Other questions will be in John's mind also. For example

- How do Donald and Heather manage conflict and disappointment in other parts of their marriage (e.g. parenting, household chores, money matters)?

- Have there been changes in the context of their marriage at this critical time, such as children going through a life-stage (e.g. adolescence), change of employment or housing, a significant illness in the family, further education or training for one or both of them?

- Is Donald's premature ejaculation a reflection of anxiety that he is experiencing about his performance in other areas of his functioning in his life?

In his initial counselling, John may find (as with Fiona and Bill) that this couple can explore their attitudes and communication, and make some changes. In particular, he may help Donald to deal differently with his anxiety, and Heather with her frustration and resentment. Simply talking in a matter-of-fact way about length of stages of inter-course, and normal variations in these, may help Donald to lower the level of his anxiety.

However, in contrast to John's approach, it is sometimes easy for pastors to think they have ready answers to very complex problems. John will not be filled with supreme confidence that what he can offer in counselling is the answer for Donald and Heather. Premature ejaculation is a common problem for couples. So is impotence. Common sexual problems usually require very skilled attention.

John recognizes that where sexual problems are intractable, the situation that they are in can elicit from some couples a very special quality of mutual love. The respect and the tender care that inhere in this kind of loving, which includes the forgoing of some sexual pleasures, might not be achievable by every couple. But some can fashion this quality of love in response to their sexual situation.

John will not continue to counsel Donald and Heather for long, nor will be buoy them up with false optimism about the likelihood of an easy solution to their problem. Referral to a competent clinician is the next step. But helping Heather and Donald attend to some emotional issues may be part of their preparation for referral and may ensure that they benefit from further treatment. As he works with them, perhaps briefly, his deepening understanding of them will guide him in making an appropriate referral.

There are questions in John's mind.

- Would medication benefit Donald, and if so, for what specific purpose? This is obviously beyond John's range of knowledge.

- Do Heather and Donald require specifically sexual counselling? That may well be the case.

- Could they use training in the squeeze technique? This is a useful and cooperative behavioural procedure which in some cases can help a husband control the timing of his ejaculation. The clinician to whom John refers Donald and Heather may provide effective training for the couple in this technique.

Some couples have found learning the squeeze technique a pleasant therapeutic process because of the approach and the personality of their trainer. The trainer is one who is comfortable discussing the method in clear detail. Simple accurate explanations, offered in an unselfconsciously direct manner with a touch of lightness, set a couple at ease. Such an approach minimizes the couple's discomfort and is therapeutic in itself.

As John gains a clearer idea of the help they need, he can consult with his supervisor, a medical practitioner, or a marriage counsellor specializing in sexual counselling, to help him evaluate the best source of help for Donald and Heather.

Cameron and Gina

A third couple, Cameron and Gina, come seeking John's help. Along with their distressing sexual problem, they bring to the counselling room an atmosphere of open, mutual animosity.

Gina: 'Cameron is always wanting sex and he is very insistent. I don't want to give it to him because it always hurts me.'

Cameron: 'Look, I think that you are just trying to put me off. It didn't hurt when we first married – in fact you seemed to want it even more than me. But now you say it hurts, even when I take great care to get you aroused and well prepared.'

Gina: 'Well it does hurt. I don't pretend. You just forget the pain I went through with the birth of Rodney, and the stitches I had at the time. And you wanted intercourse almost as soon as I came home from hospital. You said that you had been waiting a long time, and I felt I had to be kind to you.'

Cameron: 'You always go back to that. I've told you over and over again that I am sorry that I pushed you at that time. I now know that I was wrong, but I don't see why I should be punished over and over again when I have repented for that.'

Gina: 'I'm not punishing you. I still hurt, and I'm very upset that you think I'm pretending, when I'm not. You try to bully me into suffering so that you can have what you want.'

In so far as Gina and Cameron are aiming for the mutual healing that sexual loving can give, they are certainly missing the mark with each other. They are, moreover, talking about their sexual intercourse as if it were some procedure detached from their mutual personhood, and a vehicle for their present hostility. Their marriage bed seems to have become a battleground of demand and resistance.

It is possible that Cameron is just an insensitive ignorant man who discounts Gina's vaginal pain and is focused on his own sexual needs. But John will not make such an assumption yet. He will aim to attend early in his counselling to the high level of resentment and hostility that is obvious between them.

Aware that Gina's pain may well be caused — as she seems to suggest — by the presence of scar tissue resulting from vaginal repair after Rodney's birth, John remembers that Rodney is now four years old. Has Gina not received proper gynaecological care for her vaginal pain? If she has not, what are the reasons? Do she and Cameron know that such care exists? Is Cameron frustrated because Gina has not sought this care? Does he suspect that by not doing so she may be punishing him?

Cameron's and Gina's sexual difficulty is very real and requires attention. However, it looks to John as if this difficulty is also a symptom of long-term resentments between the marriage partners. Who could imagine Cameron and Gina melting into each other's arms affectionately and becoming gently helpless with the urgency of their sexual desire for each other? Not even Barbara Cartland or Mills & Boon. The warmth and loving tenderness that should precede sexual arousal is not within Cameron's and Gina's current repertoire.

But what was the quality of their sexual loving more than four years ago? Was sex always divorced from their personal meaning for each other? What personal and sexual meaning did their relationship have for each when (as Cameron asserts) Gina wanted sexual loving more frequently than he?

These are issues John will be exploring, as he raises first of all the matter of gynaecological care for Gina. By commenting on the need for medical assessment, he is acknowledging to Gina in Cameron's presence the reality of her physical pain. In this way he identifies indirectly Cameron's apparent discounting of Gina's physical pain. Thus he opens up the possibility of addressing their mutual resentment as he explores with them their hurt feelings and the ways they have dealt with these feelings throughout their marriage.

Considerations for the Pastor

The cases of the three couples — Fiona and Bill, Heather and Donald and Gina and Cameron — demonstrate something that those in pastoral care need to be aware of: that *sexual problems really are sexual problems* and that *many are also symptomatic of emotional difficulties like guilt and resentment.* The resolution of emotional conflicts does not usually come about quickly and easily, but as husbands and wives deal with these conflicts, their freedom for sexual satisfaction is likely to increase.

In other cases, partners need information, for in our sophisticated world where sex is openly discussed, some people can be as lacking in factual information as their grandparents are thought to have been. Along with information, many partners need antidotes to the super-human expectations that infect our present society.

There are many cases too where more specific and specialist treatments are needed. As well as corrective surgery and training in particular physical techniques that couples can use, treatments include appropriate therapy for vaginismus and phobic conditions. Compassionate concern for their people motivates pastors in counselling to ensure that they have access when necessary to information about medical practitioners, specialists and sex counsellors in their region.

Pastors need to know the level of competence of these clinicians. Of equal concern to them is the reputation clinicians have for personal attributes such as sensitivity and warmth. Like pastors, they become key people in the marriages of couples referred to them, and their effect on these couples will be for better or worse.

15

ADULTERY AND AFFAIRS

'I'm uncomfortable about the intimate looks Hugh and Karen have been giving each other at church', said Geoff's wife as he handed her coffee in the Manse. 'And now I've said that, I'll be saying no more about the matter to you or anyone else.' She stirred her cup and went back to her writing.

Geoff, who often had trouble handling his emotional reactions, felt thankful for his wife's down-to-earth approach to trouble, and her gift of a disciplined tongue. Experience in ministry had taught them both how easily destructive excitement and drama can be compounded in a parish in the name of righteousness, especially around rumours of sexual affairs.

Geoff had observed Hugh and Karen at choir practice, and had felt troubled. One of the elders had made a vague, uneasy comment to him about them. In his prayers Geoff had been asking for wisdom as he decided how to be responsibly pastoral with them, and courage to grasp the nettle rather than hope devoutly that it would die away.

At a quiet time Geoff reviewed the situation in reference to the four people most deeply affected by it. He realized that for some months Karen's husband Joe had seemed more reserved than usual. Joe had not responded when Geoff had made attempts to get alongside him supportively, and Geoff had respected his reticence. Geoff was sceptical of the popular sentiment frequently expressed in this style: 'We have to get people talking about their problem and help them get their feelings out; there's always healing in that.'

Regarding Hugh and his wife Ingrid, Geoff had taken their marriage to be affectionate and stable. He knew the couple had worked with Joe and Karen on several church projects, meeting in each others' homes.

An opportunity arose where Geoff was able to move beside Karen and touch her arm lightly as he said: 'Karen, how are things with you? Are you all right?' Karen gave him a bright smile and a quick affirmative reply, then moved on. Next day, while Geoff was considering the yet ungrasped nettle, Karen called. Postponing a less pressing task, Geoff was able to see her in his office that evening.

Karen: 'I don't know what to do, Geoff. I'm in a terrible spot. I'm in love with Hugh and I can't pretend with Joe any more. I know it's wrong but I can't do anything about it. I've tried to stop seeing Hugh. I've told myself and we've both said many times it's got to stop. But we can't.'

Geoff: 'Neither of you manages to stop seeing each other, though you both say it must stop?'

Karen: 'We both know we should stop making love. We're Christians, we know it's wrong, but we can't bear to be apart. Every time we decide to stop, one of us rings the other and it starts again. I'm being torn apart. I can't pray. I feel a traitor in church. I think you've known about us – haven't you? – and that's why you spoke to me yesterday.'

Geoff: 'I've been concerned about you Karen; but I haven't known what you've just told me.'

While he listens to Karen, Geoff's heart is sinking. Karen is confirming the worst of his fears about Hugh and her. They are in love with each other, and they're having a sexual affair which they feel helpless to stop. Geoff is sad, and also very angry that two people who work actively in the church and worship there each Sunday are messing up their lives and their marriages. They are also giving a very poor example, and this distresses Geoff; but his anger is primarily with what they are doing to themselves, and to Joe, and to Ingrid.

In his distress Geoff finds himself praying silently an old prayer he suddenly recalls, 'Lord Jesus Christ, Son of the living God, have mercy on us all', and mentally aligning himself with Karen as a sinner like himself who requires mercy. This helps him deal with his desire to rebuke Karen at this point and call her a poor Christian and a sexually immoral one. He disciplines himself enough to stay with her situation and put aside his feelings for the present.

Geoff notes Karen's theme of helplessness: she *can't* stop, *can't* bear to, *can't* pray. (Her last 'can't' could entice him into an apparently spiritual focus on prayer and God's grace, but that would be tangential piety.) He notes that she implies not just that she cannot stop her feelings for Hugh, but that she is helpless to stop her behaviour and do something else. She believes she cannot stop seeing Hugh: her behaviour is not within her volition. 'Every time we decide to stop . . . *it starts again*', she says. This indicates that she experiences their affair, not as behaviour that she and Hugh do together, but as something that has a life and volition of its own. So in her state of helplessness she does not express the reality, which is '*We start the affair again*'.

When he hears Karen say that she knows her behaviour is wrong, she can't pray and she feels a traitor in church, Geoff hopes these statements reflect a useful sense of guilt. He recognizes that they may do so, but he needs more evidence; otherwise he might respond to her at a level that is not meaningful to her. Geoff would like to use his authority as a minister to tell Karen firmly that she must stop her relationship with Hugh right now (not '*It* must stop', but '*You* must stop'). He suspects that if he did so, she might agree quickly and try to obey him.

Geoff will not direct her in this way. Unless she has a well-internalized and healthy sense of guilt, her conforming to Geoff's direction will not represent a genuine repentance and a turning away from sin.[1] Geoff sees the importance of Karen making the decision in

[1] Readers will note an inconsistency between Geoff's response to the acknowledgement of adultery and the response of another counsellor to the acknowledgement of marital violence (chapter 12). When clients decide from a ready positive will rather than from mere compliance, they are more likely to succeed in changing their behaviour. (Their marriage partners will want them to choose their new behaviour

such a way that (this time, unlike past attempts) she can carry it through.

Part of Geoff's pastoral function at this stage is to make some sort of assessment of Karen's approximate stage of moral development, such as that suggested by Kohlberg's system of six stages.[2] It is just possible, though unlikely, that much of Karen's functioning is only at Kohlberg's Stage One, where a person's behaviour and judgments of right and wrong are determined by the amount of power wielded by those in authority. Having soberly considered his own level of moral development, Geoff understands the concept of stages as something not to be slickly applied to people. He knows also that, like Karen, he needs to function under the grace of mature guilt to be a faithful pastor and counsellor.[3]

Thinking ahead, Geoff is acutely aware that Karen cannot have a pain-free solution to her dilemma. If she decides to end the affair, she will experience pain and grief as she mourns its loss. If she decides not to end the affair, but to end her marriage to Joe, her pain and grief will be great. (Mourning the loss of her marriage will not be less simply because she is the partner who decides to move out.)

So Karen will experience a sense of great deprivation if and when she ends her affair. Geoff knows that being in love and committing adultery are the end of a *process*, and that if he is to help Karen get her life straight and make a real repentance, he has to take seriously the steps in that process. In other words, he can expect to find that there have been deficits in Karen's and Joe's marriage for some time.

Just possibly, the main defect could lie in either Karen's or Joe's style of personality. Joe may seriously lack emotional depth, so that he is not available to anyone (let alone Karen) in a satisfying way; or

---

rather than be coerced.) However, as marital violence is rightly considered a criminal offence in our society, waiting for a ready positive will is not a counsellor's option in cases of violence. Adultery is not a criminal offence, though it is an offence against God and the partner and the community. A counsellor's reasoning and discernment guide the choice of different responses in ambiguities that present themselves.

[2] See Kohlberg, L., *Stages of Moral Development*, cited in Maccoby, E.E., *Social Development*, Harcourt Brace Jovanovich, New York 1980.

[3] See Tournier, P., *Guilt and Grace*, Hodder & Stoughton, London 1962.

Karen may live consistently at a shallow thrill-seeking level. More likely, Karen and Joe have each been contributing to the impoverishment of their marriage: Joe perhaps being very strongly defended against awareness of any need within, and Karen living with a vague sense of emptiness for which she has been seeking (probably unconsciously) the filler of excitement and self-affirmation through her affair.[4]

Geoff thinks that probably Karen and Joe have each failed to meet the normal needs of the other, so that the liveliness has gone out of their marriage. It has become an un-nourished relationship.[5] With his personal feelings of distress to manage, Geoff's task is to be empathic at this moment with Karen, a needy human being.

Geoff: 'Yes, you are in a terrible spot, Karen.[6] You're saying you know what you should do, and you feel you can't carry it through.'

Karen: 'I feel so guilty. Joe has been a good husband to me in many ways, and I'm married to him, and I know I should love him. And in a way, I do. But Hugh is so wonderful to me, I feel alive with him. It's exciting and I feel really loved when I'm with him. It's wrong, but I can't do without it, however hard I try.'

Geoff is tempted to remind Karen that Hugh has a wife Ingrid, who is supposed to be Karen's friend. He could say 'Where do Ingrid and Hugh stand in all this?' but decides not to. *He is careful not to indulge his own anger by expressing it*, recognizing that Karen needs her minister to move slowly, and to also accept the reality of her present distress.

[4] Regarding their affairs, many clients say something like this: 'I wasn't looking for it. It just started out with someone to talk to. My husband/wife never had time to listen to me or be with me.' Or 'It started with being with a friend who just liked me and didn't make constant demands and talk at me.'

[5] Couples say 'We just grew apart and the marriage died.' Often the reality is that they have not known how to keep nourishing it, or have not even understood that a marriage relationship requires nourishment to flourish.

[6] It is too early for Geoff to express it as 'You've got yourself into a terrible spot'. Karen will hear him if his response reflects her own perception of her spot, but may hear 'You've got yourself into it' as too painful a reality to face just yet.

Geoff is seeing two sets of forces at work in Karen:

- her sense of *dullness* in her relationship with Joe, pushing her to look outside her marriage, and

- her sense of *excitement* with Hugh, drawing her toward him and away from Joe.

The timing isn't right to describe his perception to Karen. Instead, he encourages her to say more about her dilemma.

Geoff: 'You're feeling guilty about your excitement with Hugh and you know you should love Joe.'

Karen: 'And I can't do anything about it.'

Geoff: 'Say more about loving and not loving Joe, Karen.'

Karen: 'Joe's such a good man and a responsible worker, and I was in love with him once. We had really good times together. But now I don't even want to be with him.'

Geoff: 'You were in love with him in the good times you had, and now they're gone.'

Karen: 'Well, we get on all right still. But it's the spark that's gone. We're good friends still. We're pleasant to each other, mostly, we don't quarrel a lot. We don't make love much any more, and when we do I have to admit to you I just put up with it.'

Geoff: 'You're stopped enjoying making love with him.'

Karen: 'Well, I pretend a bit, but my heart isn't in it. I even think of Hugh then, I may as well tell you, and I wish I was with him. And that's when I resent it's Joe who's with me.'

Geoff notes the readiness with which Karen describes her inner thoughts and feelings.[7] Angry on behalf of Joe, and on behalf of Ingrid also, angry with Hugh, dismayed at the situation, Geoff tells

[7]Rather than assuming that his empathy skills are inviting a client to be 'open and honest' in a healthy way, a counsellor asks himself questions, e.g.: Does readiness of this kind stem from initial relief and release from tension at finally articulating a problem with a tried and trusted counsellor? Does it indicate lack of self-boundaries in the client?

himself that Karen is the one to whom he has a pastoral responsibility right now. He stretches his spine to release his tension, and without taking his attention from Karen, he consciously breathes more deeply and slowly.

Karen: 'I feel so fulfilled with Hugh. He really loves me. It's wonderful. I know I shouldn't feel this way, but it's like what I said before, the spark with Joe is gone.'

Geoff: 'And when did the spark with Joe seem to go, Karen? Go back and remember what was happening around that time.'

In beginning to explore with Karen the loss she has experienced of loving intimacy in her marriage, Geoff uses her words – 'the *spark* is gone' – and asks her to think about it as part of a process. Some people link such a loss to a significant event in their lives. Others do not. The loss may be related to a birth, a death, a change of employment or moving house. It may even be (for someone like Karen who is closely connected with a church) an event within the family of the church: perhaps a change of her status or her role there.

In such significant events, one spouse may not meet the needs of the other very adequately, and – realistically or not – the expectations of the other are disappointed. Insufficient comfort and understanding is received. Resentment from the actual loss is then displaced onto the spouse. This resentment has in part been triggered by the situation of the loss and is external to the immediate bond between wife and husband.

However, such crises of loss and change are not always involved. The lessening of affection and intimacy in a couple's shared life can be gradual, related less to particular events than to the intensity of a personal and known characteristic. A wife may say 'I don't love him because he doesn't talk much about what he feels', when in fact he never did so. A husband may explain his loss of interest in his wife by saying 'I have to work too hard to arouse her sexual interest in me', when their difference in ease of sexual arousal has always been marked.

Geoff is working on some expectations concerning Karen:

- Karen can accept her difficulties with Joe as partly her responsibility;[8]

- She can consider these difficulties and find some realistic solution;

- When she and Joe can enliven their relationship – and this may be possible – then the attraction Hugh has for her will be less powerful.

Geoff is not assuming that these three abilities will be easy for her to access (i.e. find within herself) and exercise, nor that the exercise of them will be sufficient to renew her marriage. Rather, his faith is that it is possible for her to do what many women and men manage to do. And he sees that his priority in counselling Karen is to attend to her marriage difficulties, Karen's awareness of these having now been heightened both by her adultery and by her telling Geoff about them in this counselling session.

Stop Seeing Hugh?

Does Geoff now urge Karen to stop seeing Hugh? Our answer is: Not at this stage. The reasons we have for that answer are based in our understanding of how God's grace works (he never forces us), as well as in our experience of how human nature operates.

The pastoral decision of when and how to focus on Karen's relationship with Hugh is difficult. It requires much thought and clinical appraisal. In Geoff's place, some pastors would want to stop the extramarital relationship right now, telling Karen to keep away from Hugh. *A pastor's need to fix things up, however understandable, is not the basis for pastoral decisions.*

Karen has said that she has been telling herself to stop seeing Hugh. But note that she hasn't yet managed to obey herself. Her desire to continue is strong enough to withstand the telling. This indicates that her values (her 'shoulds') are not strongly and

[8]For example, perhaps in trying not to upset Joe, Karen did not tell him what she actually felt; thus Joe had no information on which to reconsider his behaviour.

sufficiently internalized, and not integrated with the rest of her personhood, enough to stop her adulterous behaviour.

If she obeys her pastor, it will be obeying an external 'should' – perhaps a revered one, but with hardly the power to stem the flow of her desire toward Hugh. The void within, resulting from obeying her pastor, just might push her to try working things out with Joe; and that would be out of loneliness (for Hugh), not out of having chosen from a will directed by mature values. At this stage she would not be ready to stay with a decision externally driven. She would very likely go back to Hugh soon – with additional guilt and, just as importantly, additional distress for everyone.

Jesus responded to the wealthy young man's question 'What must I do?' with information, but he did not urge him to obey. Our heavenly Father, who never seems to be in a hurry and never forces us to do what is right, knows what he is doing. Karen is very aware that Geoff (like her) knows what she should do. Geoff's task is to proceed in such a way that she will have opportunities to be *able to do* what she knows she should, opportunities for realistic repentance and new behaviour that she can maintain. Amendment of life is part of true repentance.

On the other hand, if working on her marriage doesn't result in Karen's releasing herself from her affair with Hugh, Geoff will be mindful that there may be a time when Karen is still putting too much energy into her relationship with Hugh and not enough into her relationship with Joe with whom she intends to stay. When Geoff sees this, he will confront Karen with what he perceives, and suggest that she stop seeing Hugh. He will need to be sensitive to Karen's response to this, watching both for resistance and for vulnerability, each of which may be powerful at this stage.

Thus far Geoff's thinking and work has been with Karen alone. He will need to decide when to involve Joe in the counselling. He will take into account how much Joe knows, and the degree of desperation Joe might feel. Geoff is aware that Karen is the one who has to make the major decision: What does she want to do? What is the outcome that she sees as right for her? How does she see her responsibility for herself, for Joe and for the children? Once she has made that decision (even tentatively) her counselling can go on usefully as she has a goal to work towards.

Counselling with Joe

Karen now has some clarity about what is wrong with the marriage and what she wants to achieve. But when her adultery and the state of their marriage are out in the open, Joe has a long way to go before he can think clearly about their situation. He does not yet have Karen's relative clarity of perception. Feeling confused and desperate as he talks privately to Geoff, Joe pours out his distress to his pastor.

Geoff requires all his skills in empathy to stay with Joe's turbulent and contradictory emotions. Joe swings from anger to self-blame as he talks to Geoff; sometimes he reaches a state of temporary calm, then he becomes desperately angry again. He describes to Geoff his behaviour at home, where at one moment he reproaches Karen bitterly, and at another he is swearing to forgive her everything. Geoff recognizes that his reactions are those of a man whose previously well-practised defence of reticence has broken down, so that he can no longer keep anxiety at bay.

Feeling betrayed and hurt by Karen, at times he rejects her in disgust; then in guilt and shame he becomes smothering and pleading, blaming himself for her affair. These confused emotions stem from his grief reaction. Joe has suffered a grievous loss: the loss of his identity as an adequate man and marriage partner. While Joe's turmoil is running its course, Geoff continues to see him on his own. He expects that in time Joe will be ready to deal with what is wrong in the marriage, and to identify realistically the part he has played in its impoverishment over the years.

If Joe were to maintain a self-righteous position, blaming Karen entirely and appearing unable to acknowledge the mutual difficulties leading to the crisis, Geoff might ask the couple earlier than otherwise, to have a joint counselling session. His purpose would be to set the agenda – for Joe to hear what has concerned Karen in the marriage. Geoff would observe how Joe responded to Karen's explanation, hoping to link on to Joe's response in a way that would help him move from self-righteousness. This is not to place blame on Joe for Karen's affair, but it is acknowledging that one element in her motivation was her dissatisfaction with their marriage and her inability to turn it into a mutually nourishing relationship.[9]

Geoff's task is to encourage Joe to acknowledge Karen's dissatisfaction. Joe doesn't have to agree with the factual details of her complaints, and he is certainly not expected to condone her affair. But Geoff wants Joe to gain

- some sense of what Karen was doing that contributed to his own dissatisfaction, and

- some sense of what he himself was doing that resulted in Karen's judgment that the marriage had lost its spark.

Crucial to this process is Karen's acknowledgment of the destructiveness of the affair to the marriage. Sometimes one hears a comment about an affair having a positive effect on the couple's relationship. This view glosses over the meaning of sexual commitment as part of marriage.[10] A minister has, as part of his calling, a responsibility to help people reach a place of genuine repentance for real wrongdoing. In fact any good counsellor invites a client in Karen's position to a sober response of genuine remorse and amendment of life — though not to an exaggerated display of soap-style sorrow!

When Karen and Joe each have a sense of responsibility for their part in the marriage's problems, their counselling can proceed more productively. Its productiveness will involve Karen and Joe together acknowledging and facing

[9] If Geoff sees signs that Joe is interpreting his care for Karen in her dilemma as condoning her adultery, he will say something like this: 'I don't condone her adultery, but I believe the best chance for real repentance and a new commitment to your marriage comes by facing up to her dissatisfactions in the marriage'. Or he could simply say: 'I don't condone her adultery, but it is important that she wants to remake the marriage for good and realistic reasons and not just because she should or she feels guilty.'

[10] The shock and drama to a marriage that an affair causes does sometimes trigger a radical reassessment of the relationship by the couple and evoke a new quality to the marriage. But this is not to say that an affair can in itself be good.

- their resentment toward each other;
- the reality of Karen's betrayal of the marriage;
- the loss of Joe's self-concept as an adequate husband and sexual partner to Karen;
- the need for development of a new, mutual trust and (in some senses) a new marriage relationship between them.

It is important that full recognition is given to the difficulty Joe has in forgiving Karen's adultery. Betrayal of a marriage commitment is not quickly and easily forgiven, and like some other great griefs, Joe's may never be entirely resolved. By the grace of God resentment and bitterness can be let go. There are some very beautiful marriages which were once marred by adultery and in which the partners still share the grief it caused. The old grief may still surface occasionally.

A wise counsellor is able to say to someone in Joe's position, gently and reassuringly: 'You don't have to forgive all at once. Take your time. Recognize that you can begin to trust again and build a new relationship with your marriage partner, while you are going on with your forgiving, and before you have done all your forgiving.'

Ingrid and Hugh

Ingrid had been uneasy about Hugh's involvement with Karen for some time, but she told herself they were Christians and about the Lord's business. The devastation she felt when her suspicions about the affair were confirmed was intense, and she went to Pastor Geoff for help.

Geoff welcomed Ingrid. As he listened carefully to her story, he was wondering what to do. (Though sometimes we may find it difficult, we can listen empathically and consider at the same time what to do). Geoff was aware that as he was already counselling Karen and Joe, there would be many difficulties for him and for all four parishioners if he counselled Ingrid and Hugh also. How would he remember exactly what he knew from whom? Maintaining confidentiality would be a master task. How would Karen and Joe not hear him bringing into their counselling information from his sessions with the other couple – and vice versa?

Geoff knew his limitations! Though handling his emotions might not be his greatest skill, his reality-testing was very adequate. So Geoff decided to refer Ingrid (and Hugh if he would go) to Helen, a marriage counsellor whom he respects both for her competence and her value-stance. We will consider Geoff's process of making a referral in the chapter on that topic.[11]

The Partner who Wants to Move Out

Partners of the two marriages we have considered wanted their marriages to work even though they were facing real difficulties and real attractions. However, not all persons involved in adultery want to work out their marriages. The adultery may be one move in a process of disengaging from the marriage, perhaps a determined action to deal with an unsatisfactory marriage. In such a case, the spouse who is disengaging may agree to see their partner's counsellor, but usually comes with reluctance. The counsellor's task is to make a realistic assessment of the likely outcome of any counselling interventions.

'Don't flog a dead horse' Geoff reminds himself on occasions when reluctant spouses sit defensively in his counselling room, expecting to be judged and urged to return to the marriage. Geoff isn't into flogging. He recognizes that some men, and some women too, act callously toward their spouses; they have affairs and leave their marriages (and often expect to return) at their own convenience. These people have not developed a stable conscience and an ability to value others.[12]

[11]Chapter on Referral, No. 19.

[12]Ministers and Christian counsellors tend to be very ill-informed about personality disorders, and to lack discernment in judging people's levels of moral development. So they can be taken in by the earnest charm and the apparent vulnerability of those whom the more astute would quickly dub 'con-artists'.

However, Geoff recognizes also that good people do wrong things and that all of us have a capacity to suspend informed moral judgments at times. Even for people who love God very much and seek to serve him, sometimes wrong-doing can seem the right thing to do. (On these occasions people tend to be functioning out of their third belief systems, telling themselves that what they are doing is the right way to survive.)

Faced with a disengaging spouse – let's say a husband – Geoff may remark early in their discussion: 'I guess that in some ways it seemed right for you to take that course.' The husband is initially surprised by this genuinely understanding comment. After his surprise, his next response may be a recognition of Geoff's acceptance. He describes for Geoff *what has been wrong for him in the marriage,* and *what attracted him into his adulterous relationship.*

With Geoff listening to him and taking seriously both sets of forces, this husband may just possibly begin to review his marriage and his affair in fresh terms, and engage in constructive marriage counselling. However, Geoff's remark 'I guess that in some ways it seemed right for you to take that course' (i.e. the affair) is not made as a cheap trick to bring about a particular result. Its purpose is simply to be with the man, accepting the ambiguity of the motives he had as he searched for relationship and sexual satisfactions.

Marital Breakdown and Separation

If this man has made a firm decision in favour of his affair and against his marriage, the breakdown of the marriage is already in progress. Where an adulterous affair by one spouse features in marital breakdown, the other spouse finds the resolution of bitterness very hard to achieve. But all couples whose marriage was once a deeply loving, committed relationship feel a sense of betrayal and bitterness when it ends.

Marriages do not end without bitter hurt and animosity; unless of course, the relationship has been a shallow one – something like the stereotype presented in magazines about the marriages of stars in the world of actors. These stereotypical marriages seem more like a public performance between two persons than a marriage bond between a man and a woman who initially committed themselves to each other for life – for better, for worse.

There was once a simple card game called Happy Families. Recent decades have seen attempts to promote, as an easily achievable goal, Multiple Happy Families. In this image, the previously married couple, their subsequent spouses or sex partners and all the children involved are mutually tolerant, warm and caring. While the goal of letting go old animosities is a good and true one, the Multiple Happy Families image is as illusory as any other house of cards!

It is an image that does not take account of the nature and intensity of marriage and family relationships, or the human tendency to territorial rights, or the grief and dysfunction of parents and children following rupture of the marriage bond.

In the case of the disengaging husband referred to above, his move out of the marriage is an emotional one for him, even though he has chosen to leave. Separation counselling can be the next step for him, for his wife, and ideally, for both in joint sessions if they are willing. However, at this stage she may be in a state of grief similar to Joe's, one that manifests itself in confused and intense emotions. In that case, individual sessions for her and for the husband will be appropriate at first. Later, when some of her grief and bitterness has abated, joint sessions could help these two people achieve a good separation.

Separation counselling is a subject too big for us to cover in this book. Briefly, however, we may say that a 'good' separation is one that has the following characteristics:

• The level of hurt and animosity between the two people has lowered sufficiently for them to come to necessary though painful agreement about access to children and settlement of property.[13]

---

[13]Such agreements are never going to be 'fair'. The separating spouses are doing well if they manage together to safeguard the interests and welfare of their children and achieve the optimum in adequate material circumstances for all.

- The partners have been able to gain some understanding of what went wrong, and to have some discussion about their past relationship; each accepting responsibility for personal limitations and even making admission of personal wrongdoing.

- They are able in some measure to let each other go, neither clinging out of dependency nor tying themselves with a chain of resentment to the other.

- They have grieved over the loss of their marriage and are beginning to say goodbye to it, taking up separate lives with some acceptance of the past events.

Those who undertake the skilled work of separation counselling understand that letting go takes time and patience, and that in so far as each partner is gradually able to express appreciation as well as resentments of the other, they let go a little more. And in marriage breakdown where affairs have been a feature, the counsellor understands that even adultery, like other forms of betrayal, is finally forgivable.

16

AFTER A MARRIAGE BREAKS

Conventional wisdom says that a person chooses, in marrying a second time, either someone very similar to their previous partner, or someone very unlike that partner. While this is over-simplified, it can be a useful starting point in considering some aspects of second marriages.

In the sense that marrying is something that people continue to want to do, marriage is still extremely popular. In spite of the level of marriage breakdown in Western society, a very large percentage of adults is of married people, most of them living in first or second marriages.[1] The majority of those who divorce do not give up on marriage: they soon enter a new marriage, legal or de facto.[2]

The issues a minister encounters with people in a second marriage are largely those of a first marriage: two people are living in a close relationship, each having limited ability to meet the other's needs. As ministers recognize, this limitation in ability is common to all human living, and common to all marriages. It is the severity of the limita-

[1] In Australia in 1992, of all families with dependent children
80% had registered married parents
  7% had de facto married parents
13% had a sole parent   — *Australian Bureau of Statistics*
[2] A de facto marriage is an 'in fact' marriage, which we take to be committed, monogamous and meant by both partners to be permanent. Not all de facto marriages fulfil this definition.

tions in ability and the way any particular couple face up to them that make a difference.

There are issues particular to second marriages. These tend to arise when an ex-spouse, in choosing a new marriage partner, is trying blindly to resolve the difficulties of the previous marriage.

Bringing Same Self and Same Needs

If I enter a second marriage, nothing is surer than that I am going to bring my self and my needs with me. Am I also bringing unexamined assumptions about those needs and about that self of mine? Am I choosing this new partner on the basis of my unexamined needs? Am I willing to understand, assess and admit to the strength of these needs? Was I disappointed in my ex-spouse because I assumed he or she could meet most or all of my needs?

Brian took himself into his first marriage expecting to be dependent. Anna, his first wife, was able to meet his need for dependency, and he enjoyed being almost subservient to her. Initially Anna enjoyed Brian's dependency. Later she found it burdensome and finally she left the marriage. Now Brian is hoping to marry Clare. According to his friends, Clare seems remarkably like Anna before Anna changed. Brian's story describes one situation in which people repeat a marriage choice because they have not understood and assessed why they are so strongly drawn to such a partner.

On the other hand, a Brian may respond to the breakdown of marriage to an Anna by choosing someone very childlike and dependent. In the second situation, Brian tries to overcompensate or bend over backwards trying not to repeat his choice of partner. He consciously looks for someone different from the earlier partner, because consciously he desires a very different marriage. However, the pattern of the new relationship may still be blindly determined by the experience of the previous one. People bring themselves and their unassessed needs to a new marriage.

The Brians who choose a new partner with a very different personality from the previous partner's find that their second choice brings its own set of problems. They may initially be delighted with their choice of a wife who does not invite and encourage dependency and instead, likes to be dependent and childlike. But such a Brian has not resolved his need for dependency: he has brought it into his new marriage, and he will be looking for ways to be dependent.

Staying in 'Good-enough' First Marriages

Throughout this book there are frequent references to ways in which much of our behaviour is habitual, learned in large part from our families-of-origin. We need to recognize something positive about this, and recognize it clearly. If we grew up in 'good-enough' families,[3] we learnt many modes of behaviour and attitudes that serve us well and productively. They serve others well, too.

Some of our habitual behaviour and attitudes – our third systems – do not serve us well. Their chronic and unassessed aspects can mar our current functioning. It is these aspects we need to attend to, recognizing that we all respond to people and situations in patterns that are more habitual than we usually like to think.

Dan, a member of a therapy group, had felt terribly derided as a child and had adopted a critically assessing attitude which, while helping him defend against the derision, made him a superior, distanced and fairly friendless man. Devastated by his wife's leaving him, Dan learnt in the group that others including the co-therapists found his super-critical assessing of them unpleasant. In the nonetheless accepting environment of the group, Dan was gradually able to let go some of the destructive power of his third system.

Our habitual patterns are often modified in a first marriage (sadly, Dan's were not). We learn there to tolerate to some degree the differences from us that we find in our spouse, and to extend that newly learned tolerance to others, especially if there is plenty of need-meeting for us and our spouse in our marriage. As long as the marriage is a safe place and a relatively need-meeting place to be, as

[3]In the 1950s Winnicott's concept of 'good enough' parenting came as a relief and a release to some people working in child and family guidance clinics who had adopted doctrinaire, perfectionistic attitudes to what families should be.

long as ours is a good-enough marriage, it can be a place to reassess our third system less-than-good attitudes.

And that is an important reason why many a first marriage remains the wife's and husband's first and only marriage. It continues to be a safe-enough place. The partners' different and habitual ways of being, even their less-than-acceptable ways of reacting, present a challenge. Often enough the challenge they present can be accepted as something positive and exciting. It doesn't have to be viewed as negative and therefore defended against and rejected.

Rebounding into Second Marriage

Some first marriages do not remain a safe place for one or both spouses. Whatever the reasons, the marriage becomes one where each partner's less-than-useful third system attitudes and behaviours are reinforced and exacerbated. A divorce takes place. Then, all too often, a partner quickly enters a second marriage, rebounding from the breakdown of the first marriage.[4] Marriage counsellors expect rebounders to have difficulties: they have not taken time to allow the negative and habitual patterns built up in the first marriage to be modified and so allow for a less destructive relationship.

Cara joined a therapy group not long after her marriage broke down irrevocably. Quite soon in the group she was making frequent references to a male friend who was interested in having a romantic relationship with her. As Cara described him, group members commented on the similarities between the way she viewed him and her earlier description of her husband. Cara was strongly attracted to this man. Some months later he faded from her life. One reason was his keenness for a sexual relationship with her. Despite her sexual desires she rejected this, on the grounds of her Christian morality;

[4] Just as disastrous as rebounding into a second marriage is embarking on a series of sexual relationships in the hope of finding healing of hurt there. In contemporary times, when the message not only of society in general but also of some church people that such relationships are acceptable, it is very difficult for lonely separated spouses to go against this permissive aspect of Western social *mores*.

but also on the (connected) grounds that in her life-reconstruction, she had other goals to achieve.

Another reason why the friendship faded was that Cara had used the group to develop stronger reality-testing. She began to speak appreciatively of other friends, old and new. By changing some of her concepts (and strengthening others) about quality relationships, Cara widened her range and variety of friends and thus enriched her life.

Many marriage counsellors believe that a recently divorced and even more certainly a recently separated person is unlikely to make a constructive choice of a new partner. A delay of two years is likely to be helpful in giving such a person time to grieve over and assess the broken marriage.

Churches can provide a safe place while people are doing this. It is sad that some churches do not provide a safe place, sad that some church people coming from a broken marriage do not feel acceptable to the church they attend. The human limitations of Christians explain this sad situation, and we need not hurry to condemn such churches on this account. It remains true that there is a great ministry to be offered by mature church people and their pastors as they can provide a safe place – the church – for people whose marriages are over.

Such people, lonely, disappointed and grieving, are likely to come feeling already humiliated by their perceived failure as a spouse. They are likely to feel angry with their marriage partner. They are therefore sensitive to real or perceived rebuff by church members.

Living – as we all do – in a sex-obsessed society, people who have come out of a marriage are very open to the temptation to enter a new sexual relationship, even a passing one. In theory, who better than the people of God, committed to biblical theology, can offer such needy people an alternative? They can offer respectful and personal acceptance, a message of hope, and the possibility of an ongoing life in Jesus Christ and among his servants.

Such an environment can offer those whose marriages are over a loving alternative to hastening into a relationship to fill a marriage gap. It can offer them what it offers every one of us – a chance to practise ordinary good-enough friendships with other people, mutually trying to be forgiving and to tolerate each other's differences. But churches can only do this well if Christians who have not suffered a broken marriage understand that those whose marriages are over have much to give and to teach them in many areas.

Relating to Stepchildren

After a marriage breakdown, people who are now sole parents can feel strong internal pressures to couple-up with another partner. These pressures may come from their desire to have someone share parenting and practicalities like household expenses, as well as from the desire to receive consistent attention from someone.

Being in a very lonely situation, the sole parent often feels the urge to restore, somehow, the family system that existed – a system which, despite its familiar marital miseries, is missed. An attempt to somehow restore known systems is understandable. Frequently, then, sole parents face the pressure of a temptation to couple-up without adequate evaluation of the possible and likely outcomes. The relief seems too great for relevant questions to be asked.

Separation counselling and post-marital counselling can be helpful to sole parents. Group counselling and support groups can also be valuable. However, skilled group leadership is required so that members avoid using groups to reinforce their identity as injured spouses and sole parents. The task of members of groups is to let go enough of the past marriage and the unfulfilled hopes so that they are affirming themselves and one another as people who are moving on and out into membership of their wider community. So, rather than having 'separated' or 'divorced' in the names of such groups, it is better to call them *and make them* 'life reconstruction groups'.

When parents make a second marriage, the new domestic situation possibly consists of a husband and a wife who are on their own except for access visits from the children of one or both. Much more likely, it includes children from the prior marriage of one, or the prior marriages of both. Thus, while learning to be a new married couple, the partners cannot do this in a leisurely unencumbered way. Much of their energy and focus has to be on the child or children they have in their custody.

Fairy tales focus on the difficulties stepchildren have with a cruel step-parent. Counsellors of people in second marriages are, however, dealing with the difficulties of an ordinary human and fallible step-parent and an equally human parent, as they struggle to do well with children in a new situation. These children, hurting and feeling helpless, are in a new domestic scene that is not of their making or choosing.[5] It may seem sometimes that, rather than having any investment in being part of a blended family, they are intent on making it a curdled family. They seem to be trying magically to remake their original families.

With a domestic situation involving children and stepchildren, a couple in a second marriage tend to have issues to contend with:

- Patterns of behaviour in the children which irritate the step-parent and seem normal to the natural parent.

- Protectiveness toward one's own children against the real or perceived sentimentality, harshness, jealousy or resentment of one's partner.

- Access visits and other perceived intrusions on the new marriage, by an ex-spouse or two ex-spouses. And sometimes there may be a further issue to contend with:

- Alleged physical abuse or alleged sexual abuse of children by a step-parent or by their other parent on access.

Maya and Neil

Maya has persuaded Neil to come with her to see their minister Frances about the difficulties they are having with their children.

[5]See Wallerstein, Judith S. and Blakeslee, Sandra, *Second Chances*, Corgi Books, London 1990, p. 40. Wallerstein, counsellor of divorcing families in California, describes the life stories of divorcing parents and their children of whom she made a longitudinal study over a period of many years. She presents sobering and compelling evidence of the long-term effects on children of divorce.

Each of them came into the marriage with two children. Maya believes that Neil doesn't back up her authority with the children. She says he isn't fulfilling an agreement they made about this when they married, that each would support the other in the disciplining of the four children.

Frances acknowledges the commonness of the conflict and asks Maya for an instance of it in their marriage.

Frances: 'Yes, many couples in second marriages have difficulties over the discipline of their children. Will you describe a situation you've had recently – or, to be more specific, how you, Neil, and you, Maya, get into conflict about it.'

Maya: 'The worst time is when the kids come back from access. My two are noisy and aggressive after being with their father Jamie, and Neil's are sort of superior when they come back from Jodie's. They're dismissive of me. They go off to their room and pull out pictures of their mother and pictures of Jodie and Neil and themselves together. And they put them all round the walls with Blu-tac. And all Neil says is "Well, she is their mother."'

Frances keeps in mind that she is involved with a complex set of systems:

- The system of Maya, Jamie and their two children. This system has been partially disrupted by divorce, but perpetuated through custody and access, and by the thoughts and feelings the parents still have about each other and their children.

- The system of Neil, Jodie and their two children. It is in a similar situation.

- The system of Neil, Maya and the four children, with regular interruptions for access and with incursions from the ex-spouses directly or through the children.

With this complexity, Frances decides to concentrate primarily on the parental subsystem in the household of the presenting couple. She reasons that with Maya and Neil working together as a team the welfare of the children as well as the marriage will be enhanced.

In her previous marriage Maya saw herself as a victim. As she perceives the present situation, Jamie is still persecuting her in her new marriage by encouraging their children to give her a hard time. Neil also seems to her to persecute her, by letting his children display photographs of his ex-wife.

Habitually Neil's response to Maya's distress takes this form: 'Just ignore Jamie's behaviour. Don't get upset about your children's behaviour when they come home from Jamie – they soon settle down.' As for his own children, his response to Maya is 'Maya, you just have to realize that you are their mother most of the time. Don't get annoyed when they flaunt Jodie's photo. It's natural for them to do that after they've been with her.'

As Frances gets a feel for Neil's attitude and Maya's negative reaction to it, she asks Maya and Neil to turn their chairs to face each other and discuss their plight.

Maya: 'I'm upset because you don't take me seriously about this. You are not even angry with Jamie for stirring my kids. You let your kids get away with flaunting those photographs. You don't stop any of the four of them from playing their tricks when they come home after access.'

Neil: 'I am taking you seriously, but you get too excited about it all. I do what I can. I know the kids will soon settle down. I wish you would settle down too.'

Maya: 'There you go again, denying it's important. You're really telling me I'm sick. I don't know why you married me. Or maybe I do – you just needed a mother for your children. And don't keep saying I'm their mother most of the time. You know Jodie's their mother and always will be.'

Neil: 'That's not-fair, saying I married you for their sake. I love you. I married you because I loved you and I still love you as much as I ever did. But you make it pretty hard with your criticisms and your accusations.'

Frances: 'You're both in a very sore spot. Maya, it seems to you Neil doesn't take proper account of you, and Neil, you think Maya doesn't take what you say seriously. It seems that the four children have really got you two split.'

Neil: 'I suppose they have. That's exactly what I don't want. That's what I get desperate about. I'm afraid we'll break up.'

Maya: 'No, it's not the children. It's Neil. If he really cared about me he'd stop them putting me down. He doesn't really love me.'

Frances doesn't respond to Neil's 'I get desperate . . . afraid' or to Maya's 'He doesn't really love me'. She will not be deflected from the notion that Neil and Maya allow the children to split them as a team. She will return to these later.

Frances: 'It seems the kids are controlling you both. That's really bad for you – and it's not good for them. You need to be team for each other – and that's likely to be good for them too. It's important you don't let them split you.'

Neil: 'That's what I mean. I want us to get on, not to fight.'

Maya: 'But that's the trouble! You don't want to fight the kids, so I finish up yelling at them because you won't. You snap at me that I shouldn't yell, and I know you dislike me. Then you turn round and say you love me. I don't believe you!'

Frances observes Maya feeling unloved and let down, and Neil frustrated by Maya's inability to *be sensible* and realize he loves her. Frances sees that Neil's frustration – his helpless anger when finally he snaps at Maya – compounds Maya's sense of her own unlovability. Maya isn't seeing something that becomes pretty clear to Frances as she observes them together and looks for the positive motives behind their negative responses.

Frances sees that Neil's way of expressing love to Maya is to offer her his sensible reasoning accompanied by his long-lasting patience (and it's not a phoney patience). This loving of Neil's is making absolutely no difference to Maya, and finally Neil expresses frustration. Maya interprets Neil's frustrated angry outburst (snapping) as further evidence of his *true feeling*, not of his loving, and she uses it to confirm her sense of unlovability.[6]

⁶Note the circular process of Neil's and Maya's interaction. See chapters 4 and 5.

For Maya, who wants very much for Neil and her to be a well-functioning team, there is a further positive motive in her negative responses to Neil. She is crying out 'Meet me! Meet me!' or in other words 'I love you, I want you to be with me in a way that assures me of your love for me.'

Discounting and Resistance[7]

Frances recognizes how doubtful Maya is about her own lovability, and how in consequence she discounts the reality of Neil's love for her. Maya is likely to resist the process of letting go her sense of unlovability. She will also resist assurances of the reality of Neil's love for her.

On Neil's side, Frances notices the defensiveness of his reasonableness: he is a peace-lover rather than an active peace-maker, and discounts the very real need to grasp nettles in his and Maya's situation. He avoids their sting and discounts how painful they are for Maya to handle. He also discounts her need to have him understand how she experiences the situation.

In consequence, he will resist the demand to change his actions because he experiences the demand as all-encompassing; he fears that any action will never be enough for Maya. With the Neils of the world discounting and resisting in this pattern, the risk is that the Mayas of the world can be wiped off by the other people involved, as paranoid[8] about the situation.

At this stage Frances chooses not to take either of two courses which seem to her premature. One is to explain to Maya that *Neil*

[7]*Resistance and the discounting that supports it* are not limited to second marriages. They can take place in any relationship. We have chosen to give an account of some ways they operate in second marriages where stepchildren and ex-spouses can easily present a threat.

[8]Those who doubt their lovability can feel so discounted in situations of stress around loyalty that they become excessively sensitive to real and imagined slight and criticism. It is wise to remember that when feeling as if we are fighting alone with our backs to the wall, temporarily we all tend to be sensitive to the point of being what some would call paranoid.

gets angry because, loving her, he feels frustrated when she discounts the reasoning and patience which are his ways of reaching out in love to her. It would be difficult for Maya to hear the meaning of this explanation.

The other course which would also be premature for Frances to take is to ask Maya *what would need to change for her to let Neil's love in, and what is different for her when she does let his love in.* Maya is too frightened and therefore too defensive to think through the answers to those questions. Frances tries to help Maya confront her own discounting and resistance by putting the onus on Neil to initiate discussion between them.

Frances: 'Neil, will you talk to Maya about what it's like for you in the stresses at home?'

Neil: 'I love you, Maya. I feel helpless and irritated when you don't want my help and concern.'

Frances: 'Maya, will you tell Neil what you heard him say to you just now?'⁹

Maya: 'He said he was angry when I'm upset.'

Frances: 'Will you tell *him* what you heard him say?'

Maya: 'He heard it.'

Frances: 'Will you tell Neil?'

Maya: 'She says to tell you that you were angry when I was upset.'

Frances bypasses Maya's addition of 'She says to . . .'. She has no investment in being pedantic, but simply wants Maya to respond to Neil in what is turning out to be a risky attempt at a communication exercise. Instead, she asks Neil to respond.

Frances: 'Neil, will you tell Maya whether she heard you as you meant it?'

Neil: 'She didn't get it right.'

Frances: 'Okay, tell her again.'

⁹In this kind of listen-and-tell-back exercise, counsellors gently insist on the partner addressing the other who has spoken. Frances may have chosen prematurely to ask the couple to do this exercise, as Maya's resentful resistance suggests, but she will persist in the hope that Maya has sufficient trust in her to take part in the communication with Neil.

Neil: 'I love you, Maya. I'm helpless and I'm angry when you reject my efforts to help you.'

Frances: 'Maya, will you tell him what you heard him say?'

Maya: 'That he's angry with me.'

Frances: 'Yes, he did say that, and he said more. Will you tell him the other part too?'

Maya: 'That's what he really means.'

Frances has been *resisting Maya's resistance*, instead of *going with the resistance*. Now Frances recognizes that her own optimism has not paid off. The risks for Maya are too great. So Maya's responses are those of a beleaguered besieged child who for her own reasons will not trust Frances and enter into the communication process Frances wants to facilitate. Frances guesses that from her third system Maya is telling herself something like this:

- I have to hold onto my belief that I am unlovable because it gives me some (awful) sense of defended safety.

- If I let Neil in and believe he loves me (especially with Frances as witness), it won't be the sort of love I want, it won't be enough, it won't last.

To defend her position, Maya has to assume that *she knows* what Neil is saying or meaning; she has to refuse to be coaxed into hearing a different communication. From this position of defence, it isn't safe for her to trust the counselling process. Frances becomes aware of Maya's state of siege. Belatedly, she decides to go with Maya's resistance. But she still wants to facilitate communication between Maya and Neil, and she tries to do so by lining up with Maya's defensive energy.

Frances: 'Maya, would you be willing to tell Neil why he should be angry with you and why he can't love you?'[10]

---

[10]Frances uses the energy of her own 'child' – which involves humour – to enliven Maya's 'child' and, she hopes, engage Maya's humour.

Maya: 'No, I won't do that!' (She speaks with some defiance and a little smile.)

Frances: 'Okay. But I guess you tell yourself the answers sometimes.'

Maya: 'Yes, but that's different.'

Maya's and Frances's humour break through simultaneously. They laugh a little together. Maya seems to sense that Frances, in spite of having resisted her resistance, is in fact firmly on her side, while being also on Neil's.[11] Frances risks a little more gentle humour.

Frances: 'Will you tell Neil how unlovable you are?'

Maya: 'Oh, he knows that. Neil, you can't possibly love me. You don't even like me much. I'm angry with you – and unlikeable. I'm scared about Jamie and I'm scared about the way I carry on about him. I'm a burden to you.[12] You'd be better off without me.'

Neil: 'That's rubbish. I love you, and I'm married to you.'

Frances: 'Tell him you're not worth loving, Maya.'

Maya: 'You're kidding yourself, Neil. You couldn't love me. You just want me for your children and your bed.'

As Frances has been expecting since her invitation to Maya to tell Neil how unlovable she is, Maya begins to smile as she hears what she is saying. She knows that it is part of her self-perception, and a part that surfaces strongly when she is feeling threatened by those around her. She also recognizes the unreality in this perception of herself.

[11]Part of the task in marriage counselling is to demonstrate the message 'I am on both your sides'; and the message can only be demonstrated if it reflects the reality of the counsellor's attitude.

[12]Maya may carry guilt, realistic or otherwise, about the breaking of her previous marriage, and her remarriage to Neil. Christians do not necessarily feel guilt-free and right before God about their marital history, simply because they seem to accept comfortably community attitudes about divorce and remarriage. An essential role for the minister, in counselling people who have divorced, is in pastoral ministry and pastoral counselling around guilt, repentance, confession and assurance of forgiveness. See chapter 9, Shame, Guilt and Self-Esteem.

Frances has first identified for herself that Maya's resistance is strong, and then by allowing a little humour to surface, she invites Maya in a creative way to express that resistance constructively. A counsellor whom Maya did not experience as very much with her might also have invited Maya to tell Neil how unlovable she was — and Maya might have found it insulting or even sarcastic. Frances continues working with Maya.

Frances: 'Maya, will you tell Neil that even if you're not very lovable you realize he does love you.'

Maya: 'Yes, you love me. I can't imagine why.'

Frances: 'How about you just believe it even if you can't imagine it?'

Maya: 'Mm. All right.'

Frances: 'Say to Neil "I believe you love me, even if I can't imagine it."'

Maya does this, and with Frances's lead, tells Neil 'I believe you think I'm lovable'; and 'Some day *I'm* going to believe I'm lovable.' Maya speaks with increasing energy, and with a touch of tenderness to herself and vulnerability to Neil. She has moved from rejecting firmly the possibility of Neil's love, to allowing — or beginning to allow — his love in. The change has come as she has challenged her internal dialogue — challenged her little-child belief about her own worth.

Frances has used her skill and her empathy to follow Maya's magical, internal self-talk, and has enabled her to say this out aloud. Hearing it outside of her head, Maya has been able to hear some of its incongruity. Now, though perhaps temporarily, she has been able to laugh at it in a constructive way.

Counsellor Mistakes

With this case Frances's hunch proves to be correct, and her subsequent steps work out fairly well. Her ability to recognize when she is on an unproductive track with a couple has grown slowly, with practice. Such a track was her attempt to persist in coaxing Maya to change her discounting stance by telling back to Neil what she had heard him say.

A skilled counsellor recognizes when a potentially useful technique is proving unproductive in a particular case, and is able to change it for another. A skilled counsellor is not one who doesn't make mistakes, but one who knows what to do after making a mistake.

Every couple is unique. Every counselling case is unique. That is why it cannot make for good counselling to read dialogues (of the kind that are used in this book to demonstrate processes) and then use the words of the counsellor's interventions in imitation. The task in counselling is to flow with the persons being counselled, not to use stock words and phrases: to be with them where they are, attuned to the internal self-talk with which they discount themselves and others, understanding the very real reasons why they use resistance.

Staying on Track Within a Broad Context

In the case of Maya and Neil, Frances has been careful not to side-track into dealing with the children's behaviour. Her focus has been the couple's subsystem, for the benefit of their marriage and the demanding tasks they have to accomplish with the four children. Frances is working on the hypothesis that if Maya is free to feel less threatened, she will be free to acknowledge and trust the reality of Neil's love. Then she will be freer to handle the alleged stratagems of the children and of her ex-husband: stratagems to which she has responded with fear and distress.

Frances will stay on track by keeping in mind that Neil's habitual ways of reacting, discounting, and resisting are as much a part of the marriage and the wider context as Maya's are. They present a challenge equal to that of Maya's, and Frances still has to engage Neil in confronting them in himself.

Frances keeps in mind also the wider context. Each of the four children in the household has a point of view and needs. Each has the sense of deprivation that comes with the break-up of the marriage of their parents, and the formation of a new family that includes a step-parent and step-siblings. Each has lost familiar and daily contact with one of their parents.

The wider context includes also Maya's ex-husband and Neil's ex-wife. They too are people with a point of view, needs and losses from the break-ups of their former marriages and families. When Neil tells Maya that she is the 'mother' of his and Jodie's children 'most of the time', he is discounting the reality of their relationship with Jodie. When he tells Maya to ignore Jamie's behaviour, he is discounting the reality that Jamie and Maya continue to be linked by their past relationship and their children, just as he and Jodie are linked by theirs.

Frances has been weaving her way through a very broad context, and yet keeping focus on the central relationship of Maya and Neil. While being aware of many conflicting themes, she has concentrated on the parental subsystem within the larger multifamily system. There are many directions she could have taken, but her knowledge of systems (their interdependence and their resistance to change: homeostasis) helped her to decide which part of the system to choose and to influence. She knows that she will need to keep her energy pitted against the natural resistance to change in order to maintain the small gain she has helped Maya to make. She will stay with Maya to reinforce her new perception of her self-talk, and she will help Neil to bring his magical self-talk into the open, so that he can modify the negative aspects of his peace-loving. She is helping each of them to modify their 'safe defensive' positions to take the risk of more intimate and vulnerable meeting with each other. This is the beginning of building a more satisfying marriage for them, and there-fore a more constructive relationship for their children.

17

PRAYER AND SCRIPTURE IN COUNSELLING

'We've come to you, because our last counsellor wouldn't pray with us, even though he said he was a Christian counsellor' were the opening words to Kerry as she met a couple looking for help with their marriage. They were implying that the essential criterion of Christian counselling was prayer by the counsellor, and so seemed to imply that considerations of competence in theory and practice, of soundness of moral values and knowledge of biblical theology were all secondary. Or perhaps they thought that if the counsellor prayed, all these factors would follow.

While Kerry rejects the particular way her clients define the place of prayer in Christian counselling, she firmly believes that prayer is a part of her counselling, as of any other activity in her living and working. She prays with some clients sometimes; with some clients not at all; but she prays for all her clients regularly and carefully. She sees prayer as acknowledging the energy of God in the interview and in the life of her clients; as something that helps to keep her, and all things she thinks and does, under the Lordship of Christ.

Often she will choose to pray with clients when she sees they need particular support in staying with the pain of facing what is wrong in their relationship. Her prayer will be for them to have the grace and the courage to keep the situation in focus, so that in time they will find a way to change what they do to and with each other. Clearly she will be careful with her timing of this prayer. She may be tempted to pray from her own driven desire before they have reached that vulnerable spot. If she is expressing her need for them to be where she thinks they ought to be, she will be preaching at them rather than being with them in their current situation. If she prays at this time, it is better to pray 'Be with your servants as they try to face what is really wrong in their marriage, and grant them the grace to see clearly the issues they face.'

At times, she chooses to make a prayer of thanksgiving when they have made significant changes in their behaviour toward each other, and as they are in process of reinforcing those changes. At times, she will pray both in thanksgiving and for courage to hang in there. While Kerry acknowledges the power of prayer in counselling, she is uncomfortable with her clients' restricting view of her as a counsellor who can do Christian counselling only if she prays with them. She believes she is required to be discriminating not only about what and how to pray with them, but also about whether and when.

She chooses not to pray when she sees a couple using prayer as a way of denying the reality of the struggle between them. However carefully she prayed for them to have the grace and courage to face their differences, they would probably *hear* her prayer as denying those differences, and putting a pious veneer (or Band-aid) over the beginning openness or vulnerability achieved in the interview.

She may choose not to pray if she sees a marked difference in Christian commitment in the couple. The risk in praying with such a couple is that both partners might see her as aligning with the more committed one.

Use of Prayer

Prayer is an essential part of Christian counselling. While all ministers who are counselling members of their particular church will have a regular pattern of praying for all parishioners, each will also have a particular method of praying for those being counselled. Emma (chapter 6), whose main ministry is in counselling, has her own pattern of praying each day for her clients, particularly for those she will see that day. She will also be praying that she will know the grace of God in all that she does, so that she will be free to work creatively with her clients.

Emma, like Kerry, does not always pray with those she counsels, and part of her prayer is that she will be discerning about this. She believes that the Holy Spirit guides her in deciding when to pray and how to pray. She also appreciates that the Holy Spirit works for her clients through the understanding she has of them because of her professional discipline.

Emma does not pray with those clients who would see prayer as a violation of their position or as a misuse of her power over them in the interviews. While she sees prayer as an important part of her discipline (and she may well pray silently at some point in the interview) her respect for her clients will guide her in not imposing prayer on them.

David is careful not to pray with those clients who use prayer as a way of escaping responsibility for their will and their behaviour. He helps Tim and Sally, and Una and Vincent (chapters 4 and 5) to realize and acknowledge what each does to the other and how they justify these actions to themselves. So his prayer with them might include some sorrow for their destructive patterns, and later a request for courage and sensitivity as they try out new patterns of behaviour. In this way David avoids giving the impression that he is using prayer like a lucky charm that might magically solve problems without pain and effort.

When he prays with clients, David is careful to use the same tone of voice and the same type of language that he has been using throughout the interview. The Lord has been with them throughout their time together. A change in tone or language could suggest that David had suddenly brought God into the room, and needed a pious tone and language to invoke and sustain God's presence.[1]

There are principles on which counsellors will exercise their choices about praying with clients. Prayer will be

• consistent with the issues being faced in the counselling

[1] Dorothy Sayers remarked about clergy she was familiar with: 'At the name of Jesus every voice goes plummy.'

- supporting clients in their struggle and in their attempts at new behaviours – it will be where the clients are

- consistent in tone and language with the rest of the interview.

Prayer will not be

- jumping ahead of where the clients are – expressing the counsellor's needs for them to be where she thinks they ought to be

- imposing something on reluctant or unbelieving clients

- supporting a lack of responsibility for behaviour

- providing a lucky charm or other magical solution

- applying a pious Band-aid to a messy interview.

It is important to remember that in the emotional intensity of the counselling interview, clients will often *hear* a counsellor pray what they expect her to pray, rather than actually attending to the words and meaning. This is specially so if the counsellor has been missing them somewhat through the interview, failing to be with them.

Use of Scripture

Some clients and some counsellors think that counselling without quoting from the Bible is not Christian counselling, but this brings a very restrictive view of Christian counselling. It is important that a counsellor be discriminating about the use of Scripture on very similar principles to those set out about prayer above.

While David uses scriptural stories, parables of Jesus, Jesus' own words, Paul's or Peter's teaching as part of counselling, he does so selectively. Usually, he uses Scripture to support some work the client has already done: for instance, when Karen (chapter 15) has decided to ask forgiveness of God and Joe, David might refer to the action of the prodigal son (Luke 15) going back to his father with a well-rehearsed speech of repentance, while the father is waiting and watching, ready to go quickly to him with forgiveness. David might add that God is wanting to forgive her, but that Joe would probably find it more difficult in practice, and that Joe might understandably find himself in the elder brother's role for a time.

If Karen has been struggling to gain the courage to ask forgiveness, David might debate inside his head whether to encourage her to confess by the example of the prodigal son and the eager forgiving father, or whether to stay with her doubts and with the process by which she is shrinking from confessing. He will make this judgment on the basis of where he sees most of her energy is invested – to confess or not to confess. If he sees her as mainly wanting to confess and resisting a little, he might support her with the account of the prodigal son. But if he sees her mainly resisting, he will empathize with the resistance.[2]

Care should be taken in the use of Scripture that the client shares the same meaning as the counsellor about a passage. One client (who taught Scripture in schools) was considering in a counselling session the parable of the prodigal son as she dealt with her value as a person. It became clear to her counsellor that even though she knew the parable well, emotionally she didn't make the journey back to the Father, to forgiveness and reinstatement. Emotionally she stayed in the far country, rehearsing repentance but never putting it to the test, never finding forgiveness, always bereft. The counsellor will attend to the inner meaning of the Scripture passage for the client, and not assume that the client has incorporated her cognitive understanding in her living. He will stay with her in her stunted understanding until she can complete the story.

When Dierdre said (chapter 3) that Scripture can be used like a brick, she was referring to the inappropriate use of Scripture in counselling people. A counsellor who is using Scripture well will be so empathic that it will always have immediate relevance to the client – either supporting the client's insight or enlarging his understanding of the moment. The client will perceive the Scripture

[2]See also Frances and Maya, chapter 16 pp. 206ff.

as *on his side* whether in support or in confrontation.

Sometimes Scripture can be used to correct assumptions or platitudes which are assumed to be Christian or biblical. Many Christians think that it is unchristian to be angry, while others believe that the Bible says 'Forgive and forget'. With these and similar assumptions it is not usually sufficient to confront them verbally and cognitively. They are usually embedded in a family (or church) tradition with a deep emotional involvement. The confrontation then must be at an emotional or magic-thinking level as well as cognitive.

Problems arise when the counsellor thinks that she *must* use Scripture, and in the urgency or pressure will tend to *use it as a brick*, or will use it tangentially (either off the point, or leading the client away from the theme he needs to follow). It is difficult enough empathically to stay with the client; it is much more difficult to be empathic while searching the memory for a Scripture that is suitable for the moment. Sometimes it comes more easily when the main counselling work is done in the interview for the client and counsellor to reflect theologically on what has happened. In other words, to think through which scriptural passages or incidents might enhance or correct in spiritual terms what has been done – largely in the psychological mode. Such reflection will be continuing the spirit of the interview where the counsellor is seeking to bring a cognitive understanding in scriptural terms of the psychological process; the sort of understanding that can move easily into thanksgiving or prayer.

18

TERMINATION

You have been counselling a couple with whom you will have future contacts. Perhaps they are members of your church, perhaps they are a clergy couple from another church in your area. The couple believe they have achieved what they want from counselling, and they come to their final meeting with you as your clients in counselling. What will you do in this terminating session?

You do much in this terminating session that you would do if you were a private practitioner in counselling who expected not to meet the couple again unless they returned later for a few more sessions. There are some added factors in your situation which we will discuss later; but in the main, you will follow the principles and the process in your final session that apply to the termination of counselling by any counsellor.

The purpose of this session is to make a clean and clear conclusion to the work you and the couple have been doing together. One part of your task is to reinforce the empowering you have done in the past sessions with the couple by focusing with them on the fact that it is they who have made the changes in their relationship. Help them reflect on how they themselves have achieved their changes, emphasizing that whatever skills you have brought to the counselling relationship, it is they who have used the counselling to effect their changes.

You make sure that they identify and articulate those changes. Then you get them to make connections between the changes and their initial presenting problem. (They may have done much that is good for them, but it is still important that they and you are sure they have done sufficient about their presenting problem.) The next step is to help them identify the processes by which they have changed their thinking, their feeling and their behaviour. To the extent that they are able to make such an identification, they will increase their awareness of how to deal with similar difficulties themselves in the future.

Your next task is to have them acknowledge with you that there is quite a strong possibility that they will have similar difficulties in the future; and that what they have done in their sessions has taught them something they can use in resolving future difficulties. They also need to hear you say explicitly that every marriage has a cyclical quality: that we don't live constantly on an even plane; that there are forces external to us and forces within us that affect the level of our sense of joy, loss, excitement, dullness, disappointment and success, of our energy and our weariness and of our tolerance and intolerance to stress.

You need not introduce and follow the above steps in sequence, you may range, rearrange and reiterate them according to your couple's leading. However, it is your task to ensure that the steps are accomplished. The following questions to the couple are a guide for you as you seek to ensure completion of the process.

- What changes have you made during your time in counselling?
- How do the changes you describe relate to the problem that first brought you here?
- How have you made the changes you describe?
- How are you going to slide back – supposing you do so – into your bad spot?
- How will you recognize that you are sliding?
- What will you do then about the sliding when you recognize you're doing it?

Wonderful Counsellor?

It is important that clients do not terminate their sessions thinking that the counsellor is wonderful. As indicated elsewhere[1] idealizing holds the risk of image splitting in relation to a client's parent or partner out there in the everyday world, and this does not help the marriage. Whether the counsellor is removed from other contacts with clients or whether the counsellor is their pastor, transference issues need to be dealt with consistently through the counselling process so that idealization is kept in check and does not have to be dealt with only near the time of termination.

The fact that through the process your couples have had other contacts with you and therefore presumably know about your feet of clay out there in the everyday parish may be an advantage. Their view of you in the counselling room may have remained a more rounded, realistic one.

However, it is with the 'child' of the husband and the wife that you have to a large extent been involved. By taking on the role of marriage counsellor with them you are *in loco parentis* in a particular way. Like all ministers, you have a church role that in itself indicates authority and leadership. Your task with the couple as you terminate counselling is to move to a relationship where the special dependency and vulnerability they have had with you gives way to a normal degree of interdependence between you and your former clients.

That's what needs to be re-established — a normal social relationship with give and take, each being appropriately responsible for the self, and with the couple now giving to as well as receiving from you. Thus for you and for them there is a return to a normal power balance between minister and people.

In this process — which is one of deliberately handing back to the couple authority over themselves — you ask them near termination about any unfinished business that you think may need to be finished

[1]Transference, chapter 22.

between you. 'A few sessions ago you and I were at odds because I seemed to be siding against you/pushing you both/under-rating your level of stress. Is there something you need from me around that issue before we finish?' . . . 'So when you think back on our sessions there may be a sore spot or two as you remember how I wasn't able to make that easier for you. And I couldn't.'

Finally, as the couple describe the changes and achievements they believe they have made during the counselling period, it is important that you genuinely accept their appreciation of your work with them, as well as genuinely remind them that those changes and achievements are their own. And if the three of you together give thanks to God for his grace in all this, so much the better.

19

MAKING REFERRALS

Many of our foregoing case examples present ministers who are considering referral of couples. John's concern[1] was with aspects of sexual counselling, Geoff's[2] with management of emotional and professional complications in ministering to two intertwined couples. Using a therapy group as the preferred treatment for an abusive husband was the referral aim of another counsellor.[3]

All ministers and all other counsellors have a set of questions to ask themselves regarding referral. Consideration of these questions is relevant not only in the first counselling interview, but also at various stages during the continuing process of counselling. (The questions are relevant also to counselling individuals and families.)

- Is it appropriate that I see this couple, or are they the responsibility of someone else?

- Do I have the time and energy to counsel them well, around this particular issue?

- Are there emotional and professional complexities and ambiguities which would seriously limit my effectiveness in attempting to counsel them?

- Are my training, experience and supervision adequate for quality counselling of this couple, and can I recognize, let alone treat, the

[1]See chapter 14.
[2]See chapter 15.
[3]See chapter 12.

extent and kind of personality disorders apparently present in this couple?'

There are simple types of referral that take place at the time of receiving a request for marriage counselling. They involve *redirecting enquiries*. In the light of one or more of the questions above, the counsellor may consider it appropriate at first contact to suggest that the enquirer seek another counsellor. Sometimes it is necessary to listen for a while to the enquirer's explanation of a specific need, so that a particular source of help can be suggested. (This listening does not develop into a counselling process.) Such simple referrals as these are as important a part of ministry as any other.

Sending them On: Early Referral

A different kind of referral consists of *referring after some personal involvement accompanied by evaluation*. This can be viewed as 'counselling for referral'. An example is Geoff's decision to refer Ingrid and Hugh.[5] His pastoral responsibility is complicated by a practical reality: an attempt to counsel them, while in the same time-span he counsels Karen and Joe who have been entwined with them, would present insurmountable complexities.

It is for this reason that Geoff takes time and care with Ingrid. He listens carefully and pastorally to her before introducing the idea of referral, giving himself an opportunity to evaluate her situation. He hopes the referral will include her husband Hugh, and he keeps Hugh in mind; but it is to Ingrid in her predicament that he gives his primary attention.

In this session, when references are made to the affair between Ingrid's married friend Karen and Hugh, Geoff expresses what he says in terms of principles, not personalities. By refraining from any

'For an introduction to the importance of such recognition, see Esther Schubert, 'Personality Disorders and Overseas Missions: Guidelines for the Mental Health Professional', *Journal of Psychology and Theology* 1993, Vol 21 No. 1, pp. 18-25.
[5]See chapter 15 Adultery and Affairs, p. 189ff.

hint of derisive and censorious comment, he maintains the dignity of all concerned. It is not to Ingrid or to any of his church people that he expresses his personal indignation (though in various ways they may invite him to do so). It is with a professional colleague that he deals with his emotional responses if this is necessary.

Geoff does, however, let Ingrid see that he is moved by her predicament. He enters into her sadness and grieves with her in her sense of shock and loss. He empathizes with her in her disappointment, her anger and her sense of betrayal. Finally, it seems to him time to introduce the idea of referral.

Geoff: ' . . . and you're not sure what to do at the moment. Give yourself time, Ingrid. You can really use some support right now. And I guess that's why you've come today. Ingrid, do you realize that the kind of support I can give you won't be marriage counselling? You say you know I'm already counselling Joe and Karen, and –'

Ingrid: 'But if them, why not us? Or me, if Hugh won't come?'

Geoff: 'The complications would be too great. There wouldn't be any way I could avoid the risks of confusion. I mean, Ingrid, even remembering whether I'd heard something from you or from them would be beyond me. So I'm suggesting you see another marriage counsellor – with Hugh, I'm hoping – while I support you with other kinds of pastoral care.'

Ingrid: 'But isn't there a way you can counsel us? Or me?'

Geoff: 'There isn't, Ingrid. Even giving it my best go, there'd be risks. I could so easily make a mistake that would seem to break confidentiality.'[6]

Ingrid: 'But I know you and I trust you, Geoff. And you know Hugh, and he respects you. I wish you could find some way to give us marriage counselling.'

---

[6]The pastor stays with one practical, simply-expressed reason for his decision not to accede to this request for marriage counselling. The reader will be conscious that his rationale includes awareness of a number of complexities, and that he is wise in choosing not to load Ingrid with their full extent at present.

Geoff: 'And there isn't a way that would be satisfactory. I do understand your reasons for wishing to continue with me. But I want your counselling to work for you – and for Hugh too. Would you be willing for me to arrange for you to see Helen? She's a marriage counsellor and I find her values very trustworthy. I know she's good at her job.'

Ingrid: 'It's going to be harder to get Hugh involved.'

Geoff: 'Perhaps you're right. It may be. On the other hand, it may be easier for Hugh to go to someone outside our church. It will be a big step for you but I really believe going to Helen will be a positive step for you. I'll still be available to you as your pastor.'

Geoff has felt the pressure of Ingrid's plea, and the distress he feels in his concern for her is apparent.[7] Ingrid also sees in him a sureness and a purposefulness: he is not browbeating her; he is not wanting to manipulate her for his own benefit. Ingrid may need more time to accept Geoff's decision. He tells her that if she agrees to see Helen as counsellor, he will speak to Helen and pave Ingrid's way before she rings Helen for an appointment. He explores with Ingrid the likelihood of Hugh's agreeing to go with her, and they discuss how best to persuade Hugh to do so.

Referring after Considerable Counselling: a Later Referral

A case example of later referral is that of Donald and Heather, whom John decides to refer for specialist treatment that is not within his scope.[8] (He will continue with their marriage counselling while they are receiving specialist help about one aspect of their marriage relationship.) While they go elsewhere for assessment and treatment of Donald's premature ejaculation, John continues to help them find

[7]It is natural in this situation to cling to a trusted person and plead for more than that person can give. The pastor contains his own distress, seeing a broad perspective of pastoral responsibility and holding to a measured decision as he does the best he can for this parishioner.

[8]See chapter 14, Sexual Counselling, p. 171ff.

- clarity in their communication;
- adequate ways of dealing with their disappointment and resentment;
- satisfying ways of affirming the positive aspects of their marriage.

There are many reasons for referral of a couple to another counsellor after doing a considerable amount of work with them. Instances in which John makes such a referral include these:

- His skills are insufficient in a particular case;
- the couple cannot use well what he has to offer them; he and they don't make a good fit;[9]
- information emerges about factors in a couple's situation such as violence, a medical condition or a psychiatric illness, and some forms of current or childhood sexual abuse.

Co-Operating with Medical Practitioners

As counsellors, Geoff and John are usually interested in consulting with the medical practitioners to whom they refer couples. They believe it is important that counsellors and doctors check with each other that they are keeping their respective roles clear, and that to do so is in the interests of accurate and co-operative treatment of couples referred. However, this is a delicate area for both counsellor and doctor.

Many medicos are happy to consult with the counsellor of someone who is their patient; and there is always the professional question of what information may be appropriately handed on.

---

[9] They may feel positive toward him, and he is a competent counsellor, but he and they are unable to shape themselves to each other's mode of operating. While John will see such a referral as constructive, he will not be satisfied with his inability to join with this couple, but will explore with his supervisor how he might have been more useful.

Counsellors, too, when consulting with their clients' doctors, have also to consider how much information it is proper for them to pass on. Discretion is necessary in both professions; so is consistent respect for clients' privacy. The fact is that counsellors tread delicate ground, that sometimes dilemmas arise, and that this is only to be expected.

It is also a fact that medicos are afforded a particular role and responsibility in society. To counsellors who value their own practice skills and their own accrued wisdom – and also the breadth of perspective they have gained – it can seem sometimes that regard for the medical role in society takes precedence over regard for counsellors' skills and function. This may be so, but counsellors and doctors are finding that usually they can work very well together for the benefit of clients.

The amount of counsellor–doctor co-operation will always vary with the individual counsellor and medico. It will depend too on the esteem and trust in which each holds the other's integrity. Further, the particular marriage case and the way the couple's situation is viewed by the two professionals influences the amount of consultation each can expect from the other. Couples are best served when neither counsellor nor doctor is defensive about status and role: not proprietary about the couple, nor about themselves as the chief source of knowledge and healing!

The Messianic Don't Refer!

Referring a couple can be a very constructive act of ministry and ideally it should not be viewed as failure. It is easy for any of us when we are faced with a task beyond our competence to feel that we have failed and are therefore failures. We can catch ourselves working on the fantasy assumption that we are messiahs: superpersons who should be able to manage everything.[10] We ministers and counsellors

[10]Such an assumption can come from a low, simplistic view of counselling which disregards the skills and complexities it entails, as well as from a messianic view of the self.

do well to practise an attitude of true humility; that is, an accurate acknowledgment of our strengths and our limitations, with not too high a view of self, nor too low! Then we can get our preoccupation with self out of the way and address somewhat more realistically the advisability of referral.

The counsellors in the case examples given above are clear about this aspect of their counselling ministry. And they suggest referral in a caringly human way so that the couples concerned will not see it as a rejection. When failing messianic counsellors eventually have to refer, their personal sense of failure can filter through to their clients as a message of rejection or reproach. Their behaviour and demeanour can be interpreted as 'Go away, you are too tough for me', or 'You won't use my ministry'.

When suggesting referral, it is useful to have a pattern of previously worked-out words in mind: for example, 'The best way I can care for you right now is to refer you to . . .'[11] This sets the referral in terms of positive ministry. It is useful also to have a list of procedures that a counsellor follows in the task of referral, and to make a running mental check of such a list:

- Make clear the purpose of the referral, specifying the requirement you and the couple are wanting the referral to fulfil.

- Manage the change-over, discussing with the couple details such as how much information about them needs to be provided by you for the referral person, and who will arrange for the first appointment.

- Help the couple deal with their resistance, if any, to referral; and discuss with them any practical obstacles in the way, such as appointment time constraints.

- Define for the couple the type of continuing ministry you will be able to provide while they are seeing the referral person.

[11]Prepared forms of words can be used as slick formulas, but they are also part of the caring counsellor's skill in genuine communication.

- Discuss with them the limits and extent of the information they would like to request the referral person to report back to you.[12]

Where to Refer

You like Geoff and John may have confidence in referring to a marriage counsellor and to a medical practitioner because you have already had contact with these people. You asked fellow ministers and counselling colleagues about the skills of various professionals in your area. This was part of a process of building a network of helpers who could co-operate in providing a better service for their clients and patients.

You could invite someone like Helen, a marriage counsellor, to one of your clergy group meetings and talk with her about her work, and the possibility of co-operation. To another meeting you could invite a medical practitioner to give a medical perspective on some issues like depression, anxiety and on sexual difficulties.

In such meetings you and the other participants can assess the values of the invited consultant and ascertain their areas of expertise. The outcome of these meetings may be that the ministers clarify which consultants they feel confident in referring to. Another outcome may well be that the consultants may gain a new confidence in referring their clients and patients to the minister in appropriate situations.

After you Refer

Are you good at letting go? Sometimes a professional marriage counsellor finds the referring minister tiresome. Such a minister wants to keep checking with the referred couple or the counsellor to find out

---

[12]This discussion demonstrates to the couple that they have control over the confidentiality of their private information, even from you. They need to know also that the referral person may choose not to give you information that they may be willing for you to have.

how things are going. He usually becomes part of the problem.

It is, however, his responsibility to check with the couple that he has made a useful referral. He can do this after they have seen the new counsellor a few times, by asking 'Are you getting what you need?' It may become his task to help the couple hang on in with the counsellor when they begin to find the going hard – as they probably will.

Sometimes a minister becomes concerned because the counsellor doesn't seem to be 'saving' the marriage, or (in his view) taking seriously enough their spiritual beliefs. He won't trust the couple to her. He expects her to treat him as a co-counsellor and to give him information or explain herself; whereas her code of ethics (even if not her inclination) prevents her from doing so. She won't exactly delight in a couple saying 'We were talking to our minister and he wonders if you should . . .'

The minister's own ethics require that he refer a couple to the best source of help he knows and then bow out – except for continuing to pray for them. People who are referred by their minister sometimes have their own agenda in wanting to keep him involved inappropriately after referral. It is his responsibility to resist, and to stay properly detached; and sometimes this is far from easy to achieve.

20

THE PERSON OF THE MARRIAGE COUNSELLOR

Can a Single Person be a Marriage Counsellor?

Our answer is yes. We have known single people to do marriage counselling of high quality, whereas some people who are in loving, mutually need-meeting marriages have not been able to master the skills of counselling.

However, there is more to be said in our answer. The term *single* as used in contemporary society has broad connotations. It is a term that includes permanently separated spouses, widowed people, members of religious orders under a vow of celibacy, and people who live celibate lives but who have not taken formal vows. Among all these groups there are some whose work is in marriage counselling.

The range of single persons includes also people who are actively homosexual; people who perhaps once had a marriage but do not now consider sexual commitment to a spouse a goal for themselves or even a positive life style for many people; and single people who are involved in sexual relationships from time to time. From all these groups, which are not mutually exclusive categories, come some who work in marriage counselling and have a mandate to be marriage counsellors.

We believe that all marriage counsellors bring to the counselling room whatever understanding they have concerning what marriage is about and what marriage can be. The understandings they bring affect couples they counsel for better or worse. The implications of this are profound and complex, and cannot properly be opened for discussion here. For the purposes of our present consideration we limit the question to this: 'Can a single Christian living a life of celibacy and chastity counsel a Christian couple effectively?' The answer, as we have said in chapter 1, is that it depends on the extent to which the single Christian can translate his or her Christian dimension into counselling skills.

A wife and husband enjoy a physical familiarity with each other that belongs in marriage and is intrinsic to it: a sexual relationship, and the freedom for a physical companionship and a physical awareness of each other. However, the differences between celibate and married people can wrongly be emphasized, as if they were people from different planets. Let's look at the similarities between the relationships that celibate people have, and those that married people have with their spouses. The requirements in both sets of relationships are largely the same.

Much of what is required of a celibate person in his or her close, demanding and mutually need-meeting friendships is also required of a husband and a wife in their marriage and in their other relationships also. The challenge in each case is to so own oneself – and at times stand for self against the other – that one can then authentically die to self for the other.

That may read like a counsel of perfection, and a pious one at that. But in fact it is the basic requirement of all who would have a good relationship, and it's what Jesus Christ was on about. Although neither the married nor the single person meets the challenge perfectly, it's this challenge that offers us the pattern for living in relationship.

We never get away from having to drag our fallibilities with us through our lives. Let's say that in another way: In all our significant relationships – those that are not lived simply at a social level – we don't manage ourselves in relation to the other person as well as we would wish. St Paul had the same problem.

In our relationships we experience the pull of our third systems.[1]

[1] See chapter 3.

They influence the way we see the other person and react to them, especially under stress. We also experience the pull toward our straight-out self-centredness, covetousness, competitiveness and timidity in the face of conflict. Constantly these results of our fallen nature mar our desire and our ability to manifest fully the fruits of the Holy Spirit in our relationships. Yet to manifest them is the call to all of God's people, single and married.

There is an interesting variable to be considered regarding a possible limitation in the marriage counselling done by a single person. It relates to domestic stresses. In contemporary Western society a single life does not require the sharing of a household with others, whereas marriage does. It is therefore valid to ask whether the marriage counsellor who is single understands these stresses.

In married householding, there are shared areas of intimacy and irritation, like bathroom hurly-burly, television programme choices, and child management. These are intricately bound up in marriage stress. Managing the irritations of living cheek by jowl and having one's space invaded is a requirement in marriage that cannot easily be denied or avoided. However gregarious and community-loving one may be, the stresses of this are felt.

Single counsellors may understand the stresses of a couple's intimate sharing on either or both of two counts. First, they may have childhood experience in a family to relate it to. Second, they may also have adult and current experience of opening their homes to others in a way that allows invasion of their space in rather discomforting ways.

Much is made of the argument that celibacy precludes people from understanding married life. We're suggesting that it's more important for them to understand – from the inside as it were – areas of intimacy other than sexual intimacy. Celibate people, like married, have to live in an intensely sex-conscious society. Like the married they have to live with their sexuality and manage it.[2]

It is the stresses that impinge on marriages like bulls in china shops that single marriage counsellors need to understand – blasting radios,

[2] This is not to underrate the importance of sexual intimacy, or of sexual counselling as part of marriage counselling.

mud prints on carpets, pantyhose on shower screens and suddenly empty biscuit tins. Experiential understanding of these stresses – external stressors – is a criterion far more important than experiential understanding of sex within marriage.[3] Some single people do understand the stresses of home sharing because they don't live their lives carefully buffered from them. And of course some spouses manage to control their environments – including people around them – so stringently that they limit the normal household stressors impinging on them instead of learning to tolerate them.

In answering the question above we have ranged widely, making these essential points:

- The kind of counselling each counsellor does is influenced by personal values and beliefs about marriage: by an understanding of what marriage is and what it can be.

- Each counsellor requires personal skills and experience in ordinary human relating; and an appreciation gained from experience of the stressors attendant upon domestic or household living.

Surely being Interested in People is the Main Criterion?

It is a mark of our humanity to be genuinely interested in other people. To be warm and compassionate and capable of putting ourselves out for others are human attributes. But if we are to keep the quality of our interest in people wholesome we need to be aware that some forms of interest in others are neither healthy nor healing. These forms of interest are exercised by the following styles of people.

The people-curious It is easy to have an over-interest in people of a quality different from the interest we have just described.

The specifics of sexual intercourse as an issue form a very small part of marriage counselling.

Curiosity about people is certainly an interest of sorts. However, our interest can be intrusive, and we can be busybodies. We are wise to keep a check on the quality of the interest we feel in other people.

A writer of strange and interesting novels in the 1930s had a character say ' . . . it isn't my business to have more opinions than I can help about other people'.[4] In such reticence there is a rare wisdom and in contemporary times few people possess it. We are in an age of analysis. For those who would be counsellors, over-interest in analysing other people's personalities and motives is something to be guarded against. It's not the gift some assume it to be.

The people-discusser   In everyday life, the same over-interest is commonly displayed. Have you been at dinner parties where guests are ready to discuss people who, though not present, are known to those present? Condescendingly, kindly, knowingly, the absent ones are assessed in terms of their characters. Those who indulge in this party game might justify their behaviour as 'a natural interest' or 'harmless gossip'. But it is a violation of another's right to privacy.

The prayer-grouper   Another field of low-quality over-interest can be prayer meetings. There we can exercise it as if it were spiritual and virtuous. 'I think we should pray for Alice' can be the prelude, not only to disclosures about Alice's circumstances that are not the speaker's concern, but also to opinions about Alice as a person, perhaps offered in grave tones of authority. And what a buzz we all get out of this fugue, reverently holding Alice up to the Lord and imagining our prayers are music to his ears!

The marriage-curious   There is another target of intrusive over-interest, and that is a couple's marriage. This interest is indulged in by a third person, and it is different from an attraction toward one of the partners in the marriage and an envy of the other partner. It is a curiosity about the couple's actual relationship, offensive to the

---

[4]*The Place of the Lion*, Charles Williams © 1930. Copyright 1950 Pellegrini & Cudahy. Reprinted Eerdmans, Grand Rapids, Michigan 1980, p. 88.

couple and hard to rebuff without appearing to be rude. The interest expressed may seem kindly and friendly, but it has an intensity and intrusiveness. The intruders are likely to be married people who are failing to direct their energies into their own marriages.

Healing is needed in the intruder's marriage, and it can come only by redirecting the misdirected energy back where it belongs. Awareness of the possibility of this kind of wrongly directed energy can help marriage counsellors keep a check on both their level of interest in the couples they counsel and the health of their own marriage. It can also provide one criterion to those who have the task of selecting candidates for training in marriage counselling.

The people-possessor There is a further kind of over-interested person whose attentions are not healthy and health-giving. An extreme example is given in one of C. S. Lewis's stories.[5] The character depicted tries to bargain with heaven for possession of someone's soul, admitting in desperation 'I must have someone to do things to'.

This is the expression of a natural love unchecked till it turns into a hellish desire without human quality. If we let ourselves become so preoccupied with counselling that our identity is bound up in it, we run the risk that our over-interest in others is veering towards that desire. If we cannot imagine ourselves not counselling, it is time for us to return to an understanding of who we are.

'Who am I? I am a minister (or a counsellor) – one who does things for others.' There's the trap. The identity 'one who does things for others' can veer in the direction of 'one who has, needs, and must have others to do things for'. Or even 'to do (good) things to'. Ministry or counselling is my current role in my pilgrim journey. It is not my identity.

The examples we have given of over-interest are not pleasant ones. The concept they embody is power over others; need of others, not care of others. In the nature of every one of us resides

[5]C.S.Lewis, *The Great Divorce*, Geoffrey Bles, London 1945, (Fontana Edition 1991, p. 81).

the potential for desiring such power, and none of us is free from it. Part of the marriage counsellor's litany might well be 'From possessiveness, curiosity and intrusiveness, good Lord, deliver us.'

The well-boundaried Refreshing it is, to have as close friends people – counsellors and non-counsellors alike – who have the health that comes from an absence of over-interest! These people relate to others without the compulsion to form opinions about them. They enjoy person-to-person discussion about all manner of subjects from gardening to Grieg, from politics to Pelagius. They argue. They have plenty of opinions about the *ideas* that other people express, but they don't readily make assessments of the *personalities* of others.

People who behave in this way have an identity that comes from living inside their personal selves. They have, then, no need to live in and through other people. They are wholesome people because they are whole, with personal boundaries across which they relate to other people, respectful of these others' boundaries. Personally available to others, they are not intrusive.

Who then is the Ideal Marriage Counsellor?

The ideal marriage counsellor? There isn't a model, any more than there is a model of an ideal minister. But there are some characteristics that point the way. Effective counsellors tend to have a clear structure for thinking about what they do, and their thinking is also flexible. They are fairly comfortable with their emotions and those of other people. They have firm self-boundaries, while at the same time they are personally available to others.

Effective marriage counsellors show also that they are

- optimistic about the ability of most people to change their behaviour, at least to some extent;
- optimistic about marriage – even if they themselves have experienced a separation or a divorce;

- able to learn and change by reflecting on their own experiences;
- sturdily and consistently facing the difficulties that arise in their own relationships.

This last point is important. All relationships are flawed – not perfect at their best, only good-enough. All ministers are flawed. (Who else does God have but flawed people like us to call to community, to marriage and to ministry?) We can spend an interesting lifetime working on our significant relationships, and we don't have to become solemnly earnest and perfectionist as we do so.

While living with the many difficulties of a relationship, we can enjoy its satisfaction and lightness. This is true in reference to any friendship. Those who enjoy relationships with others, and who tolerate the imperfections of their relationships, make good candidates for training as marriage counsellors.

Sometimes people think 'I would make a good marriage counsellor because my own marriage is a successful one'.[6] But however we define success, it is not the criterion by which we as Christians are allowed to assess ourselves. What is a successful Christian? Surely recent prosperity theology and triumphalist theology have taught us by default that we are to be wary of measuring our *success* in God's eyes by any of our real or imagined achievements.

People who make good counsellors do not (we suspect) think of themselves in terms of *success* – either as people or as counsellors. Their focus isn't on themselves as the central figure. When a counsellor sees a husband and a wife achieving changes together, with courage and perseverance, she feels a warm respect for them. Of course she gets a kick out of being part of the process, of having hung on in with them and facilitated skilfully; and of course she grieves when she hasn't managed to facilitate as well as she wished. But she's very aware that it is the wife and the husband who have done the work of changing.

[6] Such people may have very good potential as marriage counsellors, if by 'successful' they mean they are facing stresses and resolving conflicts in their marriages. People who do not experience stresses and conflict in their marriages do not make effective marriage counsellors.

In all aspects of our life, including counselling, we are called to be faithful, not successful. What status and success can you and I claim? The highest status we can have and the best we can be is *forgiven sinner*. None of us is successful enough not to need Jesus Christ as Saviour, Redeemer and Strengthener.

And given this status, it still remains true that of all people, counsellors who are Christians should feel the challenge to excellence in their work. The picture of an ideal counsellor, then, is related not so much to a particular model as to a readiness for challenge.

21

TRAINING IN
MARRIAGE COUNSELLING

You have decided that you are the sort of person who might make a marriage counsellor, or you are in a position of ministry where you seem to have no choice but to have a go and do the best you can. What sort of training will you seek and where will you look?

Throughout this book we have presented effective counselling as a combination of theoretical understanding, learned and developed skills and a stance of hope and of respect for people – all this informed by a biblical faith. The interplay between these aspects is vital: sound theory will guide the use of skills, developed skills are the way that sound theory is worked out in practice, and hope and respect bring energy and enthusiasm to engage people in the task. A pastor with excellent theory (psychological and/or theological) who has not developed skills will not be very effective. One with highly developed skills but an inadequate system of theory will be like a ship without a rudder – there is no sure guidance or direction for the use of the skills. One who has little hope or enthusiasm is not likely to encourage people to work and change.

You may find a training course that includes all of these aspects, but you may find that you have to settle for components from different places and auspices.

Basic Counselling Skills

The basic skills in any counselling are listening and empathy and these are required whatever method of counselling is used. Counsellors need training in these skills even if they already have a reputation as good listeners. There is an added discipline in the quality of listening required for effective counselling:

- I am attending to the other – giving myself and my attention to the other.

- I am putting myself aside for the time being – not attending to my desires or needs.

- I am wanting to understand the feeling, thinking and the inner world of the other.

- I am suspending the impulse to solve the issues being presented.

- I am seeking to stay with this person – in their world.

To translate this discipline into practice, several skills are required. In his excellent text on basic personal counselling, Geldard[1] names six micro-skills that apply to all counselling.

- **Making minimal responses**   I make brief responses aimed to facilitate the client's talking.

- **Reflecting the content**   I paraphrase what I have heard the client say, to communicate that I have heard and to check with the client the accuracy of my understanding.

- **Reflecting the client's feelings**   I communicate that I understand, to validate the client's feelings, and again to check the accuracy of my understanding.

- **Reflecting the content and the feelings**   I bring together

---

[1] Geldard, D. *Basic Personal Counselling* – training manual for Counsellors, Prentice Hall, Australia 2nd Edition 1993. See also Egan G., *The Skilled Helper*, 2 Ed Brooks Cole, California 1982.

what the client is thinking and describing and her accompanying feelings to encourage her to develop a sense of meaning.

- **Asking questions**   I ask open questions which invite further exploration, description and reflection; not closed questions requiring yes or no responses.

- **Summarizing**   I draw together a number of reflecting statements which form something of a theme, or a process of action and behaviours.[2]

Courses in these basic counselling skills of listening and empathy are offered by various institutions and groups in most areas, and competent trainers are available to teach these skills to groups who wish to learn.

Theory of Personality

Every counsellor uses a theory of personality as he seeks to help someone. Every person who seeks to influence another person uses a theory. In many cases, this theory is not thought out, but might be expressed in such assumptions (believed as axioms) as 'If I tell him, he will change', or 'If I love her enough, she will do what I want', or 'If this person and I pray in the right way, their inability to make good relationships will disappear'.

Rather than working from such assumptions, an effective counsellor requires a realistic and systematic theory and will learn a coherent theory of personality:

- how persons think, feel, behave and decide;
- how personality develops;
- how persons use reason, fantasy, feelings and defences in their living and relating;

---

[2]The reader may like to review the counsellor's responses in the case examples in this book in the light of this list of micro-skills.

- how a person gets into trouble – doing what she doesn't want, provoking responses she doesn't like.

Theory of How People Change

An effective counsellor also has a theory of the process by which people change some of their attitudes and behaviours. In other words, a counsellor requires an understanding of the conditions and interventions that enable people to make the changes necessary to live more closely the lives they believe are true and right, and to enhance their relationships with others.

Theories of personality and theories of therapeutic change tend to come in packages:

- Behaviour modification theories. These purport to be strictly theories about behaviour change; however, many of them seem to have personality theory implicit in some of their assumptions and practices.
- Psychoanalytic theory of personality and the practice of psychoanalysis and psychodynamic counselling.
- Subsequent expansions of psychoanalytic theory. Object relations, Gestalt therapy, Transactional analysis, and Rational emotive therapy are often viewed as combinations of the two packages above.

Effective counsellors will have a thorough grasp of at least one of these packages of theories, and some understanding of others. They will have reflected on their own lives and relationships in the light of their theory, so that their understanding of the theory will be from the inside. Their learning of such theories is best gained from experiential workshops; lectures and textbooks provide understanding, and perhaps personal therapy is available and possible. Prospective counsellors will need to search around for suitable courses at tertiary institutions and other teaching bodies or agencies.

Marriage Counselling Theory

Marriage counsellors require theory beyond individual personality theory as they focus on the relationship between two people living together in a marriage. Such theory will include many topics discussed in this book – the circular nature of the partners' interaction and systems theory; the giving and receiving of communication in words; feelings, postures and gestures, symbiosis and detachment, mutual need-meeting; dependence and dependability, conflict and negotiation, as well as violence and sexual issues.

While a marriage counsellor will use all the disciplines (e.g. empathy) of individual counselling, he will need to learn additional skills – joint interviewing, communication strategies, helping couples to give feedback to each other (not in defensive blaming ways but in ways that invite and encourage change), and dealing with escalating feelings during an interview.

Courses teaching the theory and practice of working with the marital dyad are more difficult to find. They are now available at a few universities and other teaching institutions, and through some marriage counselling organizations. The best way for you to find courses available in your area is to enquire from marriage counsellors, a marriage counselling agency or a family therapy centre.

Alternatively, you could gather a small group of clergy together and invite a trainer to work through the topics of this book, helping you to review your own experiences and your practice in helping other people. It is important that the trainer has considerable skills in marriage counselling, and if he or she shares your faith position that is a bonus. While such a trainer may not share your values, it is important that you do not allow the difference in values to inhibit your learning of the theory and skills that they can teach. The same applies to leaders of any tertiary course you may take. Whether or not a trainer or a lecturer shares your faith position, you need to be engaged in theological reflection. In learning the art of marriage counselling so that it is part of your own thinking and doing, you will internalize and digest what is taught (and perhaps you will eliminate some of the teaching in the process). Reviewing and revising in the light of biblical values will be part of your learning task.

For optimum learning, the process seems to be something like this: Learn voraciously from your trainer, get all you can from them without filtering. Enter into the theory and practice with enthusiasm and risk-taking, and then consider, review, filter and integrate later, so that *your practice accords with your best understanding, under God, of eternal truth and of the way life is.*

Supervision

The most productive part of training is the supervision of your own practice. This is where you review what you actually have done with the people you counsel and how far your learning comes together in your practice. And it is not going to all come together the first time! But some of it will. At the very least, your training will be helping you to attend to them in a way that is therapeutic. Novice counsellors (aware of their limited skills) tend to forget that apart from the counselling room their clients do not have another place where they are listened to so carefully for an hour.

The choice of a supervisor is critical. One who is also skilled in *marriage* counselling is best, and supervisors who are skilled only in individual counselling are less useful. The tasks of the supervisor cover three areas – support, education and administration.

Support A supportive supervisor identifies and reinforces the good work you do and encourages you as you face difficult counselling situations. Confronting and correcting you strongly may sometimes be necessary in your supervision sessions, and it is a mark of your personal and professional maturity to view it as part of genuine supervisory support. It is also a mark of your supervisor's maturity when he or she is able to correct and confront in a supporting way. It cannot be stressed too much that supportiveness as a continuing, habitual attitude is very important in your supervisor – and also that the supervisor who fails to confront you is letting you down, not supporting you.

Education   Your supervisor helps you to

- sharpen your understanding of theory as you apply it to the particulars of your cases, so that you are able to see aspects of theory in practice terms;
- choose actual words and strategies to enhance your actions with particular clients;
- identify gaps in your knowledge of theory and practice;
- identify transference and countertransference issues in your counselling;
- recognize when the direction you are taking your clients is inappropriate, unrealistic or just plain wrong.

Your supervisor is thus guiding you in what you do in counselling, guiding you in your continuing learning, helping you to be self-aware in your attitudes to your clients, and assessing when and how you are going off track. Supervision is a different skill from counselling in some important respects, for in your supervisor's eyes you are a counsellor, not a client in therapy. While an occasional supervision session may take on, briefly and in a limited way, a therapist-client flavour, your supervisor will expect you *not* to expect to be treated like a fragile client, but as a professional colleague.

Administration   If you are working in a marriage counselling agency, your supervisor is part of the agency's management team and accountability structure. He or she is accountable to the agency's director to enhance the quality of your work; to you for the quality of the supervision; and indirectly to the couples you counsel, for they are the agency's clients. For a realistic standard of care for the couples you counsel, you are accountable both to them and to the agency through your supervisor.

As a parish minister who counsels you may find your supervisor, while being outside the line of church accountability, is useful in administration matters that relate to your responsibilities to your denomination, church council and parishioners. Issues such as time management and confidentiality may be part of your supervisory agreement or contract. There are other relevant issues related to administration with which your supervisor helps you; for instance, a supervisor's function is to help you

- decide whether particular cases are within your competence, and when and how to refer those that are not;
- monitor your expenditure of energy and expectations of yourself;
- monitor your general case management, which includes the keeping of records.

Keeping a log-book or journal of the process of supervision can be a very useful aid. Here you record the cases and issues you bring to supervision, and then add what you have learnt from the supervision hour.

Professional Development

While most professional marriage counsellors have weekly or fort-nightly supervision throughout their careers, ministers who do some counselling may see this as something of a luxury with their small case-load. Only a minority of clergy seek supervision of their minis-terial tasks. Perhaps it is not so much that they reject it, as that they do not consider the possibility of supportive learning and correction being available to them. However, a minister who has had extensive training in marriage counselling will have experienced the value of supervision of his counselling work (and seen the flow-on of this value in his other work). He will want to continue to learn and grow by this process, and to have a place where he is accountable for the quality of his work. He will work out with his supervisor the frequency of meetings to balance optimum support and learning with responsible use of time.

He will also be attentive to other possibilities for professional development that may be available:

- He may be able to join a professional association of counsellors (marriage counsellors or Christian counsellors) and attend their educational meetings and workshops.

- He may be able to attend conferences of counsellors.

- He may be able to join an agency or private group for attendance at its case conference and for other continued education.

- He may choose to join a course on some aspect of counselling, enlarging his initial theory base or adding a different form of theory and/or practice, or adding to his theology of marriage or counselling.

- He may choose to invite some of his colleagues to join together to form a study group for a number of sessions to expand their theory and practice, to support each other in their learning and their counselling, and to bring a biblical theological critique to the work they do.

The Trainee's Marriage

Any intense training programme, even in marriage counselling, places a trainee's marriage at some risk. Training in business courses or general academic courses, specially for women returning to study, can change the balance in a marriage. There is the demand in counsellor training to review your assumptions about life and relationships, to review your habitual methods of dealing with those who are your intimates. There is also the demand of extended and intimate exposure to trainers, fellow-trainees and clients. These demands bring a crisis – there is risk and there is opportunity.

As trainee counsellors change some of their ways of relating, their spouses may feel excluded from the process and threatened by it. The notion of circular interaction[1] reminds us that if one person changes, the other is receiving an unexpected stimulus. That partner then has to succeed in pulling the other back to the status quo, or

[1]See chapters 4 and 5.

else make some personal change. In either case there will be stress on the marriage as the trainee and spouse work out the changes in their marriage which have been triggered by the training. Trainers and trainees will be wise to consider this process and take steps to ensure as far as possible that the outcomes will be for better and not for worse.

22

WHEN CLERGY
GET INTO TROUBLE

Counter-transference

We want to begin our discussion of transference phenomena by relating it to sexual attachments that develop between clergy and parishioners, or clergy and those they counsel. Not all such attachments can be explained — and certainly none are to be explained away — in terms of transference phenomena; sexual exploitation is too often the result of deliberate wrongdoing in those clergy who have not understood and practised chastity as part of their obedience to Jesus Christ.

It is a tragic blot on the image of the Christian Church, and even more importantly on its mission, that many ministers get into inappropriate and wrong sexual behaviour with people for whom they have pastoral and professional care. A number of studies confirm that sexual exploitation is widespread in all denominations.

These studies relate to male clergy. As far as we know, there has not yet been organized research and consideration into sexual misdemeanours of female ministers and into the direction and forms these are likely to take. While we, like other counsellors and supervisors, have some experience with female ministers, our focus in this discussion will be sexual exploitation by males that comes from counter-transference to females.

In our experience, the majority of those who develop a pastoral or counselling relationship into a sexual one begin the process as concerned pastors wanting to do a good job of pastoral care. These men are horrified when they realize what they have done, and not just for fear of being caught out. They are shocked at the destructive results of their initial attempt to care. Their behaviour all along has been *ego-dystonic* with what they believe to be right.

The published code of ethics of any professional association of therapists and counsellors specifically prohibits sexual contacts and exploitation of patients and clients. This kind of explicit code has not existed for ministers, perhaps because churches have in the past taken for granted (however naïvely) that wrong sexual behaviour was unthinkable, given the light of biblical truth that ministers possessed. In any case, a few practitioners in professional associations with codes of ethics would argue that their own sexual behaviour with clients and patients is not unethical because it is a matter of mutual consent – or even part of the person's treatment and healing. Such an attitude fails to recognize that ethics statements are based in this reality: that in professional care there always exists a power imbalance, and that clients require protection from the temptation of practitioners to misuse their greater power. Clients are vulnerable and suggestible. All people with responsibility for the care of others hold power and can misuse that power.

There are clergy who do not experience horror and remorse at their own sexual wrongdoing with parishioners, and those they counsel. Their personalities are disordered so that their behaviour seems to them acceptable: it is *ego-syntonic*. When they are confronted, they use avoidance techniques, slipping sideways in their responses. Or their responses are attempts to shift discomfort back to the confronter: they may reproach the confronter for being judgmental or for being a bourgeois puritan; or they may ask in an interested counselling tone 'What is it about my normal sexuality that offends you?' or 'What about love in all its breadth and depth?'

Such clergy may go on to justify their sexual behaviour by claiming that it was initiated by the client or parishioner, or a matter of mutual consent: and therefore, they argue, they have not exploited anyone. They are ignoring the power imbalance when they make such claims.

A Positive Counter-transference Goes Wrong

Kevin is rector of a suburban parish. As a consciously planned part of his ministry, he shares with his wife the task of supporting the marriages of young couples. He knows that empathy is an important part of pastoral care, and he has attended one experiential workshop on listening skills; but he does not receive clinical supervision of his counselling with parishioners.

Kevin lacks information and awareness about the emotional forces that can be unleashed by effective listening on its own. These forces are related to the depth of parishioners' neediness and their consequent vulnerability, and also to the driven intensity of a pastor's compassion when it stems too much from his need for intimacy, his need to care, and his need for personal significance. Kevin is shocked when he finds himself in bed with Priscilla, a lone parent for whom he has been caring pastorally.

While delivering goods from the church's emergency foodstore, Kevin has been responding to Priscilla's plight as a sad and needy person and he has begun to visit her regularly. His intention is not only to bring her some cheer along with the foodstuffs and the church's goodwill. He has also been telling her about the love of God and about forgiveness and new life through Jesus Christ. Oh yes, he has hugged her several times because she is lonely and sad – and in return she has clung to him. But he is her pastor and he wants to stay with her empathically in her need.

What has gone wrong, that sexual passion takes over from pastoral care? Priscilla has appreciated Kevin's visits with the church's practical gifts, his personal comfort, and his message of hope through the Gospel. It brightens her day to feel his strength when she is helpless, and she looks forward to his visits. He notices that she is taking more care with her appearance, and is pleased at what he sees as a sign that she is recovering from her depression – through his ministry.

Kevin is unaware of the attractiveness to Priscilla of his care and his strength. She does not have to make a very conscious contrast between Kevin's loving behaviour and that of the estranged husband who seemed so unaware of her except as a provider of his practical and sexual needs. And Priscilla's account of her husband's readiness to use her has triggered Kevin's anger toward the man and increased his concern for her.

The comparison Kevin makes between Priscilla's husband (as she presents him) and himself does not have to be a very conscious one for Kevin to begin thinking how much Priscilla needs someone who can love well, and how good it would be if she could feel really loved. Between them sexual attraction grows quickly and takes over. Kevin's motivation has seemed good to him: he hasn't meant to exploit Priscilla, and he is shocked when he realizes what he has done. That Priscilla was expressing her transference in attraction to Kevin does not excuse Kevin's behaviour.

Here we have a classical split image. Kevin views Priscilla's absent husband as bad – selfish, rejecting, exploiting; he sees himself as good – caring, giving. By losing sight of the reality that Priscilla's husband is (like Kevin, like Priscilla) a mixture of good and not-so-good, he encourages Priscilla to split her images of her husband and her minister into bad and good. The dangerous aspect of their perceptions is that together they share a fantasy: that she is a victim needing to be loved and that he is the ideal carer.

The relationship that develops between Kevin and Priscilla is an example of a situation where a minister's positive counter-transference goes unmonitored and unchecked. We do not give an account of Kevin's dealing with the breach of his ethical code, his repentance and forgiveness; but part of his amendment of life is to obtain consistent supervision on transference issues.

A Negative Transference

Some months later, after he has obtained supervision, Kevin is counselling another separated wife, Nicky. He is puzzled that Nicky is becoming sullen and resentful toward him, for no reason that he can see. He thinks he is consistently accepting and respectful of her, he has evidence that she often appreciates his ministry, and yet increasingly she is showing resentment. When he asks gently 'Nicky, you seem angry with me today, will you tell me why?' she says she's well aware that he disapproves of her for having left her husband, and that since he is being helpful out of pity for her, of course she is angry.

For a moment Kevin is hurt and wants to defend himself, telling Nicky indignantly that she is misjudging him, responding to her resentment with resentment, and reproaching her for seeing him as judgmental. He makes none of these responses, and thus he avoids reacting to her negative transference with a negative countertransference. Kevin simply says in a reasonable tone that her expressed perceptions surprise him, and that they don't fit him and his motives; that he believes she believes what she is saying, but that he doesn't believe it; and that her anger with him won't make any difference to his hanging on in with her as her pastor during the tough time she is going through.

In the relationship between a pastor and a parishioner (or a counsellor and a client) there are likely to be some characteristics in each that realistically draw out from the other a positive or a negative response.[1] It is unconsciously driven (third system) reactions to each other that are involved in destructive counter-transference and transference.

Nicky may have realistic reasons to be angry with Kevin at times, simply because Kevin, being human, has irritating characteristics. But Nicky appears to be responding to Kevin as if he were a judgmental figure from her past. She carries this figure around with her in her head, and it is part of her internal dialogue. In the dialogue she judgmentally attacks herself and then reacts to her own attacking self, who was originally a significant and judgmental person in her external world, and is now her internalized (introjected) judge.

---

[1] A pastor who says 'I treat everyone alike' is failing to pay attention to the fact that each person draws out of and responds to unique aspects of each other person. For many ordinary conscious reasons, each of us feels more affinity with some people than with some others and we do well to admit it. Having done so, it is easier for us to treat everyone with equal respect and consideration, and so avoid the charge (often deserved by pastors) of having favourites and non-favourites.

It is this judgmental figure, introjected, that she first transfers out onto Kevin and then responds to with her attacked self as if it were Kevin who judges her. Kevin's reality-oriented response takes account of the fact that only empathic, straightforward information is likely to lessen Nicky's negative transference. Reproaching or pleading will only reinforce the transference phenomena.

If Kevin has had a significant person of power in his early life who read his mind and accused him of base attitudes and motivations, he will find it harder to deal reasonably with Nicky's accusation. He will more likely respond either from a fearful stance, accepting discomfort and searching himself for the attitude Nicky accuses him of, or he will attack her judgmentally for her accusations. In the first instance he will be transferring to Nicky the early significant person's power over him; in the second instance, he will be playing out that significant person's attitude in an attempt to defend himself.

Thus Kevin could be tempted to make counter-transference responses to Nicky, distorting the reality of their relationship further in response to her transference distortion. His reasoned response, undefensive and understanding of her position, is a way of dealing with transference/counter-transference phenomena.

Split Image

With Priscilla, Kevin's counter-transference and his distorted images led him into trouble. Lester's image of a young married parishioner he is counselling leads him into a problem too: the result of not overtly sexual exploitation, but the inability to set up constructive marriage counselling with a couple.

Lester consults an experienced marriage counsellor, asking 'When should we counsel for separation?' Recognizing it as a rhetorical question, his consultant waits for his story about a marriage problem. The wife is a recent convert to his church. He has been responsible for her conversion, he says, and she is beautiful in her love for the Lord. The husband is into a bad way of life – no, not violence, just wilfulness – and he is resisting the Lord, says Lester.

Although he has seen only the wife, Lester feels sure that she should begin a new life and that her faith is at risk while she is in this bad marriage.

The consultant notes that the evidence Lester has of the husband's defects come mainly from hearsay and not from Lester's direct observation. As she listens, the consultant notices also that Lester seems to be viewing the husband as the marriage's bad partner, and to be aligned with the wife as the good one. Aware of the complex dynamics in spouses and their interactive patterns, the consultant asks Lester to consider what is keeping the wife in her marriage. 'It's because she loves the Lord' is Lester's prompt reply, and he is unable to explore alternative perceptions of this marriage.

Her failure to help Lester see that he has become part of the couple's marriage problem prompts the consultant to remember a wife who had once been referred to her by a parish priest. The priest seemed to view this wife as a dear little woman with a brute of a husband, and for several sessions she resisted the consultant's request that her spouse be invited.

When he did come, he turned out to be a good-natured man, not over-sensitive, who liked his pub mates and his horse-racing a lot and who was an affectionate husband. This had not been the image of him that his wife had presented, either to her priest or initially to the consultant. The husband proved open to change, and so did the wife, and the outcome was an increase in the wife's goodwill toward him and in his awareness of her needs.

It seemed to the consultant that the wife held a split image of two significant males in her life: her idealized priest was good father, her rough-and-ready husband was bad father. Through his attentive listening and his excellent intentions (laced with sentimentality), the priest had inadvertently reinforced her disgruntled view of her husband. The priest's image of the marriage seemed to suffer from a good spouse/bad spouse split. The consultant was glad he had referred for counselling the wife of a marriage that turned out to have genuine strengths.

Splitting images is a tendency that all of us share, and marriage counsellors do not eliminate it for ever even with the advantages of experience and training. The playwright Eugene O'Neil had a character speak of 'the curse of always having to see both sides of every question'. Sometimes it can be a burden (though it is not a curse) to see both sides of a marriage with all its subtle complexities. But that seeing is a potential blessing for couples we counsel, because it protects us from image-splitting and it is a fairly effective guardian keeping our counter-transferences in check.

Defining Counter-transference

Some readers will note that we are using the terms 'counter-transference' and 'transference' in a fairly loose way compared with their original and classical meaning. Commonly in contemporary thinking and in case discussions, marriage counsellors find the terms useful to refer generally to attitudes of counsellors towards husbands and wives in counselling, and vice versa.

They are useful terms too when applied to everyday pastoral care given by a minister to parishioners. As suggested above, an appealingly dependent person may elicit in me, the minister, a response of parental protectiveness (positive counter-transference) while toward a critical, unco-operative parishioner, I may take up a defensive, irritable attitude (negative counter-transference).

When transference and counter-transference are discussed, the assumption is easily made that it is the client who always brings into the counselling relationship attitudes, appealing or otherwise, that come from childhood; and that it is only in response to these third system attitudes (transference) that I the counsellor produce my third system attitudes (counter-transference). As a counsellor I had better remain aware that I am very well placed in my position of power to trigger off clients' third system responses to me. If I need to be needed and admired, or if I relate from my role and its persona rather than risk the vulnerability of being myself, genuinely and transparently, I give messages that invite clients' third system responses. Even if I am as transparent as I can be, I still invite some transference responses from my clients.

Counter-transference and transference, in the way these terms are now commonly employed, do not necessarily interfere with the goals of the client or couple. Both can be used advantageously. We can enjoy a couple or feel strong compassion for them, or even express our exasperation to them at well-chosen times. They need us to be real people with them. But they also need us to be people who can quickly move to an assessing position that we don't take up with our friends in our everyday life and relationships (that is, if we value our friends).

'You're both a bit sore with me this session?' 'I'm not doing too well with you two today and I'm a bit disconcerted because I don't know what's going on between us.' 'Yes, I am shocked by your treatment of her as you describe it – but I'm on the side of you both and your marriage, not against you.'

In this way the counsellor remains free from the complementary behaviour that the transference invites, and so the clients are free to examine (from a new perspective) the outcome of their transference behaviour, and to start considering more realistic options. In doing so they begin to use the transference relationship to empower themselves to change their behaviour, to redecide their ways of coping. When one partner, in the presence of the other, is attending consciously and actively to the meaning of his/her transference to the counsellor, it can have exciting results for both. Transference aspects of their own relationship, which have puzzled them in the past, come into focus or suddenly have meaning.

Freedom to deal with transference and counter-transference enables the counsellor to maintain an attitude of warmth and positive regard toward parishioners and is a gift that comes with both emotional and spiritual maturity. It is based in ability to trust and in truth that sets us free. These maturities combine to give the freedom to meet people and be with them where they are, in their sickness and their health, their richness and their emptiness, their antagonism and their friendliness.

23

MARRIAGE AND MINISTRY

The majority of clergy are married, apart from those in the Roman Catholic communion. So far, counsellors' involvement with clergy marriages has been mostly with those in which the husband is the minister: the ordination of women is still a comparatively recent phenomenon for some denominations, so the amount of accrued understanding of the influence of church context on ordained women's marriages is still very limited.

This chapter focuses primarily on the situation of men who are ordained pastors or priests and their wives, particularly those who with their children live in church houses, among the people to whom the husband ministers. If you are a minister and also a married woman, there is relevance to your situation in the issues raised here, even though our examples are of male clergy and their wives. You will be able to extract what applies to you as a minister and a marriage counsellor. For married lay leaders in the churches also, and indeed for all Christian couples, the same or similar issues are crucial.

If you are an ordained person and counsellor who is single, a chapter, even in a book on marriage counselling, that focuses on the marriage of ministers may seem to discount you. Our intention is to highlight some specific issues and not, as Christians can easily do, 'exalt marriage above single life in such a way that it undermines single people who have chosen to be celibate'.[1] We are indeed aware

---

[1] *Embracing the Single Life*, Payne, Robin A., Acorn Press, Melbourne 1994 p. 99.

that 'the married or single state is not a matter of "better" or "worse". Both should be held in high esteem. Whatever good marriage offers is only penultimate, for marriage is not the ultimate goal for humankind'.[2] And it may well be you, a single counsellor, who at times could have the task of counselling a minister and his wife with some of the issues we highlight, so that they grow toward their shared and penultimate goal of a good marriage.

Loving God and Loving one's Spouse

The lonely depressed wife of a high-profile minister confesses with guilty tears, 'The terrible thing is, I resent that he loves God more than he loves me.' She is seeing the difficulties between her husband and herself in a tragically distorted way, and he is concurring in her false definition of their problems. The two are colluding in a fantasy based on false understanding and false piety.

In the nature of loving there cannot be competition between the love a minister has for his wife and the love he has for God. Unless I as a minister love my wife, I can't love God with the love that he is wanting to call forth from me. Unless I am seeking to love God in God's way, I can't love my wife in the way he wants me to. I believe I understand the greatness of the love God has for me, God who has called me to be an ordained minister. Do I also understand that part of loving God is to love my wife? In the loving of both God and wife there is corollary, not conflict.

The husband of the lonely depressed wife would say he understands this, and it is true that he appears to treat her with patience and courtesy. In the wider church people who admire his preaching say that the fruits of the Spirit are very evident in his life, and those who haven't the privilege of understanding something of her spiritual journey tut-tut about his neurotic wife. Impressed with his piety, they are not uneasily aware as some of his colleagues are, that his expressed love for God has a somewhat euphoric quality. He is

[2] Ibid, p. 38.

personable, able, and seems warm and emotionally available to others.

However, the kind of contact he makes with people is through a very personal charisma and charm; he is unaware how much he depends on it, and unaware of the degree of his self-reference and his inner detachment from others. Only in his home where there can be no substitute for ordinary, genuine and mutual relating do his deficits surface; and there they are falsely defined in terms of 'loving God more'. And because he is so 'successful' in his public image, this minister is disinclined to accept the challenge to assess his concept of love: of God, self and wife.

He continues to bask in the adulation of his admiring public. And then it seems that he reaches a point where he considers himself not subject to God's laws. Serious wrongdoing by this minister comes to public knowledge, and those who have adored him are bewildered and shocked. Now the question is whether this turn of events will force him to a sober revision of his assumptions.

Though situations of this kind make sad stories, they help us take a clear-eyed look at the worst of directions that marriages of ministers can take and they needn't stop us rejoicing in the best of directions they take. We are personally thankful to many clergy couples who have taught us much about the art of loving and of being loved. Some of these couples we have come to know and appreciate through counselling them, and they belong to a range of denominations. In our understanding of marriage we draw on these couples as one area of involvement on which we have reflected. A second area is our experience of our own marriage, where the husband is ordained. And our discussions with friends and colleagues in similar marriages provide a third area.

The experiences have sharpened our awareness of some subtle traps for clergy couples, just as they have sharpened our sensitivity to the fine possibilities that clergy marriages hold. The same traps and possibilities exist for couples who are lay people exercising leadership in pastoral care and counselling.

Making Marriage Holy

A beautiful name for marriage that sounds archaic and quaint, but has been retained in at least some revised prayer book services, is 'holy matrimony'. A gift from God, holy matrimony comes in response to the desire of a man and a woman to live out their life together in obedience to what God wants for them. And each case of a couple seeking to do this is unique, because each person is unique. The marriages of those who seek – consistently, and inevitably in a stumbling way – to live out a holy marriage do not turn into identical little gift-wrapped boxes. God's gifts are not like that. The marriages that spouses seek to make holy tend not to fit stereotypes; for instance, they are not all made up of personable wives and husbands who are invariably sweet to spouse and children, whether they are lay or clergy couples.

When parishioners hear a vigorous argument wafting through vicarage windows or a clergy wife is observed after morning service snapping at her husband, it doesn't necessarily mean that the holy has dropped out of their matrimony. On the contrary it could even mean that the wife is doing her best to make an effective and godly protest about her husband's neglect of her and their children: neglect which clergy, focused on the demands of their church work, are often tempted to fall into. (The church, or church involvements, can be a seductive third party to any marriage between Christians.)

Two committed Christians working out their holy marriage day by day are at times acutely aware of being forgiven sinners together; and there are some days when they feel at breaking point, disappointed and fed up with each other. Many of these are good, or at least good-enough marriages. In other marriages between Christians, basic honesty and commitment are lacking in either or both partners. In others again, environmental pressures combine with some deficit in the ingredients essential to emotional maturity, so that the ability to grow together in relationship is not achieved. In all these types of marriage, some are clergy marriages.

Presenting an Image

When we who are clergy couples become aware of presenting an acceptable and impressive image to the church and to the world, we can do some soul-searching and ask each other if we are fitting neatly into some kind of stereotype. In so far as we present a shared persona we risk losing our understanding that, whatever God is calling us to be as spouses in some specifics, he is primarily wanting us to be two real people who are growing in grace together. That growth seldom fits well with a church's image of the ideal clergy couple (or counsellor couple), let alone the general community's image.

There are norms of behaviour placed on all people, whatever their occupations. And there are some appropriate expectations of behaviour that come with the roles and functions of both a minister and his wife. There is no virtue in flouting these out of a compulsion to 'be myself' or 'be really me'. To do so may well indicate that the 'me' is still tied by rebelliousness to some concept of authority that lies in the 'me's' third belief system. On the other hand, there is no virtue in our conforming to expectations of behaviour without first assessing the genuine value to others of these expectations and to us as God's servants. We can at least search out whether we are chaining ourselves by mere compliance to apparently imposed norms – or perhaps by the desire to get on in the Church.[3]

We have said that holy matrimony is a gift God offers us as couples. If a marriage between two committed Christians is to yield up its authentic fruits, it has to be consciously lived out from within. And we can expect it *not* to fit the stereotypes we impose on it.

Christian couples can be strongly influenced by popular views including contemporary ones thought to be liberal, enlightened and sociologically correct. To the extent that we are so influenced, we adopt stereotypical views about relationships just as much as when we are influenced by what some Christians describe narrowly as

[3]In the compulsive quality of our chronic rebelliousness, compliance or ambition, our third belief systems (see chapter 3, pp. 21ff.) are involved.

'truly biblical views'. Both views, though conflicting strongly, arise from an authoritarian dogmatism that intimidates people into conformity and even ridicules those who think differently.

The high view of matrimony – to be real people growing in grace together, a commitment deliberately lived out from within, not conforming to nor rebelling against stereotypical expectations – may seem to be impossibly idealistic and to come from an other-worldly naïveté about life and relationships. Yet this apparent perfection-seeking in relationship by Christians is part of the vision which we are called to see and follow. We realize we will never reach a point where our marriages are really great vehicles of divine revelation. We recognize that to outsiders looking in we will seem to be ordinary mundane (even dull) and very flawed couples. But the high vision has to be there, and the high calling pressed toward.

One further way that clergy couples get trapped into presenting an image has to do with 'the star factor'. This factor is a concept of Rediger's, and while he develops it in relation to the use and misuse of power by ministers it is equally applicable to clergy couples.[4] The minister is an identified spiritual leader in the church, a known moral leader in the community, and a performer in the spotlight of regular worship services. These three factors, combined in the clergy role, together form the star factor. The star factor, seen in the case of the minister with the lonely depressed wife in our story above, may also be observed in some clergy couples who are committed to each other and to the service of God. Where a husband and wife are a double act – upfront spiritual and moral leaders and also in the spotlight, performing – there are star factor pressures both from their church people and from within the couple themselves. One such couple moved from being upfront stars to being the only leaders, and then to feeling they owned the church!

The sense of power that accompanied the star factor in this couple led them to become possessive, first of role, then of church. Initially it seemed natural to everyone that they should take precedence over

[4]Rediger, G.L., in *Ministry and sexuality: Cases, counselling, and care*, Minneapolis Fortress Press 1990, uses the concept in discussing the misuse of sexual power by ministers.

others ('You do it all so well' they were told), but a consequence of their star factor was that the spiritual and moral leadership that could have been exercised by many parishioners was restricted to the minister and his wife, whose role in public prayer and worship was also paramount.

In the process, the couple lost the plot: they were not living out their marriage from within, toward each other. The church was their stage. Their energy was focused away from their intimate relationship onto the busyness of their joint activity in the church. As a result they were unable to show forth to their church people a genuine model of one companionable, ordinary (but precious) marriage; so while initially the brilliance of their star factor was admired, bewilderment and disillusion developed in the parishioners – for it became evident that this couple's joint role had taken them over.

While we have emphasized the uniqueness of every marriage, we want to go back now to a similarity between all the couples that our chapters on counselling have pointed up. Our 'child' needs are an essential component of both our falling in love and our staying in love, and these needs are for better as well as for worse. Two people can scarcely be so disengaged that when they marry they do not yearn for their 'child' needs to be met by their spouse. A normal marriage with its normal bonding has, inevitably, aspects of 'child' yearnings as an essential element.

Initially in marriage, spouses are unconsciously expecting that they will be able to reconstruct in their relationship the magical image of a love in which each will perfectly satisfy the other. Of course, even before they married and particularly when the minister preparing them for marriage told them about it, they gave strong intellectual assent to the reality. The reality is that two people working out their holy marriage have the task of recognizing (as part of the holy) that they have to settle for less than they want from the other. The realization of what this means comes gradually, and at times very painfully. The 'child' yearning lingers on, never quite goes away, and sometimes surfaces very strongly.

Living Out Marriage

A minister and his wife are living out their Christian life together at a time when ethics and morality are at a low ebb. The media presents sexual activity and promiscuity in a way that seems to give permission to many to act on these models. What are couples to do in wanting to have a Christian marriage and give a model of right relationships to their children?

A challenge for us is to accept and value the people we serve, and still stand for biblical truth in regard to honesty and integrity, and against greed, cheating and dishonesty, for care and concern in a culture of self-centredness and self-reference, where aggression is portrayed as a virtue, and the enjoyment of genital pleasure as an end in itself. In recent decades genital orgasm has become increasingly an end in itself, rather than being a part – the ecstatic part – of becoming one flesh in the union that is a lifelong commitment.

Clergy face the question of whether they can and should speak out against common destructive sexual behaviour of young people, when their own children accept society's norms. It takes courage to do so. There is a temptation to use embarrassment and personal discomfort as reasons for revising what the church and the clergy should stand for.

Our sensibilities have become so blunted, and a false pressure to be accepting has become so strong that we no longer have confidence to stand against what is happening in our society. For many, acceptance seems to have slipped into condoning the behaviour.[5] The attempt to stand for truth about sexual behaviours is often daunted by emotional intimidation and by fears of being scoffed at as judgmental.

There is so much to value in our society, and the notion of acceptance and the non-judgmental attitude are so vital to counselling and good relationships that it is difficult to stand for truth, as it is so easy

---

[5]Much better in the long run was the approach of parents who risked a rift with their children and said 'We are sad about what you are choosing to do, we believe it is wrong. We also understand that just now it may be the nearest thing to right that you can manage to do.'

to be daunted by being labelled judgmental or not accepting – this is particularly true where we have a tendency to living in our persona (where performance and the socially right way to be are paramount) rather than living in integrity from within.

We need an inner strength, both individually and as a couple, to stand in appropriate judgement; and to be really accepting we need to be firm in our understanding of what is true and right, and yet to know that each of us falls short of that truth. We stand as forgiven sinners, knowing both our failures and forgiveness.

As married ministers our integrity is likely to be buttressed by the experience of a good marriage – a good-enough marriage where the tough love of loving confrontation and loving support are experienced. In this way couples can be helped to live in the genuineness of personhood rather than in the performance of persona.

Praying and Being

Prayer together is a special way in which this relationship can be strengthened – there is something different about a husband and wife who pray together. It's not much good for a pastor to be marvellously pious and to be seen publicly as a man of prayer, if he and his wife do not pray together. It's not so much the words that are used, whether they are extempore prayers or the words of a prayer book daily office; it is in yearning together, in adoration of God and in confession together, in thankfulness together for sins forgiven and for the good things that have happened, in supplication together for each and for others, that their faith relationship is strengthened.

Another source of strength in the marriage is physical affection and good healthy sexual intercourse which can be nourishing and nurturing in a couple's mutual giving and receiving. A tendency to focus on performance and persona will detract from the mutual vulnerability necessary for a good-enough sexual relationship. Friends with whom we do not have to be pastorally responsible, where we don't have to be professionally disciplined but can share readily our frustrations as well as our joys, can be a further valuable source of strength. A supervisor for the minister or counsellor is a special case in this category, with whom the minister can review in a supportive framework his successes and failures, and find ways of enhancing the wholeness of his ministry.

There is a close parallel between what happens in the day-to-day life together of a clergy couple (including the degree of their open, unpretentious, imperfect coming together before God), and the struggling together in counselling in an open, unpretentious, imperfect seeking to work towards a more authentic relationship. In each we feel our helplessness, our powerlessness: and then a different kind of power emerges through, and in, and because of our powerlessness. It is in seeking divinity in the cross of Jesus, rather than seeking divinity in the spectacular or the miraculous quick fix, that we live our lives as Christians, as marriage counsellors and as clergy couples.

INDEX OF CASES

INDEX